MINDFUL SPONTANEITY

Moving in Tune with Nature: Lessons in the Feldenkrais Method

RUTHY ALON
*with an Introduction
by Dr Bernard Lake*

PRISM
PRESS

Medical Disclaimer
This book is not intended as a substitute for orthodox medical treatment of disease.
Readers suffering from potentially serious medical complaints should also seek
medical advice relating to their condition.

MINDFUL SPONTANEITY

This edition published in Australia in 1990 by:

INTERFACE
Upper Level, 108 Pacific Highway,
Roseville, NSW 2069, Australia

and in Great Britain in 1990 by:

PRISM PRESS
2 South Street,
Bridport,
Dorset DT6 3NQ,
England

and distributed in the USA by:

AVERY PUBLISHING GROUP INC.,
120 Old Broadway,
Garden City Park,
New York 11040,
USA

ISBN 0 947311 07 6 (Interface)
ISBN 1 85327 050 4 (Prism Press)

Typeset in Australia by Netan Pty Ltd, Sydney
Printed in Singapore by Kyodo

A note to readers: permission for illustrations
Any material or illustrations from this book can be freely used for enhancing the
well being of people. Please acknowledge the source and notify the author c/- the Publisher.

CONTENTS

To Moshe, the great teacher who shared all his inventions with us in such a way that each of us has been inspired to re-invent it all from the beginning.

Acknowledgements

This book came into being during a period of travelling. I wish to thank warmly my family, my friends and my students who encouraged and helped me all along the way.

The translation from Hebrew into English was the hardest project. My thanks to Ziona Sasson from Jerusalem, for her help, and especially to Professor Ruth Miller for her language and supportive spirit.

Preface

Learning: the freedom beyond the barrier

When you roam around San Diego Zoo you can't help feeling the care with which a sense of open space has been provided for the animals. The giraffes, for instance, have extraordinary privileges: they are not locked behind fences at all. On three sides they are surrounded by huge rocks and in front only a narrow trench separates them from the visitors.

The guide explains that giraffes are very apprehensive of any risk to their ankles. With the peculiar assignment to balance their body on top of such long legs, the giraffes are cued to go around any obstacle. They never dare cross over the trench to freedom, even though it is just a footstep away. This is a psychological barrier, the guide says.

Aren't we all, in varying degrees, captives in our own personal prisons, bound by our limiting habits? And although we are conscious human beings and see the absurdity of that self-limitation, we don't know how to cross over that trench to freedom.

Awareness Through Movement is a method concerning how not to give up freedom. Dr Moshe Feldenkrais, the founder of the method, had a genius for improving human capacity, inspiring people to get in touch with their organic wisdom of coordination in tune with Nature's intent. Feldenkrais created a learning process through which you can train gradually and patiently, safely and gently, in hothouse conditions, far from the threatening trench, how to move in and out of pitfalls in varying and changing situations. When you are aware of your expanded options, the psychological barrier loses its hold on you. You arrive at the other side skilled in creative resourcefulness, having crossed over the barrier spontaneously. You feel not only the wider expanse of freedom, but also the dignity of being the sovereign of your actions, able to choose the way of life you desire.

The horizons this method opens for you become ever-widening as you approach them. I devote this book to just one narrow trench — backaches — through which you may come to know some of the Feldenkrais ways of thinking and moving that guide you across the barriers, leaving them behind you with a higher level of functioning than before.

I call this learning process the Grammar of Spontaneity.

Ruthy Alon

Introduction

We are all addicts — the creatures of our habits. We acquire and are fitted to them through repeated exposure. Thereby we are both individualised and collectivised by them. We do not give them up without anxiety and distress. Direct denial of habit is threatening and invasive and we go through similar convolutions and paroxysms of the denied drug addict. We invent and parade a whole armoury of excuses and devices to keep our habits free from scrutiny and untouchable. They are felt to be the sacrosanct part of our identity.

What began as opportunism, in response to specific events or traumas and served as quick-fix solutions at the time, become embedded in the neural repertoire and embodied in our musculo-skeletal capacities. They are the framework of our routines. In that we do not have to waste time and energy preparing novel responses to the multitude of changing circumstances they serve us well and we become hooked on them. But the trade-off is that we forsake our rich capacity to creativity and spontaneity. What saves us from the absurdities of unnecessary invention also closes off access to refinement, sensitivity and diversity. We set ourselves up to restrict responsiveness and so we trigger ageing by invariance.

The difficult choice between the order induced by habit and the possibilities offered by change can be greatly assisted by educating our continuing awareness to match the available to the appropriate. Only at its highest level is this automatic. In between is a lifetime based on patient observation and training.

We are all watchers of the great kaleidoscope. In this mode we have a continuously changing set of images which we implicitly trust our nervous system to sort out and define response. Observation is watching supplemented by the conscious discriminative powers of our system. It requires attention, play-back with memory, thinking through and an openness to discern as many features of the kaleidoscope as feasible. It should not be bothered or distorted by 'I'-ness (ego) as it operates. That factor is only superimposed later as we finalise our response.

The best laboratory to regain this power of observation is any unhampered infant working through its still unhabituated reactions to the environment. Its search and trial efforts access numerous diverse patterns of movement uncluttered by time

Awareness and Spontaneity

restraint and social imposition. Finding solutions is exciting and reinforcing and the infant is ready to go on tackling more complex problems. One is struck by the infant's perseverance, willingness to repeat and experiment freely and the intentness of its pursuit. Of course, it is not without frustrations and failures. But these are stimulants to try again and again. The drive to self-determination is built in to the normal system. Our sense of adequacy derives from the success of mastering the transition from helplessness to the survival requirements of being able in a basic variety of ways, not least that of standing on our own two feet. Getting there is a struggle but the reward is in achievement. This taking charge and making it is the original source of fun and pleasure.

Folk sayings often have classic insights sprinkled in with the clichés. In the folk song *Sixteen come Sunday* there is a wonderful throw-away line near the end when the overeager boy is outwitted by the girl he hopes to have — 'If you will not when you may, you shall not when you would'. What a succinct summary of lost opportunity! The thrust of this line is also contained more directly in the adage about capacity, 'Use it or lose it'. It is inevitable that the infant's innocence becomes blurred and subverted by social coercion and traumas as it progresses. The infant's carers have a great responsibility to interact with the child in a way that acknowledges the child's needs so far as is possible and not from some habitual arbitrary and pre-set override. The opportunity to be open to learning can be mutually nurturing.

Indeed, by sixteen come Sunday, for virtually everyone there have already been many lost opportunities beyond personal control. Habitual patterns are firmly in place. Part of adolescent turmoil springs from an intensely focused realisation of the insecurity which drives the world and their lack of resource to deal with it. It may be wishful thinking but it could well be that the explorations of the Feldenkrais Method such as Ruthy Alon details in this book can provide a substantial base for centering and grounding these concerns. In place of stolid habits the developing person would find both strength and flexibility to cope with the many stormy changes from child to adult.

The later decades of life have always been characterised as inevitably leading to involution; an inescapable decrepitude with fragmentation and poverty of response both in feeling and action. We are compulsively driven by the solidified limitations of the habits so assiduously cultivated and clung to. Increasingly battered by change and with a smaller and still smaller range of adaptation we become bent, twisted and cornered into immobility. We are clever at belated *ad hoc* responses — sticks, artificial joints, intelligent wheelchairs. Is this scenario really inevitable? I think not. We can be equally clever accepting challenge as we meet it. We are different from the sum of our parts; let us not be indifferent to this fact. Instead of watching our decline, by observation and awareness we can use the simple skills outlined by Ruthy Alon to find specific solutions to our problems. One milligram of aware shift through a movement pattern is worth an ignored kilogram of distortion.

Introduction

In formulating rules governing the relation of our complex biology with the environment, traditional educational methods have opted either for an all-out fixed onslaught on the developing organism or have completely bypassed the hunger for fundamental self-awareness. This has had to be won by the individual with enough curiosity and drive left as a personal aside. We have acted as if personal human development were insubstantial and lightweight, left like a weed to force its way to the sun no matter what. We always get the society we pay for. Humans are too diverse and unstable for cloning techniques to work and the end result is that we get neither richness, life-satisfaction nor cohesion. In the current age of the information revolution we distil confusion without direction. This is because knowledge of facts and techniques is baseless without the grounding of direct self-knowledge. We are desperately short on delivery in this area.

Moshe Feldenkrais was one of a small group of pioneers in this century who had the dedication and strength to address their life's work productively to this end. But only he literally had the Feldenkrais Method at his command and fingertips. What he left was an open legacy, a special mirror reflecting the paradox of human commonality and individuality. This means that every person who studies and uses his offering must bring to it creative interpretation. It is no surprise, therefore, that the trainers now dedicated to teaching the Feldenkrais Method contribute the stamp of their own individuality. The few simple rules which are at its core act like a prism allowing them simultaneously freedom in teaching and yet together they manifest the overall focused coherent strength of the method. Because it is experiential it bypasses the traps of abstraction. One can only gain and there are no losers. It is a tool for tapping into and honing personal awareness like few others. And it can be started at any age and by those who are disadvantaged or disabled. It has something for everyone.

A longtime associate of Feldenkrais, Ruthy Alon has developed her own unique way of teaching the method. She is an exemplar of how one can develop along an individual path without deflecting in any way the spirit of Feldenkrais' teaching. Her gift is that of poetic empathy, a rare skill of transmitting the intentionality and beauty of action, for it is only through movement that we are known and can be in the world. Her deft tuning of the essentials is accompanied by a deep understanding of how best to present them. At every turn in the lessons of this volume one captures clear, fresh insights that are the product of her diligent refining.

The Feldenkrais wizardry is to start with the mundane and leave you empowered to face no matter what. Ruthy's magic is to lighten and enliven the partnership of feeling and movement so that this journey has the kind of flow-on from a holiday that does not ever need to end.

Through participating in what she offers, each person has the opportunity to kick the addiction to habit in a pleasurable non-confronting way. By aware, maturing observation one is led gently and securely into a new life path with access to and release of imprisoned spontaneity. The result is the ability to become increasingly sure in taking charge of the direction and dimensions of one's life. Go for it!

Dr Bernard Lake
Consultant physician

1

Functional Honesty

Your version of why you have backache

If a deep curve in the lower back structure was the cause of all back troubles, then millions of people the world over would endure constant suffering.

If the pelvis connected to the spine as a continuous extension was the right structure, then the models for freedom from pain would be those stiff people with backs straight as a board, who move their bodies as a single unit, shifting their feet while turning.

If a flexible back were the answer, then dancers, athletes and acrobats would never be afflicted with backaches.

If the goal was a strong back, then muscular men doing hard physical work would be immune to back misery.

If lifting heavy loads was the source of back pain, then anyone who carries a load, from water-drawers to weight-lifters, would be unavoidably harmed.

If soft stomach muscles were the cause of a weak and painful back, then every child would complain of backache, and each adult who would allow the stomach to relax could expect back pain.

If walking erect — seemingly humankind's unsolicited invention — was the root of the trouble, then generations of human beings since the dawn of evolution would have lived in constant agony.

If pressure on the back expressed pressure in one's soul, then all those happy with their lot would live free of all back distress.

If the back's helplessness was the penalty for exaggerated effort in sex, who would manage to stay away from pain?

Is there a formula to avoid back pain ?

Backache is the number one cause of absence from work, of leisure time wasted in pain, of disappointment in a body that betrays, of frustrating immobility and helplessness, of a declining self-image and a curtailment of our aspiration to do what we truly wish with our lives.

Backaches attack clerks and porters, scholars and illiterates, workers both indoors and out-of-doors, the rich and the poor, country folk and city folk, the fat and the thin, the young and the old, those who routinely bend while working and those who are careful never to bend, those who are active and those who restrict their movements, both men and women alike.

Those disciplined in their routine of forceful exercise believe their backs hurt because they haven't exercised enough, and continue to seek solutions in special-ised additional exercises. Those who refrain from any movements beyond their daily routine believe their backs hurt because they 'got carried away' and tried something irregular. Clerks and managers who keep to their chairs for long hours say their backs hurt from so much sitting. Salesmen and industrial workers who must work erect say their backs hurt from so much standing. Postmen declare it's the walking destroying their backs.

Those whose backs are curved, perhaps deformed, are certain their poor posture causes their misery. Yet there are some people with excessively distorted structures who know nothing of back pain, while some people whose backs seem normal, even impressively stalwart, experience constant agony.

Can there be a single, unequivocal answer to this riddle?

Can one answer solve a problem of intricate and ever varying organic life?

Is human logic, expecting an unequivocal answer, in tune with the logic of Nature?

If you're worried about your back and think all you need is to find the one specific cure, then you may fail to see how the all-inclusive reality of the quality of your life enables your pain to dwell in it. Like many others, you may find it difficult to see that the manner in which you treat your body — your functional asset and the temple of your soul — is inseparable from the manner in which you cope with other aspects of your life.

Are you aware of your approach towards your well-being? How committed are you to enhancing your life in accordance with your taste? How much efficiency and satisfaction do you dare wish for in what you do? Do you feel you need to exert and sacrifice yourself to keep up with the demands of living or do you enthusiastically run ahead of life, following the challenges beyond the hardships, not allowing any setback to deter you from seeking competence and joy? If your attitude to your place in life comes from chronic anxiety, believing life is against you, it will be difficult for you to allow your body greater ease and optimism.

It's the difference between the grinding attempt to halt deterioration and the use of intelligence to learn how to improve. It is the difference between those whose only wish is not to feel the pain in their backs, and those who dare to strive for a life as they truly wish it to be, and are ready to learn how to use their back in a way that will not prevent them from actualising their aspirations.

Have you ever considered that possibly your back's condition is a critical and clear barometer reflecting everything else about you and your stance in life: your soul's uprightness as well as your skeletal uprightness; your vista of hopes, as well as the richness and variety of your movement vocabulary; your resourcefulness to respond to ever-changing situations as well as the coordination between all parts of your body; your social assertiveness as well as your sensitivity to your body's comfort and its feeling of contentment.

Your back at the foreground of your movement ecology

Viewing your back from the perspective of movement quality alone, you will realise that your spine is the juncture of interactions and functions, through which the more remote parts of your body connect and balance one another.

What goes on in your back is evidence of the level of communication throughout your total organism. Once you realise this holistic approach, you cannot avoid taking into consideration the whole, the parts which do not hurt as well as the parts that do. To see the function of the back in the context of the rest of your body, try to recall how your back becomes crooked and rigid when your feet must cope with uneven terrain. The reciprocal bond between your back and your knees is probably familiar to you from experience: it is common knowledge that bending your torso when your knees are straight will flash a warning signal to your back. Perhaps you are less aware of how intimately your back is subjected to the mercy of your ankles. Indirectly, if your ankles refuse to bend generously, elastically, your knees cannot attain that location in space which would allow your pelvis to hang loosely and thus release pressure from your back.

Breathing also serves as a clue to the back's behaviour. Your spine is connected most tangibly to the ribs. The span of movement of each rib determines not only the volume of air in the breathing cycle and the position of the rib, but it also affects the alignment of the vertebra attached to it.

Indeed, there is not a single part or function in your whole self that exists separately from your back, or that is not being expressed through it. The state of your back is conditional upon what and how your neck is capable of moving, the options available to your pelvis, the level of tonus in your calf and thigh muscles, the way weight is distributed in your feet, and the total functional memory of your movements.

For example, when you choose to look at something on your right, does the responsibility to shift your eyes to that point fall only upon the readiness of your sight to glance around? To what extent does your torso also take part in the turning? Does each and every vertebra articulate itself and move separately from the next one all along the spine? Or does rotation take place only in the neck, and even in a very specific point of it? Perhaps you save both the vertebrae of your back and neck the trouble, and change the direction of your face by rotating your pelvis. There are people who need to shift the location of their feet on the floor in order to look sideways; for them, it is easier than bringing about differentiation between the vertebrae.

The way you organise your back is also subject to what happens to your abdomen. Perhaps as you read on you may be willing to review your ideas about the connection between physical fitness and a certain muscle tone in your abdomen, and come to wonder whether a tight belly does in fact bring about promised relief to the back.

Are you aware of the traditional agreement between the various parts of your body as to the division of labour? Sensitive observation of the work carried out by the tubelike passages in the body suggests that the concave-convex action of the lower back is part of a wave movement in which all the sphincters, such as the eyes, fists and digestive tract, work in synchronisation. Accordingly, freedom of your back depends on the tightness or slackness of your anus, and the manner in which your tongue lies at the other end of that long tube.

The feeling of comfort in your back is also influenced by temperature changes. To what degree do you trust your skin to regulate your internal temperature to its optimum, keeping you comfortable inside despite variable environmental conditions? The lower back by its nature is first to express every fear and discomfort, whether you are conscious of them or not, and it will readily express your resistance to cold by contracting.

Have people without backaches learned through conscious intervention to adapt these interactions to their benefit? Are people without pain investing time in deliberate cautiousness and planning to coordinate the many interactions between the back and the rest of the body using some ideal functional chart, movement by movement?

Obviously, this is an impossible mission. It's hard to imagine that it would be possible to monitor even with computers and a highly skilled staff such a complex of reciprocal dependencies and combinations that sustain the functions of the organism. Who then or what carries out the work of gratifying coordination for the carefree person?

The inner migration that monitors the maintenance of life perpetuates its own patterns while at the same time it has the capacity to respond to ever-changing internal and external conditions. The coordination of intricate and complex sequences of vital functions is carried out from one group of muscles to another, without interruption or burnout. The feature of this vitality is its unintentionality, a subconscious intelligence common to all creatures.

Your ability to control the overall balance of your back in the context of the organic action of the entire body is akin to your ability to control and direct your digestion, metabolism, heartbeats, hair growth, or the work of any other vital system which doesn't depend upon your conscious intervention.

Fortunately, the body's movement in space is easier to follow and to change than any other aspect that expresses the embodiment of ongoing life. Human movement in space is a communication ground between intentional movement out of conscious discernment and innate talent for spontaneous and effective self-organisation. In dealing with your back, you actually face an immense network of interactions between your back and the rest of you. Some of the pathways in this network have become impaired, even damaged, from too much use; others have been partially erased or obliterated from disuse, lying forgotten beneath a layer of stubborn habits that cover them like weeds.

The intention of this book is to reinstate the pathways towards clearing a passage for the free flow of movement; to provide you with a map to be deciphered by your own conscious intellect, and to be applied to your field of direct experience by your own sensations. One of the main things you will learn is a way to help your back by encouraging more and more of its network partners to join the cycle of activity with a greater variety of configuration and coordination. Your full range of movement may then stream through more of the pain-free parts of your body and relieve the burden on those specific over-irritated sections of your back. In healing the harmony your back begins to heal too.

It is important for you to realise that on this journey you yourself must be involved. Only you can be alert to your own inner sensations. Only you can navigate your own movement patterns.

Creative exploration versus following instructions

Healing the back is like unravelling a tangle of knots. When you try to release a single thread from the snarl, you soon realise you can gain nothing by forceful pulling. You need another strategy. It is better to find the patience to observe one thing in relation to the other, to observe the uniqueness of each knot.

You try first to pull the thread that gives easily, and at the same time you follow the effects as it drags through the whole tangle. You do this gently so that you can stop at any moment and circumvent further entanglement. Or you can retract and try another direction, taking into account what you observe in the changing configuration. The subtlety of your movements as you undertake this open-ended manoeuvre is what insures your success.

There is an old tale that describes a test of character put to a prospective bride on her first visit to the home of her intended bridegroom's parents. She is given a tangled ball of thread to unravel and as she works at the task she reveals her qualities: sensitivity, resourcefulness, the fidelity to inner grace which avoids impatient confrontation, the ability to breath through frustration and derive from it more ideas for solution.

You need this intelligent state of mind when you come to unravel the knot in your back. Blind obedience to standard exercises which lack creative exploration will leave your back in an endless struggle. Surely you are familiar with the frustration that comes from performing exercises which are meant to help you, but which leave you in greater pain, despite your faithful perseverance.

Is it not possible that the answer lies, not in the kind of exercises, not in the configurations they outline, not even in the wisdom behind them, but rather in the manner in which you execute them?

Should you seek to rehabilitate your aching back through imitation based on borrowed theories, you relinquish your individual sensitivity to all that is special about you, missing the unique and subtle sensations within yourself, sensations that change moment by moment, and can guide you in the discernment of the boundaries safe for you, the limit beyond which you can do yourself harm. When you aren't attentive to your own inner signals, you become more vulnerable to reoccurring injury, like a person lost in the dark.

It's amazing to what extent people are willing to follow strict, demanding, mechanical instructions, excercising dutifully daily, trying hard to do their best, carrying out directions as strongly and as quickly as possible, without considering the sacrifice of so much labour and the meagreness of the results. Some people are willing to invest any effort and pay any price to be free of back pain, except for this one thing: they are unwilling to give their full attention to themselves, to look inward and communicate patiently and kindly with their body.

Many of us have been raised with the dictum that life is about serious obligations, and that we must accept the toll, as if our moral honesty depends upon our readiness to do our utmost — 'utmost' meaning more power, more involvement, more in quantity. We weren't raised to value our utmost in terms of quality, of sensitivity, of loyalty to our inner selves. It is only when we mobilise ourselves to do something energetically that we believe we have done our share; we do not even take notice of the penalty we pay with our body. To be patient and attentive in the graceful and harmonious way does not seem legitimate to us, as if sensitivity were egocentric, and desire for refinement in movement were a luxury.

Perhaps we need to re-define the meaning of achievement and begin to evaluate our performance not only quantitatively, in terms of distance, but also in terms of our inner experience, assessed by our own feelings. Once we come to understand that achievement that is going against the inner sensations of our organism is actually false, we can begin a process of healing.

Denying inner signals

An entire generation was raised to equate physical fitness with the model of bending the torso forward with the knees kept straight and the hands stretching down to touch the floor. This was performed time after time, swiftly and diligently, school style.

Probably none of us could avoid investing our utmost effort and willpower, stretching our muscles to the maximum, as if not only social recognition but our self-respect depended on our success in touching the floor. To this bending was added the belief that we were doing the right thing to keep ourselves in shape. While bending we clenched our teeth as if it were some sort of emergency, we probably held our breath, and we strained the neck, not allowing the head to hang down through its own weight; not because it deepened the bend, but because the eyes are not accustomed to relinquishing control of what is happening in front. We strained our back muscles like someone about to uproot a tree in one swoop. The more we succeeded in stretching our leg muscles, forcing our hands toward the floor, the more convinced we became that we would never achieve any results without wilful pushing and struggling to overcome our body's resistance.

Our success only reconfirmed the notion that we are helpless as we are, on our own, when we don't interfere to help life along. More than ever we became certain that we could rely only on our willpower to manoeuvre and achieve results from our reluctant body. This kind of movement is like a loan — we don't own it.

Was it possible to enjoy that success, which only reminds you how weak you are, a stepson of life? We came to believe in the conflict between our desire and our natural inclination. The relationship with our body became manipulative. Self-discipline, holding ourselves in control, became the norm. If for one day we failed to maintain our quota of exercise, we feared our achievement level would flounder, further proof that our body awaits the opportunity for evasion. We didn't even take a moment to wonder whether the vigorous enforcement itself might be the factor that caused the body to overreact in withdrawal.

Such an exercise demonstrates a total disregard of those invisible inner signals by which the body broadcasts its precise complaints via the tissues and nerves. If, on the following day, the pain is too great to be ignored, this is taken to support the theory that pain is proof of the movement's value — 'no pain, no gain' — and we push on in the same style with greater determination. We are engaged in a dispute with our body, believing that the more we demand of it, the better the results. Results are measured in numbers: How close can the hands come to the floor? How many times per minute? How many bends without pause? Digits, stopwatches, and yardsticks. We assume we are objective, that we have taken the scientific approach.

Qualities that can't be measured

Such an approach does not allow you to perceive what can be known from the right side of the brain. When only quantitative results are taken into account, then the full, rich inner world of coordinative detail is lost, as are the endless possibilities of the ever-varying proportions of invested power as movement migrates from place to place. Lost is the permission to feel the grace and pleasure when the investment is congruent with the movement produced: the observation of the configuration; the tone in which you communicate with yourself; all the subtle sub-sensations that compose your attitude to movement — all the sophisticated qualities twining, as does the organic fabric of the brain itself.

When bodily movements appear to us as straight and one-dimensional, so does our thinking become superficial. Not only do we impoverish our movements within a prison of square forms, but we also dry up the inventive powers of the imagination, preventing them from playing with the manifold possibilities of ourselves in space.

Numbers are no testimony of long-term results. They impart nothing of the impaired relationship between the analytic, ambitious brain, seeking social recognition, and the frustrated organism. Numbers cannot reflect the punishment sure to come as this organism develops a prejudice against any exercise, when left to its own free will. And so, to break through your inner resistance to move, each time you have to summon up greater willpower and physical strength. This is the interest you pay on that loan.

Children are taught physical education throughout their school years. What is left of it in the end? How much readiness and enthusiasm do they have for exercises as independent adults, free of coercive frameworks?

Moving today so you'll love moving tomorrow

In your confrontation with your organism, what you are left with is not the action you have performed, but the organism's response to that action. What counts is to what extent the organism is willing to accept the direction you have given it. The result is what emerges of its own autonomous consideration in response to the action taken. This reaction is sometimes contrary to the intention of the action. A muscle forcefully stretched will react by contracting with equal intensity, as consistently as a reflex.

With this understanding of organic dynamics, you may begin to seek a style of moving which your body will be enthusiastic to repeat in the future of its own accord.

Few people consciously decide to return to a form of exercise they have started — just for the sheer pleasure of it. They have good reasons: improving health, physical fitness, shapeliness and appearance. But how many of us move for the sheer pleasure of it, from a direct feeling of loving the experience of flowing movement, with no need of a reason beyond the attraction of being carefree, for the joy of knowing that we were born to move, and with the conviction that freedom of movement is our birthright, needing no further justification?

The dynamics of getting out of bed — a choice between well-being and self-injury

After you get a taste of spontaneous harmony in the Awareness Through Movement process of restoring organic functioning, you may realise, on looking back, how poorly and disjointedly you have lived with your own body's movement until now.

Functional Honesty

An ordinary routine like getting out of bed, repeated countless times, without giving it a thought, can, if carried out consciously, become the medium for a full revision of attitude towards movement.

Do you have any idea how you usually deal with gravity when you lift your body weight from its prone position to a sitting position? Do you sit up directly or rise up through your side, and is it always the same side? What do you strain? Which is the critical moment? What happens to your breathing? What do you feel in your lower back, in your stomach, in your jaw? Which way do you turn your head? What configuration does the movement outline in space? As you learn to pay attention, a host of details begin to come to light.

Exploring this process in the context of a lesson done on the floor guides you to experiment with a series of movements and invites you to follow up on the sensations they induce. You may initiate the process of rising by drawing up your legs and bending your knees over your chest, signalling the body to curl up like a ball, to facilitate the rolling. You roll over to one side, moving slowly to and fro while listening to the inner dynamics of your rolling motion.

Observe how the pressure of your weight is transferred accordingly to that side, and how your rib cage and shoulder blades yield to the pressure and become more pliant on the floor. Discern how the direction of your eyes contributes to the flow of the rolling motion.

You may try different ways of passing your knees from the middle to the side and feel what works more easily: passing your knees together or separately, moving them simultaneously from start to finish, or allowing one to lag behind the other. You can then identify the way in which one knee has to be active and when it can simply trail along with economic passivity. You can locate that area of your back which is imprinted on the floor by the sideways motion, and also become aware of that area you avoid leaning on.

Meanwhile your head participates in the rolling motion, yet it does not lose contact with the ground. You allow your head to enter a rotation that turns your face to the floor, while its weight is still supported, through whatever point of contact, on the mat or on your arm. This detail, which is not common for most people, has special significance. The first thing most people do on intending to get up is to raise their head into the air, in a frontal forward lift. Raising the head up from a static position of lying on the back places the burden entirely on the neck, which must strain to pick up the full weight of the head while the nape of the neck is being bent backward with a sharp incurve. The weight of the head works in this way to increase compression on the cervical vertebrae, at the very sensitive and tender hinge.

On the other hand, should the head leave the ground from the sideways position, facing down, a position arrived at by rolling over, it provides a safe experience for the neck. The weight of the head suspended face-down works to release the pressure from the rounded convexity of the neck and spreads out more space between

Rolling from lying to sitting
If you are willing to accept the idea of rotation, take the time to round your back and roll on the side, turning your face to the ground and for a moment relinquish control of the world. The spiral motion raises you to a sitting position gracefully and fluently. Your neck remains comfortable and you get up with a feeling that the day ahead is going to be comfortable as well.

the vertebrae's protuberances.

Having rolled over a number of times now, you rest, and listen to the changes that have taken place. You may discover differences between your two sides. The side that did the rolling may be settled on the ground now somewhat differently from the other side onto which you rolled. Learning to discern ever-so-subtle sensations, you can begin to appreciate accurate feedback from your organism about the way you use it.

Continuing to roll, still on the same side (so that you first gain a greater clarity of the details of your movement organisation), pay special attention not to arrest the movement of the head, allowing it to wander on its rotating journey and outline a curve in space. Through this unceasing, brushlike motion, your head finds itself gradually lifting off the ground while being suspended by its weight, face-down.

The legs are also involved in rising. At the appropriate moment you may extend one leg downward and thus work to draw your head higher up on the other end of this see-saw lever. Your hands have a vital role to play in the process of coming to a sitting position. Allowing yourself to place one hand in front of you on the ground for support, you spare your neck much unnecessary exertion. That moment when your head and chest leave the ground is just one phase in the continuous round movement. It comes about effortlessly, and insignificantly, with no threat to your neck, without jerkiness in your back or stomach, and without interfering with your breathing.

While you continue to roll back and forth on your side until the momentum of the rolling lifts you gently and easily to a full sitting position, you do not place the burden of sitting up on your neck. Instead you leave that initiative to the biggest and strongest part of you — your pelvis. In rotating your pelvis, you entrust the movement to the wisdom of the spiral which lifts you up smoothly and gracefully to the sitting position.

Soon you will be ready to apply the process of arising to your other side, exploring the different personality you may discover there. Eventually you will be able to roll over and sit up with equal ease on each side. Such a symmetrically rounded swinging motion allows you a variety of ways of using your hands, and eventually you will be able to sit up without having to lean on them at all. The moment will come when you no longer need to remember the details, and you can trust your inner sense of coordination. Enriched through the process, it takes over and leads you now in flowing spontaneity.

The greatest difficulty is to believe you can move without difficulty

Eventually the process of the repetitive transition from lying down to sitting up becomes simple, clear and not at all tiring. The greater problem lies in letting go of the belief that sitting up is bound to be difficult. If, like many others, you were brought up on the myth of 'sit-ups', you probably assumed that you were okay only when you felt you had overcome difficulties, paying the penalty of strain in your neck, stiffness in your jaw, and tightness in your stomach. Thus you began your daily routine of getting up in the morning by deliberately throwing yourself abruptly into high gear, head first, just to reassure yourself that you were in good shape. And that strain in the neck confirmed for you the conviction that the day ahead would have in store for you many challenges to overcome as well, a conviction reinforced each morning by the profoundly suggestible state of the mind at the time of waking up.

Once you have realised how easy and pleasurable sitting up from a lying down position can be, in comparison to your habitual way, you'll begin to wonder whether it might be legitimate after all to choose the easy way. You may be more receptive then to the idea that the easy is simple, and the simple is right.

Right in terms of efficiency or right in terms of choice?

The lesson on the floor is not intended to demonstrate the only right way, but rather to allow you to discover your possibilities. Your habitual way of arising may not be right not because of its wasteful organisation carrying penalties, but because it binds you into a compulsive pattern, a pattern that conceals from you that another way of organisation is possible too. Habits leave no choice.

Mastering choice, you are free to decide for yourself whether you would like to sit up by raising your head forward at the risk of your neck, or whether you prefer to save your energy for something else. At this level of awareness you may see the advantage of indulging yourself, and invite the rolling motion to carry you up in pleasure. You may even begin to believe that the day ahead will have in store for you carefree leisure, support, and permission to be loyal to your own needs.

Once you've deciphered, by awareness, a pleasurable way of getting up, you will no longer be able to raise your head first and tell yourself that the reason you have pain in your neck is that your body is against you. If you persist in choosing the self-injurious way after having had a taste of the other option, it will become evident to you that it's not your neck that is so stubborn, but something else deep inside you, which refuses to let you be kind to yourself.

Encouraging the drive towards self-assertion

Beyond the re-modification of your habitual way of getting up, the process works at a deeper level to encourage the organism's right to strive for what feels more comfortable and safe for it. The intention of the process is to support your orientation towards improvising movements that are healthier and more efficient; to awaken a faculty that is designed to safeguard your existence; to develop your sensory powers of listening, feeling and exploring; and to refresh the aptitude of your intelligence for perceiving, evaluating and navigating. This innate guide has been vouch-safed to every creature launched into life.

Every movement in the process of the Feldenkrais Method, carried out with listening and awareness, provides an opportunity for making contact with your inner guide. Your innate wisdom knows how to select, among many options, the one which best supports your life.

If you suffer from persistent pain in your neck, and go on injuring yourself each morning by jumping abruptly out of bed as soon as the alarm clock goes off, lifting your head over a cramped neck, never feeling how you reinforce the damage, then no mechanical exercise supposed to make you flexible will do any good. What you need is to rehabilitate your instinct for self-preservation.

Such an instinct has guided you in the past. It saw you safely through a long line of experimental explorations that began when you were a baby. You seemed to amuse yourself by moving clumsily, with no apparent meaning or sequence, with unverbalised sensations and with no one guiding you. At a deeper level your instinct was deducing, selecting and screening what was life-worthy, until you gained mastery of your limbs and succeeded in standing up on your feet. It taught you how to fall without getting hurt, and urged you to keep trying and moving through the process of self-refinement.

As you grew into a child, your instinct guided you to coordinate your movements with harmony and grace. You ran, jumped and climbed, loving to do it over and over again with ease and with boundless energy, as a direct need of the life bursting forth from within you.

Where did you lose the compass to your well-being?

Somewhere along the path to maturity, your instinct became blunted, and lost its beneficial orientation.

Was it those classroom chairs against which, after a while, you stopped trying to revolt, that suppressed your instinct to move? Or, did you give up moving around by yourself, believing you'd be considered a good child if you stopped wriggling about? Did you lose your resourcefulness for organic coordination through being taught to obey and imitate 'the correct movements' as demonstrated by those physical education authorities? Or perhaps your resourcefulness didn't have a chance to develop in the monotonous challenges of mechanical performance and endurance that conventional gymnastics required of you.

Did you lose your grace and ease when your social status — and your self-appreciation — depended on how many times you succeeded in repeating arbitrary straight lines, exercises that shocked your system, while forcing you to ignore the protest from within?

Or perhaps you no longer sought opportunities to move, since movement became linked with the motivation of competition, leaving you with a bitter taste of frustration when you lost a race in spite of your sincere efforts, or worse still, having won and felt alone in your victory.

How did you give up the right to a rhythm of your own?

Perhaps your individual rhythm became impaired when you were told to stop day-dreaming, and in the years that followed you impeded the self-renewal that can emerge from such pauses in activity; being swept away by the sweetness of a moment's detachment behind a veil of meditation became for you a wasteful, even shameful indulgence.

Perhaps you were praised when you hurried, praised for accomplishment and achievement. You learned to perform under pressure, quick to get up, quick to answer, quick to eat — so much so that even with free time on your hands, you would no longer even recall how to do such things with carefree pleasure. If you ever allowed yourself a pause for non-doing, being tired, you regarded that as some kind of failure on your part. Instead of interpreting fatigue as a lesson in yielding to gentleness, softening to innocence, as a signal for sinking into comforting indulgence, you trained yourself to stiffen your body, investing the remnants of your strength to withstand your need to rest.

At present perhaps you may have drifted into working extra hours, committed yourself to more and more obligations, including even the task of searching for your spiritual development. You keep on accumulating your body's lack of sleep and rest, and get used to functioning at the chronic level of borrowing on life. You don't hear your organism's cry of protest. Nor are you attentive to its needs, pausing to consider it only when it collapses on you. You don't see that when you are at the point of giving either your maximum or collapsing, you have actually relinquished control, your ability to steer your life. You don't know how to intentionally reverse your accelerated involvement. You don't know how to decrease your inner tension or restore the vitality that has become impoverished through self-erosion.

Yawning — how do you accept Nature's gift of self-renewal?

You don't even allow yourself a pause to yawn, as it comes to you from Nature. You try resisting the yawn, and when you don't succeed in eliminating it, at its start, you then try to at least limit its volume and quickly conceal the gape behind your hand.

Yawning is a universal phenomenon in the living world. Through yawning, Nature pulls you out from being stuck in a shallow metabolic level. It shakes you out of the stagnation of the partial, poor utilisation of what you could have been. Yawning awakens you to collect the debt of your deficient breathing, and receive all the oxygen you dared not take. The yawn guides you to stretch out and manifest the full span of your muscles in a complete, pleasurable way which no wilful intention on your part could have attained. With your mouth wide open, its extension echoes

throughout your total organism. Through hidden pathways of internal synchronisation, all the tube-like organs, such as the passages in your digestive tract, respiratory system and sexual organs, resonate with the yawn and expand as well. In this
awakening all your parts re-connect with a more coherent and lively pulsation, and
you return to reality with a fuller presence.

In order for the yawn to occur, though, it requires a certain threshold of ease. The
yawn cannot break through tight muscles with the entire organism recruited to a
state of emergency. However, when you reduce your extra involvement, when you
let go of your defensiveness and coercion and turn your listening inward, when you
begin to allow yourself to be as you are with no exhausting pretensions, then Nature
will grant you the gift that opens up the blocked dams. Society, in encouraging only
externally manifested orientation, interprets the yawn as a statement of boredom,
and teaches you to apologise for this social offence.

Was there ever anyone who took care to balance you, teaching you that sometimes you are also allowed to be faithful to yourself, and trust the needs arising
from within?

Blame or praise — eroding your power to judge for yourself

Did you stop taking pride in your body because of frustrating criticism that repeatedly exhorted you to stand straight, as if standing straight depended on your will
and your readiness to obey? Or was it other people's admiration of your well-per-
formed tricks that taught you to realise that in order to receive acknowledgement of
how wonderful you were, you had to summon up all your resources for showing
off? You tried to excel for the teacher, and devised ways to impress your friends.
Years later, even when you were alone, your approval-seeking ego was still in
need of witnesses, to grant you reinforcement, even if the witnesses existed only in
your imagination.

In accepting criticism, as well as admiration, you gave away to others the power
of judging yourself and got used to being dependent on their presence, growing
remote from your own inner voice.

Your shape — the only thing you wouldn't do for it is accept it

What is it about your body that disturbs you — its shape as perceived by others, or
the way your body feels to you, which only you know ?

Are you one of those who see their own image according to its deviation from the
norm of weights and measures, rendering to the world your long line of failures, of
mechanical eating that has gone beyond your control? If you have tried changing
your figure through the sanctions of all kinds of diets, you know with humility how
hard it is to achieve long-lasting results when you choose the way of direct conflict
with your organic needs.

Have you ever noticed that the most dominant message radiating from you, beyond your shape and level of competence, is the one thing that is actually within your choice? Above all, what your body broadcasts and what is most perceived by others is your own attitude towards your body. People pick up what you think of yourself. And you are willing to make every effort to win their love — except for you to be loving your own body.

Clothes that make the person — a case of claustrophobia

Is it the clothes you wear that limit your movements, the too-tight pants, the elastic squeezed waist, the belt pulled in too harshly, or the pinched bra? Even your breathing gives up trying to overcome such constrictions and remains limited to a shallow compromise: you use only a part of the range of movement of your ribs, only part of the volume of your lungs, with only a small quantity of oxygen somehow able to infiltrate the barriers.

In Ethiopia, on wash day, the banks of a river are covered with rectangular strips of cloth spread out on the grass to dry. These are the natives' clothes. Such a strip of cloth, soft and pliant, is wrapped around their bodies with traditional skill. When they stride, the cloth comes alive in a game of rippling folds which conceal the structure of each separate limb, but conveys the flow of movement from within.

In contrast, in our advanced civilised culture we believe that clothes make the person. We take pride in clothes tailored to fit precise measurements relating to some static shape. If, added to that, the material is also of a sturdy texture, then such clothing implies an almost claustrophobic style, manipulating the wearer into behaving like the mannequin on which it was designed.

Perhaps the ornaments that always decorate the front of your clothing led you to believe that your possibilities extended only in front of you. Your neglected back has not been called upon to participate in planning your movements. When one bent vertebra in the curve of your lower back collapses under the compression of your weight and is repeatedly worn down in the same notorious spot, you don't know how to guide it to safety. You will push and pull and distort irrelevant areas, but have no mastery over specific sections of the spine like you have mastery in making a fist, or like a musician intentionally activating just one finger. Perhaps the long process of development of the musician's skill can give you a sense of direction for rescuing your back from its trouble.

What goes on in your back behind you is out of sight and out of mind. Imagine what it would feel like if you wrapped yourself in a Japanese kimono, having a unique and ornate embroidery covering the back. Can you figure out the revolution in the order of priorities concerning your functional orientation which could take place?

Shoes — form at the price of mobility

One glance at your feet will reveal the way in which you treat them. Do you provide your feet with a variety of challenges to encourage their wisdom for springiness, within enough space and comfort, or do you constantly beat them upon monotonous cement surfaces, placing them in the torture stocks decreed by fickle fashion that restricts your movement and gives you pain all the way up to your shoulders? The way your toes are lined up in your shoes will dictate how each vertebra will align one on top of the other. The degree of permission you give your feet to change and adjust in a sophisticated and sensitive way will determine whether the world is a pleasant, welcoming place for you, or if you must constantly be cautious, forever on guard to balance yourself over the pitfalls of life, distorting and exhausting yourself in dealing with the burden of your own weight.

Can you recall a time when your enthusiasm for this whole adventure on earth used to sing through the rich and versatile springiness of each and every one of the joints of your many foot bones?

There are shoes available today which are suited perfectly to the mould of your foot, as if they were made from the impression of a footstep in the sand. While congruently supporting the entire surface of your foot, they give it the freedom to play and manoeuvre while carrying on its dialogue with the ground in walking.

How do you cope with carrying a load?

Perhaps it was your school bag that impaired your walk and your posture, as you carried it in your hand, always on the same side, or — at best — on your back, with its straps pressing into your shoulders, provoking them to lift up in defence. Or you might have been amongst those who knew how to benefit from their school bags, and carried it on your head, in the style of water-bearers. The burdensome weight on the head triggers off the organism's response to counterthrust, thus aligning the entire spine to straighten upwards.

Have you ever tried the solution of the people in Nepal? There, the straps of the load carried are placed across the forehead, stimulating it in this way to butt upward and forward — a direction which all seekers of good posture long for. The burden itself, settled on the back, invites the hollow in the lower back to push backward and fill out, while the bent hands hanging on to the straps can with little effort regulate the pressure put upon the head.

The trouble with what you don't do

It is possible that your back trouble lies in those acts which you don't do. You probably don't crawl at all, and have forgotten when you last rolled over. You never butt; you don't suspend yourself upside down; you don't jump or skip any more. You don't curl up or swing; you don't climb, and maybe you don't even push and pull. Society expects you to have a solid and reserved appearance. Your work is being done for you by wheels and elevators. The tension from this exhausting monotony of your non-doing remains in your stressfully staring eyes, utilising them like crutches to sustain all your pent-up unexpressed involvement.

How you stopped daring

Did your parents, out of concern for you, constrict your daring to move? When you balanced, placing one foot carefully in front of the other on a narrow ledge, practising the most intelligent of your moving talents, your kinesthetic sense for equilibrium, didn't your parents say, 'Get down; you'll fall!'. Or when you spun around on your own axis, turning and turning, an exclusive skill of bipedal man, and your accelerated vitality trained your eyes to softness and flow, as dictated by the sophisticated coordination of high-spinning velocity, didn't your parents tell you, 'Stop spinning; it will make you dizzy'? You received a clear message from the people most important to you that movement meant danger, and your need to dare and experience it, to explore and decipher its sensation, worried them.

There are still some places on earth where grown-up people can quickly climb up tall, smooth trees to pick coconuts in order to drink their milk. They do it with effortless grace, with humorous joy, and with a simplicity taken for granted. You can be sure that when they grew up, no one said to them: 'Watch out'; 'Come down from there; It won't end in good'; 'How often have I told you not to climb'; 'I have no patience for your tricks', and you understood that a good child sits still.

To take risks and climb with perfect skill is inherent within potential human capacity. It was cut short by the warnings of authoritarian adults, who out of sincere concern for the child's safety, overlooked the importance of the innate drive to learn. The developing child's inquisitive urge didn't always win the parents' appreciation, nor did the need to interact with the environment, discovering by experiment strength and competence to cope with it, receive due parental respect. Such a warning attitude penetrates the growing mind, and the young person will absorb it even despite resistance to it. Like brainwashing, it will control all future considerations and reactions in a way that will not easily be given over to change, just like all the other social attitudes that children pick up on their path of growing.

The prototype of stretching

Perhaps all this began much earlier, at the very start, when you first came into the world. If you were lucky, your first experience of full stretching was a very pleasant one, emerging from you when you were comfortable and ready, supported with love. However, if you were born in a modern hospital, having just burst forth from your mother's womb with no chance to orient yourself in the different atmosphere — the dry air and blinding lights — you were abruptly pulled up by your heels, hanging in the air, convulsing with terror, and were smacked on your behind to ascertain that you were breathing.

Your softly curved back, that since you were formed was curled within in a shell-like fold, safely surrounded by your mother, was harshly dragged into a stretch. While subjected to the shock of this jerky upside-down stretch, you were exposed to the total void with the fear of falling, which is the deepest of all fears on earth.

Is this not how the civilised world introduced you to your own body? This shock was imprinted in your brain at the most receptive moment possible. Perhaps the lesson then registered in the nervous system might be that straightening and stretching involve a threat. Years later, whenever you feel upset, your body will seek solace by sinking back into that initial, rounded, enfolding position that did not have a chance to mature at its own pace, and you shorten and reduce your stature.

Injury to the spine of the personality

After all this, if your back hurts, you may still think that all you need now is to know how to properly align one vertebra on top of another. You don't realise that actually it is the spine of your personality that became injured, as you ceased feeling how deprived you are, and you weren't able to rise in protest against that which oppressed your development. The vital instinct for survival that signals warning to every living creature to avoid danger, does not work for you. You've lost the mechanism for independent judgement that knows how to navigate you to that which is best for you. You adopted approaches that were based on other peoples' views as to what's best.

This all began too early, before you knew how to assert yourself. You were helpless, fully open to learning what your patrons expected you to do, and you remained unaware of your right to consider your own sensitivities. You grew up ignorant of how to take care of your own personal ecology. You manoeuvre your body without trusting its inner wisdom. You aren't even able to differentiate any more between the voice of your own natural, original instincts and the voice coming from habitual compromise with reality.

Improvement through the restoration of sensitivity

The compass that will lead you out of the maze of your back troubles won't be another recipe for a cure, nor a revolutionary technique requiring discipline. It will rather come through the restoration of your sensitivity toward yourself, your ability to cultivate a refined level of listening to the way in which you use your own body, following the revelations of your existence while enacting them; returning autonomy to your inner wisdom of independent inquiry; renewing your talent to find out the pleasant way in every situation, sharpening your response to the ever-continuing challenges that life presents to you, experiencing and passing through them efficiently and gracefully, and moving on with a more perfected and self-reliant body.

You can find this sense only inside yourself. It is still there, present with no right to vote, hidden under the mechanical actions and habits that refuse to undergo an updated inspection for competency. When this sense reawakens, and you listen to what it has to say about the quality of your movement, as you're moving, when you observe humbly and review from the very start how you are doing what you are doing — even if you're certain you know how to do it — there is a chance that the automatic functioning, hypnotised into self-perpetuation without being aware of the price it cost you, will become open to transformation and will make room for a sensitive style, the greatest virtue of which is that it can improve itself.

Healing through progress

In order to heal the back, you must go beyond settling the conflict by a compromise of limited existence. If you're seeking only to remove the pain, then you're stuck in that same narrow-mindedness that has created the pain in the first place. However, when you are looking for progress — when you begin to enjoy discovering more and more of the rich variety of possibilities that are available to you, when you become unwilling to give up the pleasure that is embodied in the quality of grace and ease in your actions, when you choose to incorporate all the parts of your organism to function as one unified family, each giving support to the others, when you sharpen your ability to adjust, to manoeuvre, to be resourceful — you are training yourself for an organic honesty that carries within itself the healing of your back.

In order to heal your back, you have to heal the sense of your organic self-worth, to allow yourself to be more selective in your style of movement, out of enthusiasm for the possibilities that life holds for you. The healing of your back will take a free ride on the momentum of the breakthrough taking place — a breakthrough to a wider perspective for developing your body wisdom, towards a more refined and improved quality of moving, in an attitude that strives for harmony. When you can enhance the entire level of your functioning, then your back, too, will begin to recover from its depressed state. You stop using your back in a harmful way not by being careful and avoiding hurt, but by beginning to investigate the extended range of options available within the entire movement spectrum.

Awareness — the grammar of your lost spontaneity

The same sensitivity serving the mechanism which guards you against danger, accurately signalling your safe boundaries, also nourishes your search for improvement. As you become more and more aware, become sensitive to your sensations, you increase your competence in the observation of subtleties, and can point out those small details that make all the difference in quality.

It is not the movement that brings about the improvement, but rather your being attuned to its inner dynamics within you. It isn't the configuration as seen in space that generates the refinement, but rather the discovery it initiates inside, between you and yourself. It isn't the achievement measured by numbers that raises you to a level of relief, but rather the perception of the attitude required in order to produce it.

Probably you are not ready to give up the occupation which, in your opinion, may be causing you backaches. You certainly can't change the fact that you stand on two feet. You can hardly change your own unique structure, even should you wish to. However, it is up to you to change the style in which you function. You are gifted with an ability to transform the atmosphere in which you move, to alter the tone in which you communicate with your organism. You have the facility to nurture your bond with your own body by having more respect for its responses. Attentive listening to your inner self is the crossroad at which the intent of your conscious mind meets the deeper workings of your nervous system. Such mindful awareness, a unique human talent, is your tool for reviving your lost organic spontaneity.

2

Organic Learning — Learning Through Options

Are we all premature infants?

Immediately after birth, a tiny blind kangaroo joey is able to crawl up its mother's body to find the pouch intended for it.

A giraffe colt enters this world while its mother is walking around. This means that upon birth it falls from a height of 2 metres and instantly recovers, gets up onto its feet, and is able to take its first steps at the pace of the moving herd.

A human infant needs approximately a year to find the ability to stand up on its feet and begin to mobilise itself. This protracted process of gaining independence of function is reminiscent of the retardation of premature babies, whose development is vulnerable and delayed to an extent which is out of proportion to the missing pregnancy time. Being exposed to the challenges of existence before they are ready for them, the prematurely born need much more time than full-term babies to catch up with their stages of development. It looks as if the slow recovery of 'premies' from that initial helplessness is the penalty that Nature inflicts for interfering with its intended rhythm. The rush to develop doesn't pay, says Nature, because in the long run a much higher and more complex patience will be required in order to mature and safely arrive at functional independence. From this point of view, we can look upon the process of the prolonged development of premies as a symbolic example of the obstacles to human development as compared to that of other living creatures.

If I may further speculate — it might be that the Homo sapiens female who rose up on her two hind legs, had difficulty carrying her pregnancy to full term and gave birth before her time. Early birth became a collective mutation of bipeds. If this is so, all of us humans are actually premature babies who are paying the penalty of original haste.

There is another parallel between premature infants and humans in general.

It is not only premature babies who are constrained in completing the brain's growth and the maturation of their various functions when they are out of the womb, but in all humankind too the brain continues to develop and undergo changes long after birth. This is in distinct contrast to other creatures, who come into the world with a completely formed brain equipped with pre-set skill patterns with no need for a long period of training. They have the fitness to propel themselves and the ability to cope with their surroundings. Instead of the pre-learning of the collective reservoir of uniform instincts in a certain species, each one of us humans must, on his own, create his own personal repertoire of habits which he or she will adapt, conditioned by the experiences of early life. Through this process we progressively sophisticate our proficiencies, our resourcefulness in problem solving; we master the ability to learn and have the chance to strengthen our own unique characteristics.

The fact that the human brain takes its shape while at the mercy of the accidental conditions of its growth environment leaves room for individual variety, the like of which is difficult to find among other creatures. Feldenkrais used to say that if you watch the movements of cats, even for a long time, you will find it difficult to discern differences between them . . . but when you watch human beings, even if they are uniformly dressed, you will immediately observe the distinctive characteristics of each individual.

Whatever the destiny of development, when human infants are born before their due time, in actuality they are twice premature. They are premies as regards their personal fate, and premies as human beings. They are especially helpless: in order to remain alive, they need more than the endless devotion of their parents, but also the devotion of the whole team of nurses and doctors in the premature wards. In addition, they are dependent upon advanced medical knowledge, on oxygen tents and a network of sophisticated equipment.

There is also another saving factor — the senso-kinetic factor. It has been re-discovered today that in order to enhance the premies' development and to bring them more safely through their immature stages, they need touch and mobility. The more they are in direct contact with another human being, touched gently all over their bodies, and the more they are provided with soft rocking (whether by means of a waterbed or being cradled in a person's arms), the more successfully they overcome breathing difficulties, gain weight, and the faster they move on from helplessness to a state of strength. Live contact and movement recreate the sensory climate of the mother's womb. In the womb, all the surfaces of the foetus' body are held in permanent contact, and are carried in a perpetual and unpredictable rocking motion.

These two life-giving sensations — movement and touch — are in fact the field of interest and the contribution of the Feldenkrais Method.

For all of us who, from a development point of view, were all born prematurely, some to a greater and some to a lesser extent, there is a significant meaning in this method. People can satisfy their longings for gratifying movement when, in the group lessons of Awareness Through Movement, they receive guidelines for soft movement that is open to its discoveries, always within the boundaries of comfort and at their own pace. As in early life, their bodies are fully supported as they lie on the ground; or they can receive, in the private Functional Integration lesson, the touch of the teacher — a touch which reassures and guides — again, while their weight is fully supported lying on the table.

In this way, they learn to learn again, as they did in the beginning. This book is devoted to that part of the method which sheds light on the world of movement.

Early learning

Professor Bergson, Director of the Eye Department in Jerusalem's Shaare Zedek Hospital, testifies that if there is a need to operate on a baby's eye, it is necessary to remove the bandages after three days at the most, and to leave the wound exposed. It has been found that if the eye remains covered for more than three days, it will become a lazy eye forever, and the growing child will not rely on its use.

This is shocking information about the limitations of natural learning. Even though humans are the most learning of creatures, still it appears that our ability to adjust can be blocked — in this case because of a delay of no more than three days! It is clear that this delay has the crucial power to cause an impairment which remains throughout the person's entire life, only because it occurs simultaneously with a specific stage of development in the growing infant. Tracking this phenomenon can lead us to the essence of Feldenkrais' way of thought in his method for improving human function.

One of the distinctions that illuminate the Feldenkrais way of thinking is the integral approach to function. Movement in the living body does not occur as a separate and local phenomenon; rather, it takes place in the context of consistent coordination with all the other parts of the organism. Movement becomes a skilful formulated function by repetitively confirming its relationships throughout the entire network, activating some parts in a certain way while inhibiting others.

The re-education of movement utilises this organic principle of interdependence, by cultivating new correspondences between the parts of the organism. Viewing movement as a relationship between the part and the whole is one of the things that makes this method so effective in reaching the clues of habit and restoring function. In other words, to practise exercises with the eye alone may not bring results; but to differentiate eye movement from its conditioned relationships to the movement of the spine and limbs, and create new ones instead, will scramble the code of habit and bring an ever-progressive improvement.

Feldenkrais gained his insights for re-organising human function by observing the process of creating habitual patterns at the dawn of life, which Nature used when it succeeded in transforming the helpless infant into a self-mobilised person. Opening a habit to change can be attained by following the same principles which inhere when habits were created in the first place. What is this process of forming habit moulds?

Through the intensive transformations which take place at the dawn of life, development makes its way from the accidental to the organised, from the random to the orderly, from the summoning-up of all, without discrimination, to the selective differentiated act. The earlier the time of development, the more newness the infant will have to confront. The process of self-orientation in this maze earns the infant individual choices; in adapting its own style of functioning the infant is not pre-equipped with automatic solutions but has to arrive at them itself by means of experience and deduction. From these, the infant chooses for use those methods which have proved to give it satisfaction and the gratification of its desires. The preferred method of performance is the bud of an acquired habit.

The disadvantage in selecting from an accidental range of alternatives is the increased chance of error, and the trap of remaining stuck with that mistake. Therefore, perhaps, if an eye operation was performed on one eye at the crucial age when the brain was formulating its method for interpreting visual images into vision that makes sense, then during the time one eye remained closed, the other eye would acquire more competence in this skill. And the important point here is that the method of clarifying vision has already become linked to the coordination of the rest of the functions in the other parts of the body, which simultaneously become more comprehensive.

There is, for instance, a bond between the eye and the directing of the whole skeleton. A glance directed at an object located on the right side will immediately trigger a certain rotation of the pelvis towards the right, which will pull the whole backbone and rib-cage to twist with it, so that the head can more easily reach to the right and home-in its teleceptors on the object. The act elicits a willingness to stretch out the hand, as well as the setting of each leg accordingly. One leg will become the anchored pivot, and the other will be more free to move and adjust its location. Sharpening the coordination between the hand and the eye plays a significant role in orienting oneself in space and estimating its dimensions. Steering a car, for instance, will be inconceivable without this eye-hand bond.

When the baby's other eye opens — weak from its operation, having missed out on the meaningful events which have taken place among the latest innovations of development — it can evoke a sensation of alienating dissonance. When the brain has to take into consideration what the injured eye sees, to decipher and interpret that, not only will it have difficulty in coordinating the different information from each eye, but it will also confuse what the healthy eye has learned. Even if the brain found a way to adjust to the lack of symmetry between one eye and the other, the links which have been forged between the healthy eye and the totality of all other bodily functions will not allow it to relinquish easily the special way in which it has learned to organise itself to its satisfaction. Just like the giraffes and the ditch, the organism which consistently seeks the comfort of the present is inclined to choose the line of least resistance. It prefers sometimes to discard altogether the information of the retarded eye and thus rid itself of the burden of coping with the strangeness of the gap. This is a solution of compromise, a giving up of a degree of vitality, which continues to become fixated the more it is utilised. With the ever-increasing gap, the denial of it increases too.

What is more, if both the infant's eyes are covered for an extended period of time (in the case of both eyes having been injured during the crucial period of vision formulation), although there will be no problem of lack of symmetry between the eyes, the infant's ability to see will be impaired. When both eyes are uncovered, they will find a body which has progressed and learned already to draw its own conclusions, without having become accustomed to coordinating it with the eyes. Joseph Pearce, in his book *Magical Child*, writes on the phenomenon of people born blind who undergo, in their adulthood, operations which organically restore their capacity to see. Nevertheless, they have difficulty in interpreting the lights and the images which form on their retina into sensible vision, and consider them a disturbance. Who knows what other functions we have missed in this way, how many more qualities have been left lazy within us forever because they received no encouragement and were not stimulated to join with the rest of the body when it paved its pioneering ways to establish the prototype patterns of its self-activation.

For instance, do we have a chance of knowing how to feel trusting and to receive love if, during those primal days, we did not have enough opportunity to lean our weight fully, being held and cradled through changes of position, relying on a sensitive and loving parent?

Do we have a chance to know when it is appropriate for us to cease eating if, at that time, the budding of our satisfaction signals were not respected?

Do we have a chance to form a full and clear image of who we are if, during those stamping days, we were not being held and caressed again and again on each of the various parts of our body?

Do we have a chance to use one leg like the other, or a shoulder, a knee, a hand, an eye, one side like the other, if at the crawling stage we were not provided with enough opportunities for practice, to perfect through abundant experiences, sifting our non-symmetrical preferences?

Do we have any hope of moving about gracefully and leaving our neck at ease if, during those early days, our parents had the habit of helping us to rise up from the lying position to sitting via a frontal short-cut: pulling our hands straight forward, thus evoking that tension that we very quickly learned to summon up in our necks and stomachs?

Which functions have remained sealed forever by becoming lazy, comprising a part of our potential, embedded in a cumbersome habit which is not necessarily the best way for us? What is still susceptible to being awakened and developed? Where is the borderline of adult learning? Are we capable of regressing to infancy, to the place where we became stuck and held in impairment, so that we can relearn it, again without words, the way an infant learns with untiring diligence, with curiosity, with sensitivity and innocence? Has the culture which gives pre-eminence to intellectual learning cut itself off from an innate wisdom — the wisdom of submitting oneself to the hidden dynamic of experimental evolution, which carries the clue to improvement?

Style of movement: medium for opening habits to change

Feldenkrais has a message on this significant subject of the chances of intentional re-learning in adulthood. He held the vision of an ideal design of function (as was the intention of Creation) while attending, exploring and bringing to awareness the individual deviations of each person. Feldenkrais was a master artist in guiding people to find in themselves a way of moving which aimed for more congruence with their original intention. He showed that every person can, under certain conditions, open up every one of his or her functional habits to a process of improvement, to some degree. There is no situation, he said, in which it is not possible to offer a somewhat better way of organisation.

The improvement which Feldenkrais spoke of is not a correction but the rehabilitation of learning — in the context of the developing child with an innate urge to incessantly test and search for what works better and what is more enjoyable. The salvation for the person locked into habits, compromising with partial potential in the best case or deteriorating in the worst case, is a search oriented towards finding possibilities for improvement, which is characteristic of growth.

Turtles and hedgehogs are known to be the most ancient of creatures to maintain their original form. They have not developed or changed from the dawn of evolution because their strategies have served them well. They trust the strong external armour which guards the weakness of poor development within. However, their success in surviving prevented them from becoming more intelligent. Today they are getting killed on the roads because of their lack of ability to adjust to different circumstances, to re-assess their reactions. This is quite a metaphor for habits: people would rather die holding on to what once worked for them.

Entire cultures have degenerated and fallen because they were caught in perpetuating something they had once succeeded in, and ceased to develop — as F. Capra shows in his book, *The Turning Point*. Feldenkrais is about shaking you out of what you have done successfully until today, challenging you to achieve more successes every day, until you learn to develop your organic resourcefulness for creating your own successes. As a medium for self-improvement, Feldenkrais uses the individual style of movement of each person.

The only thing you can change is the manner in which you do what you do, says Feldenkrais. You cannot change your inherited structural code; you cannot help but feel the emotions that you feel; nor can you sense other than what your sensation is. On rare occasions, you may have some control over what you are thinking, over the beliefs and opinions that you hold about the world and about yourself, though it is quite difficult for you to interfere with the manner in which you use your brain. But in every situation and at every stage of your life it is possible for you — with relative ease — to bring about a change in the way you move about. You have a comfortable access to your mobility. You have a choice to put together your coordination, your rhythm, your configuration in space, the variety of your movements, and the attitude to life that your movement implies.

Movement is the essence of the meaning of what it is for you to be alive. It is inconceivable to consider any form of life without the flow of movement, whether it be recognised in space, or whether it be concealed within yourself. All the fundamental functions of life take a free ride on your mobility, whether it be procreation, or active defence in the struggle for survival, the maintenance of the organism through its internal repetitive cycles, or the fulfilment of desires in relation to the environment. The abstract improvised manoeuvres of the human brain, through which creative methods are found, are also an aspect of movement interaction. The nervous system uses a dynamic of motion which leaps back and forth between an action in relation to the environment, reaction, and re-evaluation.

The quality of coordination of your body's movements is an indication not only of your level of fitness and of where you came to a halt, but also of your character, of your relationship to yourself within the social hierarchy, and the degree of pleasure which you allow yourself in life. Your personal movement is the graphology of everything you are. When you deal with your movement you have an effective grip on your life, influencing and being influenced by it.

The human being has a particularly deep attachment to his movement habits since he created them himself. Being a kind of substitute for missing instincts, a person's habitual strategies are established according to which of his unique experiences are closest to his heart. Humans lean on the crutches of their movement habits as though they were collective instincts that have been tested by the evolution of the entire species, and attribute to them the mechanical working of instincts.

Moshe Feldenkrais reminds us that we ourselves have chosen our habits in the past, and that we are in fact able to select our habits anew. His method of Awareness Through Movement gives every human being the possibility of re-examining and updating his or her personal repertoire. The method leads us to experiment with non-conventional experiences through which we will perhaps discover a better course than the habitual one. The method shows us, most importantly, that there is no need to remain stuck even in the improved new way, as it is also possible to advance from there and develop further. In this process we not only learn specific new movements, but on a higher level we learn an approach which improves our general aptitude for movement. We learn to listen to and trust our own senses in order to navigate towards more efficient and safe movements.

The greatness of Feldenkrais was his genius for outlining the process of self-evolution. His method succeeds in returning people to the cycle of self-improvement —

Mindful Spontaneity

even people who have suffered injuries or have been beyond despair — because it follows the route of the original process through which the organism initially learned to establish the harmful way.

There is an Hassidic proverb that says, 'What we have learned to spoil we can learn to repair'. The organism responds and corrects itself, provided that its ground rules for making decisions are respected and the kind of learning in the early years of growing up is understood.

What gives Feldenkrais' perfection process the effectiveness of organic learning?

What distinguishes it from other disciplines of physical development which present us with defined and desired standards as an assignment which we endeavour to achieve?

What makes awareness of movement a greenhouse which nurtures an internal conclusion that rises from within, surprising even ourselves, as in the days of our primal development?

What is the climate which enables our nervous system to reach an updated decision, free of the conditioning of the past?

What are the conditions which return us to the primal state of mind characterised by open-ended exploration?

What convinces us to be prepared to sacrifice the familiar and secure old ways and enter the uncertainty of the new?

The answers to these issues can be derived from exploration along the same route which Nature utilises to enhance functioning during the years of growth. All processes of Awareness Through Movement aim to get in touch with this learning model and apply its principles. What, therefore, are those principles of organic spontaneous learning?

Reconstructed learning: initiated mistakes

You will have good ideas if you have many ideas. (Moshe Feldenkrais)

To always react in the same certain manner is a neurotic condition, bordering on compulsion. To be able to act in a certain way as well as being able to abstain and not do it at all is already progress; but this is still a primitive level of all or nothing, a level that has no moderation or variety, and cannot ensure the best solution. When adults function in a black-and-white manner they have little chance of attaining worthwhile satisfaction.

Man's advantage, says Feldenkrais, is his ability to perform the same act in at least three different ways. Three options are the minimum required: they will guarantee greater efficiency and begin to give you the feeling that you are a free person, the master of your life. The process of Awareness Through Movement tunes you into the intelligence of the organism which grows up to think, not in words but in stratagems to explore what is available. From the extended choice of movement alternatives you select your own individual way, that serves you most successfully, like an animal that stops from time to time and sniffs out every direction to determine how to proceed on its unpredictable path. Your exploration of movement is an intimate research into yourself, carried out by yourself. Your objective is not to produce movement, but what you can discover about it. This approach allows you to interrupt the movement at any stage, to continue it as before or to consciously alter a component of it — and of course, all along, to observe the subtle differences between one mode and another.

Errors as a challenge to autonomous learning

Feldenkrais took from the learning process that occurs in Nature the activity of exploring variations in the way a function is obtained, or, if you like, the trial-and-error methodology. Learning that occurs in Nature is totally reliant on permission to make errors. Perhaps you don't remember the many mistakes you went through when you learned to stand on your feet, to walk, to climb stairs, or to jump. You probably don't even remember how you learned 'civilised' activities such as how to drink from a cup or glass, how to hold a knife and fork, how to write, how to brush your teeth. But perhaps you do recall how you started to ride a bicycle, or the first time you drove a car.

To tune into the state of mind of primal learning, the way it happened in its original steps — learning which is clarified and crystallised from within — you just have to transfer your pen or your toothbrush to your other hand. Then you may realise that the previous concepts you held about performing these habitual tasks — even if they have already become second nature and automatic to you — does not suffice when you have to perform them under conditions which are different from the usual. A change in the context of your surrounding conditions brings you back down to the bottom of the ladder, where you begin as if from the beginning. There, at the zero point of holding the toothbrush in the other hand, you can recapture the feeling which accompanies primal learning. Only the sensory feedback that you receive from your own mode of action shows you how to adjust your judgement and your directing mechanism until, slowly, you can control your movements to become congruent with your intention.

The operating principle of this learning method is self-experimentation through errors. This process of going through various and repeated mistakes, over and over again, offers you a chance to sharpen your intelligence so as to deal more successfully with the assignment at hand, eventually minimising these very same mistakes. When you have closed the circle and succeeded in the performance of the function to your satisfaction, you are free to go forward and cope with a wider circle of functions, also initially paved with errors, which you need in order to learn how to eliminate them.

When watching a baby for a period of time, you begin perhaps to observe the logic behind what seems to be a disorder of movements. For example, recall the infant at the stage where he is learning to take the pacifier into his mouth. Can you imagine what a long, obstacle-ridden path he goes through until he gains control over this function? The intentional grasping of the pacifier, and holding it in his hand, are complex achievements in themselves. The internal organisation of limbs and muscles are only part of his organisation in relation to an object in his surroundings, which in this instance is quite evasive and unstable.

You have probably noticed how many times the infant attempts to bring the pacifier close to his mouth until he does succeed in placing it in there without missing. In this process the infant may touch an ear, a cheek, the forehead or chin, or turn the pacifier over. It may be lost on the way, when over-stimulus in a certain moment of intense need to grasp happens to trigger the startle reflex of opening up the fist. Even when the baby is bringing the pacifier to his mouth and aiming it in the right direction, he may suddenly rush and in a hasty movement snatch it out and have to start again from the beginning. Even such a basic function is not given automatically to a baby; the young human being must earn it by autonomous learning.

How does the infant learn to succeed? Certainly not by means of words and talk. Even if someone inserts the pacifier into the baby's mouth, and demonstrates how to imitate this function, in the long run this will only rob the baby of the capacity to find solutions for himself. Mistakes are necessary for developing his independence. Nature equipped the infant with the motivation to bring every object which can be grasped to the mouth, thus gaining control over himself and over the surrounding objects. Time after time the baby will err, and every error will be a new lesson. He senses the feedback of the touch of his hand on the pacifier, the sensation of bending and straightening his arm through the use of his muscles, which alter according to the differing distances in space. He feels the experience of turning his whole body, and the glance of his eyes, which facilitate the act. The baby is busy training his faithful guide, forming the judgement mechanism which will accompany his motor orientation in the future, coordinating all the rest of his functions in accordance with his character and rhythm, for precise fulfilment of his intentions. The achievement of getting the pacifier into the mouth is important not only in itself, but also in terms of developing a method which yields success. That same ability to learn lessons from mistakes, and the degree of optimism and steadfastness which accompanies it, as well as the mistakes themselves (which are the context which challenges the learning) will all be essential along the path of attaining levels of independence and further perfecting them.

During the years of consciousness you too have obtained control of your performance by means of that same system of passing through the route of errors which gradually diminish. If you ask yourself how did you begin to ride a bicycle, you will surely recall the first attempt, the experience of real riding, in which any advice or theory could no longer help you — only that which you derived from the sensation of your own body as you tried to correct every deviation so that you would not get into a more exaggerated counter-deviation; all this you did while keeping your body's balance, and that of the bicycle, as well as staying on course.

Initiated improvisation: up-dating habits

Although it may not seem to do so at first glance, Feldenkrais' learning process utilises the same principles of autonomous learning. Instead of the improvisations characteristic of the infant years, the process systematically guides the adult person to cope with a number of errors. All the guidelines in Awareness Through Movement are a series of variations of unusual movement aspects which are no longer performed by people who are locked in their habits. These variations can be considered initiated mistakes in a certain movement theme.

The instructions are not provided so that you strain to obey them strictly and compete to excel in their performance, but rather so that through them you will learn on your own to sharpen your senses — those internal senses which alone are capable of improving your coordination and the quality of your actions. Utilising variations gives you the long forgotten opportunity to examine new solutions alongside the old routine ones, and perhaps, once again, to continue enriching them through the incentive of every new variation. Coping with the initiated mistakes (or, as they are called in the learning process, alternatives) is your guarantee of success in selecting your optimal movements each day.

Don't do well: do differently

Don't make a decision before you have considered all the alternatives. (Moshe Feldenkrais)

You don't know what you don't know. Only when you allow yourself to experience a way of doing which perhaps until today you never tried will you be able to feel that something new is taking place.

When you use the language of alternatives, it appears as though you are doing strange and unconventional things. But this is the language understood by your nervous system, the language which will bring out the best in it. It has been discovered that there is one thing which has within its power the ability to halt the common course of deterioration, and this is engagement in processing new information. The willingness to cope with the unexpected keeps people young in spirit. The inner resources which are recruited when you are searching for the balance between risk and opportunity rewards you with the prize of excitement in life. However, most of us give up the taste of adventure when we can remain within a familiar security zone.

Feldenkrais respects your need for security and the hold you maintain on habits which offer you the feeling of security even though they limit you. He knows that what forces you to hold on to the status quo and hinders you from learning a better mode is your fear of failure. He knows that when you are afraid you cannot function at your best. Anxiety handicaps your intelligence. When fear takes over you feel as if you were up a blind alley, that you must break out at any cost, and so you tend to be swept into an irrelevant compulsive aggression. Feldenkrais doesn't say to you, 'Don't be afraid'. He doesn't tell you, 'This is the way out of the alley'. He creates for you conditions in which it is possible to train and discover that there is more than one way out.

Even if a certain habit does not support your well-being, it is most likely that at the time it was established it was the best alternative that your nervous system could find that was right for you. But it is possible that the alternatives which were at your disposal at that early period of habit formation were not sufficient, and were accepted under limiting conditions. Your nervous system was left from that time on with a strong inclination to compromise, and will continue to perpetuate that same limiting habit unless you address it, once more, in that same language designed for decision-making. You bring your nervous system — this time intentionally — to the primal state of mind of open search, when you avail it of information which was not previously apparent — when you invite it to again cope with the raw material of the unknown and check it from different points of view.

During this encounter with a new perspective, enriched with new options — especially if they offer more comfortable and more attractive solutions — a remarkable thing happens. Your blind alley no longer appears threatening as you begin to perceive that you have a choice of breakthroughs as you pass along it. Your hurried, self-defence impulse is replaced by a functional consideration. Your system updates its old decisions on its own. Habit loses its status of determined decision and regresses to a role, respected though not exclusive, alongside another, newer solution. It is not the process which offers the more relevant solution, but your healthy response to a wider choice of possibilities sprouting forth in you spontaneously, autonomously and beyond the control of your consciousness.

This kind of correction, by internal discovery, will differ in each person. This is what makes learning organic and gives it the power to wrestle as an equal with your stubborn habits. When your self-righting mechanism sharpens, you are oriented to progress. You are not attached to the specific progress you make, either. Your appreciation is not for the credit which you momentarily own in your functional bank, but for the method of earning it. You are actually training your sense of daring in the art of how not to cease striving towards more satisfaction, how not to relinquish vitality. Acquaintance with the method of recovering choices encourages you to continue to refine your actions. Your corrections are made with more agility and ease, and are not perceived as a special event, which requires cessation of the flow of activity. When you develop your sense of hearing, you can correct your musical performance while playing your instrument. The motivation to refinement becomes a way of life.

The true gain: biological optimism

The more your brain makes your body more intelligent, the more you arrive at a level of functioning which goes beyond the minimum need for existence. You begin to break through to what appeals to you. At this level of competence you begin to grasp where an adult human brain can reach, had it not been halted in the early stages of its development.

Thus improvement of specific movements in the process of learning becomes merely a bonus, the real gain being that your life takes on a new, positive direction. This means that with the passing of each day and each year you are able to perform every act in an increasingly better way — more efficiently, more wisely, more precisely and economically —· provided that you have not relinquished your determination to seek these qualities.

Speaking to elderly people, Moshe Feldenkrais once said: 'Curiosity to learn does not depend upon age'. He told them that they, in particular, can succeed in his method because they have no aggressiveness to waste, as do many young people who tend to rely on the power of their muscles, thus missing out on the subtleties of efficiency. Older people have almost no other choice than to be attentive as they search for the most comfortable and feasible channel. One of the unique advantages of the Awareness Through Movement method is that it has something to offer to everyone. It is not oriented towards teaching champions to win competitions, although they too can find in it a method of self-improvement which is tailored to their needs. Awareness Through Movement cares about the level of functioning of every person in the community, in every condition and at every age. Even a person whose body is losing fitness, who is limited in his imagination and has forgotten how to be creative in movement, will respond to the initiated improvisation of the process with the renewal and aspiration which are typical of growth.

Can you imagine your feelings when you discover that you are an ever-changing live organism, capable of self-correction and advancement for as long as you live? This optimism which accompanies the learning process, people's enthusiasm when they discover it, and their appreciation, are the things that make this method so attractive and inspire commitment in both students and the teachers.

Alternating cycles: the preparatory game of Nature

Have you ever had the chance to observe a cat from the moment it encounters a mouse until it cracks the mouse open with its teeth? You may have witnessed how, in this hunting dance, the cat stops the chase every now and then, listens, re-adjusts its position, shifting its head from side to side so as to perfect the precision of aligning its teleceptors; or how the cat crouches before the leap, vibrating its pelvis from one leg to the other until it zeroes in, straight to its goal. When it jumps and catches the mouse, it may not kill it straight away, but only frightens it and allows it to escape, repeating the whole process of ambush, zeroing in, and recapture, from the beginning. This can go on for an hour. What does the cat gain from this? Is it possible that Nature is prepared to waste power on amusement?

It appears that the cat acts according to a basic hunting plan which grants it consistency so that it should not stop chasing its prey, even if the struggle is not immediately rewarding. This tendency of steadfastness, of returning to the battle, is so wired into its system that the cat utilises it even if it succeeds on the first attempt. The violent operation of the life and death battle in Nature has in it more patience, planning and repetition than it would initially seem.

Have you ever heard how wolves proceed to devour the caribou? The caribou's speed is just as good as that of the wolf, and it has powerful antlers as well. When large numbers of caribou join into a unified herd, they can deter any wolf from approaching them. How, then, does the wolf's cunning enable it to succeed in capturing a caribou? The book *Never Cry Wolf* by Farley Mowatt describes the kind of group coordination necessary for such an accomplishment. At least four or five wolves manage to manipulate an entire herd so that one weak caribou is singled out to be the victim for their meal. At first, as the wolves reveal their presence, all the caribou join to form a tightly packed herd. No wolf would then be foolish enough to break in and attack them. The wolves stand still and the caribou stand still. They each listen to the other. The wolves lie in wait for a vulnerable point to show itself and the caribou wait for the sign of attack. Both groups wait. The initiative is taken by the wolves. Like sheep dogs, they begin to run around the fringes of the herd, barking and scaring the caribou into short-distance runs. Suddenly they stop. The entire herd stops as well. Imagine how each individual caribou overcomes its instinct of fright and coordinates itself in perfect unison with the herd.

After another patient and tension-laden pause, again the wolves drive the caribou off, this time in another direction. After a short distance they stop suddenly again. Each time the wolves initiate the unpredictable direction of their move. Shaken in the coordination of the herd's struggle to remain cohesive, the caribou manage over and over again to alter their formation and still remain unified. During all the intense chasing in this critical test of survival, if there is one particular caribou who is slightly less alert, less fit, with perhaps a minor restriction in one limb which does not permit it to move with the same agility as its fellows, this is the one who will be the wolves' victim. At a certain point of the cycle of the chase this caribou will be unable to remain within the herd which has changed formation and location. The instant it is filtered out and separated from its fellows, it has lost the fight. It can still struggle with one wolf face to face, but not with the other wolves behind it and alongside simultaneously.

A coherent principle is highlighted by these instances of the hunting projects of the cat and the caribou. It seems that during critical interaction between one animal and another, Nature makes use of a preparatory procedure rather than immediate and direct confrontation. In all the tumult of the struggle for life, Nature has respect for the patience involved in going through a preparatory stage — a stage which is characterised by alternating repetitive cycles of action and cessation of action. This ingrained pattern which prevents animals from succeeding straight away might be a means of allowing time to improve the efficiency of their actions and tactics.

It seems that civilised humanity has lost that primordial patience of the hunter. People approach complex undertakings as if they were supposed to prove that they know how to do them perfectly straight away. People forget that they have permission to regulate the degree of power invested, finding the trajectory and the timing necessary for performance. People have lost the humility to approach an assignment by way of an investigative stage — eliciting response, listening, and taking the feedback into consideration. Impatient people demand of themselves that they get out of bed in the morning with a sharp leap, even though the neck complains. Impatient people engage in sex without foreplay, and don't understand why the experience has proved shallow.

Lack of patience is a real problem, especially when a person is suffering and in pain. Then, more than ever, that person needs the assistance of Nature's wisdom of repeated preparatory explorations; but unfortunately it is then that one is tempted to force an immediate achievement, in a manner one assumes to be right.

Tentative sketches versus overcoming the test

How does a person with an aching arm behave while performing some everyday task like combing the hair? Civilised people will most likely attempt to lift the arm directly towards the head, the way he or she would have done when the arm was healthy. When that movement comes up against pain, either the person will relate to it as if it were a barrier which should not be passed over and will altogether give up combing the hair with this hand, or the person will try to overcome it with more forceful movements, despite the pain. In either case there is frustration.

Adopting an approach which is more in the spirit of Nature's methods, one would perhaps take permission to try a few sketches and experimental drafts first, instead of putting oneself to the real test head-on.

The Feldenkrais movement process applies this principle of Nature by giving people permission to go through gradual experiments — in this case, to explore minor movements with the arm in different directions, in different combinations with other parts of the body, at a pace that is different from the usual, and then evaluating the movement as it alternates between action and pause. The repetitions are what feed the righting mechanism and gives it the chance to select the effective action. Repetition of a part of the movement, in small doses, avoids entering the area of resistance which loudly signals the impossible. Going gradually is what promotes the feasible to its full presence. The Feldenkrais Method offers encouragement of the preparatory stage, a kind of prelude to the function.

Finding the path of least resistance

The process of Awareness Through Movement will, for example, guide the student with the reluctant arm, firstly to explore possible movement in the wrist only or in the forearm, so long as it does not challenge the pain. All this takes place while the student is lying down, where the willingness to surrender to gravity helps to reduce over-tensed involvement from the arm. Excessive tension is part of a person's defensive resistance to any movement in the arm, and removing this obstacle frees the movement. The student will repeat the same partial movement several times, within the boundaries where he or she feels totally secure — and this is already an important rehabilitation of self-trust.

In order to find a path which bypasses the defensive tendency of the sore arm, the teacher will perhaps suggest directing the hand towards the mouth. In this way the student taps into a fundamental movement, one of the most essential routines in human behaviour — and there is a chance that it will come through successfully. The student explores the possibility of sliding the hand over to the mouth without breaking the contact between the arm and the body, an act which spares the aching arm as it doesn't have to deal with the lifting of its weight into the air. However, in order to get from there to the top of the head, it will be inevitable, at a certain level, to detach the arm from its leaning position on the body. Then the process may suggest checking the possibility of various rotations which are likely to ease the undertaking. The student will discover, perhaps, a trajectory of spiral motion which begins from the little finger, goes to the wrist, passes through the elbow, turns the palm to the front as the arm keeps lifting, and reaches indirectly, dragging the shoulder and the shoulder-blade without provoking the anticipated pain. A series of varying movements will allow the student to feel what is involved in activating the arm from a position where the shoulder is fastened to the spinal cord, and note how different it is from a situation where the shoulder-blade is spaced away from the spinal cord. This offers a glimpse into the meaning of behaviour patterns, discovering where there is more permission for comfort — in the tendency towards the centre, or to the periphery. Only the student can assess in which arrangement the shoulder is more responsive, and the conclusion is an entirely personal one.

Another movement will help the student to experience how the shoulder moves in calm passivity when the pelvis recruits its own mass for the action and initiates it, when an accurate movement of the leg can create a twist in the entire spine, giving the shoulder significant lift without arousing the trauma alarm. Tracing the reciprocal interactions between the various parts of the body opens an entire world of clues and insights. The student can feel how the quality of movement in the shoulder changes when the chest bone and the ribs, one by one, yield their readiness to co-operate. This specific observation enters the realm of breathing quality, and gives an insight into how much liveliness a person allows him/herself to have in the way he or she is accustomed to utilising the rib-cage.

Another movement combination is the investigation of how turning the inside of the palm in the direction of the extended arm influences the outstretch of that arm. Backwards bending of the wrist in a right angle, in a kind of thrust set-up, receives its reinforcement from the collective evolutionary experience of quadrupeds stepping on the ground. At the end of the lesson, a winding path is outlined for you, through which your arm comes to be extended beyond your head much more easily than you supposed, and without pain. For some people, the problematic arm then lifts even more easily than the well one.

A similar exploration can be made with every other one of the arm's functional configurations. Instead of stretching the arm out to the head, you can organise the arm into one of the many forms of crawling, or cradling from side to side in a self-hugging motion. You can also walk on your shoulder-blades, lying on your back. Actually there is no end to the possibilities. Even if the nervous system was less resourceful in inventing a relevant and effective preparatory game, it would still respond to the varieties of the guided process and awaken to sort out a more sophisticated solution. If the impulse to improve is dulled, it can be stimulated through that same method of going in and out of unpredictable situations and posing challenges which are not too difficult, and in which a healthy impulse can function and succeed. This is learning from the outside in, from the action to the brain.

Walking on shoulders
The movement of the pelvis works on the shoulder blades. Thrusted into the floor, the rigid region in your upper back cannot evade altering its way of organisation and your arm becomes freer.

When you succeed in changing the method by which you use your brain, not only does the movement of the arm learn to bypass pain, but a whole vital mechanism for acquiring skill is once again available to the organism, with the same efficiency which brought it successfully through generations of evolution. Although not aggressive like the wolf attack which manoeuvres the herd to alter its structure again and again, the scanning of a variety of options is performed in the learning process according to the same principle of winnowing out the inefficient. The organism tests different methods of organisation, one way after another, sifting out those non-relevant connections, those deeply established personal gestures that cause the operation to be clumsy. The scan which undermines those routine patterns frees the brain to function with less pre-conditioning and this is expressed in a movement that is less limited.

In Awareness Through Movement lessons, every movement theme can be the subject of such a scan. In Amherst, Massachusetts, in 1980, Feldenkrais started his professional training session using the function of sucking as the theme for a process. The functioning of the mouth is one of the most intense actions in the entire organism. The movement of the mouth is perhaps the first and last in life, and is so basic and characteristic of each person that it is very difficult to change it, even though it is possible to consciously control the mouth muscles. To remind you of some of the countless options which are feasible in the sucking motion, and which are capable of clearing the sucking motion from its mechanical quality, you may move your tongue forward, ever so lightly, several times. Move your lip forwards to accompany the tongue. Allow your lips to come forward soft and full. Afterwards you may also try the reverse. Slowly and gently drag the tongue in retreat, while in contact with the upper or lower palate, with the lips still making the forward sucking movement as before. The movement is small in range, but if you haven't done this for years, it can be a revolutionary innovation for your brain. See if you can breathe in this paradox and reduce the excess tension in your shoulders, in your lips, in your eyes. Perhaps you will feel the need to yawn as a confirmation of the re-patterning.

A combination which interferes even more with your fundamental patterns would be to take the tongue ever so lightly to one side of your mouth each time that the lips continue to move forward. Distinguish the different sensation when turning the tongue to one side or the other. It is possible to vary not only the movement pattern, but also the context of your posture in relation to gravity. For instance, when you perform all the above movements while you are lying on your side, you begin to observe further subtleties such as the fact that the right half of your lips behaves differently from the left in the way it will give over its weight. If you do this long enough, the difference might be expressed later in a different feeling all through the half of your face which was closer to the ground, in contrast to the other half which was farther away. When all these deviations from the routine are done softly, repeat-

edly, without coercion or a mechanical rhythm, taking a generous pause each time
— long enough to breathe and to adapt to every combination — you will be surprised to discover what it does to the feeling of your face. Perhaps you will feel that
a very peculiar expression has spread out over your face, or more accurately, you
will feel a lack of expression — this is an experience of serenity, clear of any pretense,
and is closer to the more authentic, neutral you.

Bending Over Extended Legs
*When you see the relationship between the legs and the back you don't need to depend on stretching
the reluctant muscles of the legs, but rather you mobilise your ribs and vertebrae in non-habitual ways
and your back will release the length needed for the bending.*

Another medium can be the exploration of the movement of bending over
straight legs while sitting on the ground. The intention of reaching out and touching
the feet is a common challenge for sportspeople. Perhaps you are not aware of the

parasitic efforts which you usually activated for this attempt. The exploring process filters them out, moderately and consistently. In a series of variations you receive, for instance, instructions to start the bending when your knees aren't necessarily straight. You bend a tiny little bit forward, initiating it by flexing one elbow, and reaching with it forwards, away from your body. You will feel how the movement manages to involve your ribs and awakens them to participate in the bending.

When you raise your head and look forward to the horizon while your chest is bending, your lower back has a better chance of deepening its hollow and coming closer to your legs. Bending forward with the head lifted is possibly a combination which never occurred to you. In the process you do not argue with the theory; the result you experience in the long run will inform you which is more efficient for you. You realise, again and again, that efficiency is not found in a single better way, but rather in the readiness to dare to alter the habitual. You continue to explore another possibility, bending forward while your head is reclining too, but tilted on its side in such a way that one ear is turned more to the floor and the other more towards the ceiling. The rotation that is thus created in the neck succeeds in bypassing the attitudinal and actual difficulty in the frontal bending forward. You can hold one elbow and forearm on the floor or wherever you can reach, while the corresponding leg is also bent and the knee raised up. The other hand is extended to the ceiling, making a circle — with the cooperation of the entire torso — which you follow with your eyes, clockwise and then counter-clockwise. The circle works towards opening up a differentiating movement between one rib and another, and one vertebra and another, at a certain section of the upper spinal cord which is accustomed to being kept stiff.

At the end of the process, people are amazed to find how their original bending flows further forwards, lower, and with more simplicity. What surprises them even more is the message concerning perspective on life which is wrapped up inside this achievement: it says that if you work wisely you do not have to struggle with your muscles. You need only to interfere with the code of the operating pattern and the muscles will become organised accordingly.

Talk to the brain, not to the muscles

If you want even more convincing proof that the issue is not in the muscles but in the upper level of the headquarters, you can follow a simple, two-minute experiment.

In a sitting position, raise your head upwards and try to see the ceiling. Make a note how this movement works for you. At what point in your reach do you have a feeling of difficulty? What happens to your breathing?

Now, shift your attention to the feet. Take off one shoe and extend that foot forward, as far as your sole stays flat on the floor. Begin to slowly flex your toes downwards, dragging them along the floor closer to your heel. In this position, lift the ball of the foot from the floor and decrease the angle of bending in the ankle. All this time, the heel is still anchored to the floor. This is an unusual combination of movements involving the foot. Allow the foot to return to its comfortable place on the floor and repeat the whole sequence several times.

In the next stage, place your foot in full contact with the floor again, but this time bend the toes upward, raising them in the air while the ball of the foot stays on the ground. Alternate several times between the two movements, from bent ankle to outstretched ankle, with the heel planted all the time on the floor. The toes point to the floor when the foot comes up, and they are turned to the ceiling when the ball of the foot rests on the floor. See if you can reduce the amount of effort which you invest in bending the ankle and the toes. Notice that in order to design a strange arrangement which perhaps is totally new to you, you have to use a device other than direct physical power. Identify within yourself this quality of listening and clarification — it is this quality which makes the difference between exercise and learning.

Now bring the foot back to its usual place, and again lift your head so as to look at the ceiling. Has your scan of the ceiling now been made a bit easier than it was earlier?

You are surely curious to know how several movements in the sole of the foot can influence your neck — so much so that it surprises you, as if it had forgotten its set limitations and restraints. In this case, it is clear that the preparatory stage did not at all deal with the muscles of the neck. The activity was even performed in a part of the body farthest from the neck. How then does this work?

It appears that you are dealing with an intelligent organic system which has its own logic and traditional agreements. It might be that the alternating movements in the ankle and the joints of the toes have brought to the surface of the functional memory of your nervous system a primal, neurological clue about stride, in which the signalling in the bending foot, as it steps on the ground, is associated with the surge of a wave of response via the entire spinal cord, which arrives at the neck and raises the head towards the horizon. Or it might be that the occurrence of the non-habitual activity casts the whole brain into an atmosphere of disorientation, with a corresponding openness to change. With this reshuffle of cards the brain responds to reality without its former restrictions, the origins of which may be in old habits and prejudices. Whether it is the former or the latter case, through gaining the wisdom to form new patterns and to annul them, through this training in new possibilities, your system has the chance to attain achievements without effort, with the elegance that suits an evolved person.

Thinking, says Feldenkrais, means finding new ways of doing. In order to receive an insight of learning, your system needs a confrontation with a challenge it has not yet had.

The Awareness Through Movement method fulfils this requirement. Moshe Feldenkrais created many hundreds of processes which each time present you with a challenge which you have not met before. Every process is focused on its own theme, with its own series of steps. It is hard to imagine how one man, on his own, can have deciphered so many ways of influencing the learning of the brain. For years, Feldenkrais worked with people, observed and understood, explored and experimented, gathered and constructed principles for functioning, and created practical processes for their application. He could teach for years without repeating the same process.

In addition, the teachers whom he trained are becoming more and more creative through their involvement with the method. Around those same basic fundamentals, they add and design innumerable processes which no person has thought of before. This creativity makes the teachings into a living method that keeps growing. Every teacher creates anew by way of his or her own personal expression and area of interest. Moshe used to say that everyone writes it in their own handwriting. This was his greatness: he was a master who raised masters, not disciples.

When you begin to walk the road of Awareness Through Movement you also enter the path of inspiration and permission to renew. You improve not only your movements, but also your daring to renew — and this is what your liveliness thrives on.

Changing context: learning by contrast

Having a dialogue with the computer of your motor-cortex in its own language may sound like trying to outsmart it in countless stratagems. The list of devices utilised by Feldenkrais to stimulate the nervous system for enhancing movement efficiency is long and various. One central learning tactic is the changing of context. Have you ever arrived in a totally new environment where no-one has met you before, and a more gracious attitude of trust was bestowed upon you than you ever enjoyed on your own native ground? For some people, such a change of environment becomes a lever for thriving and self-manifestation which did not occur in home port. My journeys to the United States to teach Awareness Through Movement and Functional Integration were just this for me.

The process of movement provides you with such a setting which differs from habitual reality — firstly by the artifice of simply lying on the floor. The horizontal spreading out in itself liberates your brain from its constant engagement in maintaining vertical balance within the field of gravity. You become free to divert your resources and relate to the quality of your movement. The passive position of lying down creates an atmosphere which is more suitable to the learning of subtleties, an atmosphere which allows you to listen rather than do. When you give up operating from the standing position for a period of time you are also prepared to relinquish the state of mind that is associated with standing up, where you have a determined commitment to produce results, to get things done, and to succeed. The many coercions which constitute the social considerations in your life loosen their hold on you. Lying down, you are far from all competition or the striving to excel. There, in the posture of rest, you accept the style of slowing down and you are allowed not to anticipate what is the right way. You can close your eyes, and even though you are among people, you can go inside and be with yourself. You are in a group and you are free of any comparison with the others. Giving verbal instructions, the teacher does not demonstrate to you a model which you are expected to measure yourself against. In this atmosphere of quiet you can do your inner work and you have the opportunity to become more sensitive and to observe those hidden tones which constitute the quality of what you do.

Exploration by way of variables

In addition to the changeover to the context of lying down, the process confronts you with a sequence of different points of view on a certain theme. When you explore the same movement from alternating starting positions your ability to distinguish is sharpened and you are able to locate more clearly those details of internal dynamics which are responsible for your mode of performance. You are able to isolate them from the complex totality and you can master them at your will.

For example, take a theme such as improving your walk. All your life you walk with your own typical gait, which you take for granted, and it is difficult for you to see what can be changed in it. It might perhaps be that your pelvis, which is the handle of the whip for the entire spinal cord, repeats the same limited use in its conjunction to the spine or to the hip joints. It might be that the movement of the pelvis is somewhat more restrained on one side, or perhaps the traces of an alternating cradling of a figure-eight-like motion from side to side have faded away from it. It might be that you have understood that it is not acceptable to rock the pelvis too much in public, or perhaps in your eyes that emphasised wiggle is what makes you more attractive and you tend to exaggerate it. Whatever may be the incentive for your movement behaviour, it holds you in its grip during your adulthood, retaining those same imperfections which are characteristic of you.

It is possible that out of self-protection for an old injury in the knee or the ankle, your system became chronically apprehensive about using a certain dimension of pelvic movement. In order to propel yourself in walking, you perhaps compensate for the lack of flexibility in the hip joints or in the vertebrae by grounding your heels with a sharp emphasis which shocks your entire body. You succeed in blocking the shock by making yourself more rigid. All your joints have become adjusted to this level of inner pressure. You repeat with precision the same manner of interacting the sole of your foot with the ground and that same manner of carrying the head and shoulders, the same manner of breathing or lack of breathing in the ribs and the stomach, until it does not seem to you that there might be some other alternative which would make your walk less tiring and more pleasant. This is a habit; you have ceased to feel how you do what you do, and you are not aware that you have a limitation. Even if you have an idea what it is you would want to change, the chance of changing your style of walking while in the act of walking is no more realistic than it would be to attempt to interfere with any other automatic complex. Even if you consciously alter one detail, still it is anchored in the network of reinforcements in all the other parts of your body which will strive to return it to its former state.

In the process of movement re-education, you are trained in the dynamics of walking while you are in every other possible position, except that of walking itself. The process avails you of various starting positions in order to investigate a certain detail from within the tangle of relationships involved in walking. Take, for example, the behaviour of the spinal column as it interacts with the thigh moving towards the pelvis, while detaching the heel of your foot from the ground in the function of stepping. Sometimes the process will bring you down to lie on your stomach. You will feel there how the thigh moves back and forth in relationship to the pelvis when it is horizontal, when it doesn't have to carry the full weight of your body. The shoulders, in contrast to this, are compelled to take part in the movement more distinctly than in the open space given them while standing upright.

Or, you may lie on your side and feel the same stepping movement, where the thigh comes close to the pelvis; this time your ribs are resting safely on the ground, and at the same time the vertebrae are free to resonate and respond by bending on the frontal plane. An additional clarification will be signified in your consciousness when you attempt to lift one buttock from the seat of the chair while in the seated position, perhaps with the aid of a pillow; you will be able to further enrich the information about your leg-pelvis-back interaction.

When you perform all these movements within variations — for example with a rotation of the knee which is being dragged inward or outward, accompanied by twisting the spinal column in a way which is consistent with the rotation of the leg, or counters it — you will remind your back of the many ways it can react to leg movement, and this will enliven your walk incomparably. Sometimes, the process will invite you to fix the sole of the foot, and plant it on the floor, with the knee bent, and then manouevre the pelvis towards the foot. This is a reversal in the distribution of the labour of anchoring and movability, as opposed to what happens in the ordinary function of walking. Rich information becomes available when parts exchange roles with each other. Imagine how relationships between people would benefit if for one day — even if only in their imagination — each partner in a couple exchanged roles. Such a refreshment occurs also in your physical organisation when for once it is not the leg which troubles itself to draw close to, or far from, the constant pelvis — but instead the pelvis is revolving in space around the constant leg.

A significant understanding about how the behaviour of the spinal column is affected by the movement of the leg can be gained in a position of lying on the stomach when you draw the knee along your side. In this way you will make contact with the recoil of the hip which precedes the setting in motion of the leg while walk-

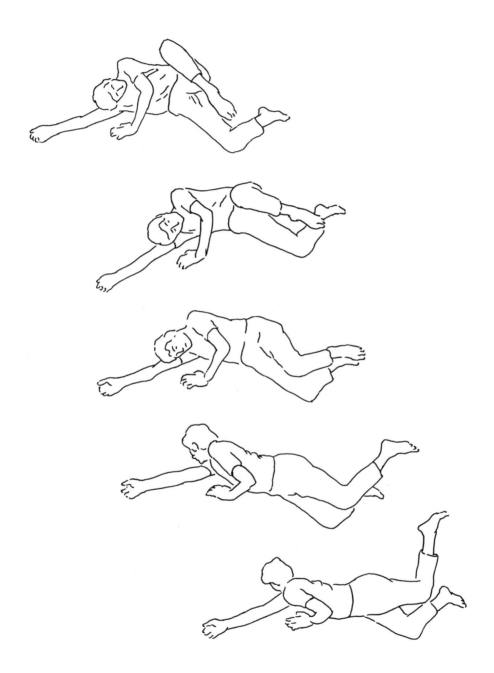

Knee In And Out In Lying On The Side
You use your leg as a handle to manoeuvre your spine, rotating the leg in and out, consistent with the rotation of the spine as well as in the opposite direction awakens in you an abundance of options in leg-pelvis-back-head interactions. You will feel the result later in walking.

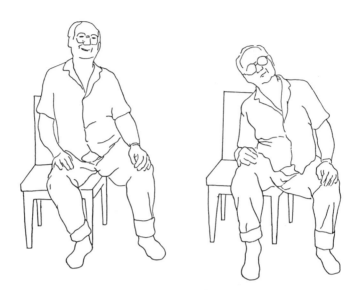

Sitting On A Chair With Half Of The Pelvis Outside
Organic bodies are not built for monotony. In order to break the routine of prolonged sitting, you can extend half of your pelvis outside the seat of the chair, or elevate one half by supporting it with something underneath. The change in the sideways plane is a refreshing novelty to the total body alignment.

ing. This detail, which perhaps degenerated during the process of walking, becomes again a necessity while lying on the stomach. As you drag the bent knee to your side, with the surface of the ground confining the leg's movement, you have no other choice but to challenge the flexibility of your hip. This reconstruction of primal creeping shows you how the relationship between the pelvis and the leg was intended to function. It reminds your entire spinal column how it should wind and spiral so as to enable efficient locomotion.

You can get another insight when you lie on the stomach with your legs fully extended and try to raise one leg into the air. Your challenge is to decipher for yourself the order, direction and timing which will make possible a gentle detachment that does not cut off the flow of the ongoing change in the knee angle or the smooth ongoing movement of the foot through space.

In these examples of exploration there is material for many lessons. In each lesson there will be a series of variations when each time one component will be altered. At first, you do the movement only on one side. Working on one side enables you to accumulate more clarity in your search for the movement plan. Your objective is not to change the muscles as much as possible, but rather to work to create enough of a difference to make an impression on the nervous system and point out to it a possibility of more efficient response. Your brain will be more impressed by the

Organic Learning — Learning Through Options

Creeping: The Primal Locomotion Prototype

When dragging the bent knee on the side, the confinement of the floor works to challenge the flexibility of the hip. Creeping reminds the entire spine how to twist, in order to provide the leg with an efficient stance for pushing off, and how to arch backwards, in order to provide the head with a comfortable position for viewing.

subtle difference on one side, which has upset your symmetry, than it would by observing a big change taking place on both sides. Symmetry is a fundamental characteristic of the organism and interfering with it can be a device to stimulate the brain to awaken and observe.

Sometimes your nervous system doesn't need anything more than such a reminder in order to be convinced of the advantage of the new proposal, and it applies it straight away for use. In making one side more intelligent, you have designed a model for new organisation. When you get up from the floor you feel that your total posture is undergoing transformation.

When you begin to walk about at the end of the process, you no longer interfere or attempt to direct this new way of walking that emerges from within you. In finally walking within the reality of gravity, you reap the harvest which grew by itself during the research of mutations you carried out in the laboratory of altered situations on the floor. In your awareness laboratory, the research itself is also the spontaneous recovery.

Linking and unlinking

A change of context can also be achieved through interference in the combination of the conditioned relationships between different parts of the body. For example, in order to lift the head towards the ceiling from a standing position, most people are accustomed to a package deal in which they also deepen the cavity in the lower back while lifting the head. Can you see the ceiling without also compressing the lower back? The meaning is this: are the vertebrae of the upper back, in between the neck and the lower ribs, somewhere around the level of the shoulder-blades, capable of stimulating themselves in a backwards bow, thus providing the head with the necessary angle to reveal the ceiling, or is the upper back too lazy to do this, leaving the job to the irritated and vulnerable vertebrae in the waist and neck alone?

Kneeling on knees and hands, you can explore one relationship and then the reverse. You look out at the horizon with your back suspended like a hammock. You repeat this gently several times. After a pause for listening, you continue to direct your eyes straight at the horizon, but this time your back rounds and arches like a cat stretching into a hunchback. You repeat this slowly, at your own pace, without having to tighten your stomach or your jaw.

You can take the combination and its reverse further through a flowing movement, coordinating them within, detaching the knee from the ground, crossing one knee behind or in front of the other, sitting between the heels after each crawling step.

After each disassembling and reassembling of the above combinations, you will discover how much farther your glance reaches when you return to look at the ceiling. What is even more important, the lifting of the head will not trigger the arching spasm in the lower back. The pelvis remains neutralised and you feel the uniform

From Kneeling To Sitting
The reciprocal coordination between the pelvis and the head in the wave-like motion of primal crawling leads to a smooth transition between crawling and sitting. The biological necessity for rounding out of the lower back in the total locomotion becomes clear by the challenge of crossing the knees.

quality of the entire back movement and how those vertebrae which were dormant have now been awakened to take their share in the journey of pulling the back backwards for the function of carrying the head up.

Base and breakthrough

Every learning tactic is derived from your recognition of the nervous system's methods of operation. A certain logic of the brain grasps that the return to home base is always easier than the breaking out. Feldenkrais makes use of this logic. For example, if you want to facilitate the rotation of your head sideways, a repeated attempt to break through from the middle to the boundary of your turning will only reinforce the limitations of this movement in your self-perception. On the other hand, try moving your head minimally to the side, within the confines you believe to be entirely safe and comfortable, and then leave it there at rest. Now, with a gentle movement which does not betray your trust in comfort and security, bring the head several degrees towards the centre, and without too much delay allow it to roll passively back to the starting place on the side. There the waiting pause will be longer.

This is the same movement which goes back and forth between the centre and the side. You alter only your attitude. In your mind you establish the attitude that the place on the side is home. Within a short time, the brain will indeed grant you there the ease which it reserves for a homecoming. This is a physical achievement which is attained without the use of physical, muscular force, but rather by the wisdom of interchanging the orientation between the base and the breakthrough.

Bringing the mountain to Mohammed

The extent to which the self-image is responsible for facts which seem objective can be learned from the movement principle of revolving the axis towards the immobilised periphery — in other words, doing the same activity from the other end.

For instance, a shoulder that hurts each time you try to move the arm can stop being problematic when you move the body in relation to the arm. In the joint which connects the torso and the shoulder, the same interaction takes place, but the division of labour is different. When you move the body in an unaccustomed way towards the arm, the central pivot, with its massive weight, takes the trouble to dance towards the lighter periphery. The advantage of using the different program is that there, the brain has not yet learned to organise recoil through inability. You come to experience the same mutual interaction between the arm and the body, but this time without the old prejudices. The movement, then, is registered in your brain as safe. What is more, if you give yourself enough opportunities to move in a more gratifying way, responding to movement as if you had no problem, then the sting of the difficulty will also be removed from the routine pattern.

The cure for a tension-laden neck through this approach can be performed, for instance, by rolling on the head from a kneeling position. The neck, which is always forced to make decisions about locating the position of the head in space, finds itself passive while you are kneeling with your head on the ground. It is the body which now comes to the head and not vice versa. The pressure on the vertebrae also comes from the opposite direction. When you do this gently, in half circles which pass between 3 and 9 o'clock by way of 12, or by way of 6 o'clock, you may afterwards find that your head floats with a more even continuity, and is more aligned to the spinal column. When you begin to heal the continuity, your neck begins to heal too.

Auxiliary movements

Of outstanding educational value is a learning tactic which is termed auxiliary movement. When movement is difficult for you, you are entitled to the assistance of various compromises, such as partial moving, all kinds of supporting pads, rhythm change, activation from another direction, assistance from another part of the body. You are invited to do anything which will pull your movement out of its frustration and elevate it to a point where it can be registered in your mind as attainable in principle. Afterwards you may realise that you can perform the movement with no difficulty — even without that assistance.

For example, rising from a sitting position on a chair straight to a standing position doesn't always come easily to people. From a fundamental movement principle you take the idea of rotation in which the back leg generates the force of locomotion throughout your body in a diagonal line that reaches the opposite arm. In other words, when one leg is moving forward, the opposite shoulder withdraws backwards. In accordance with this, when you sit on a chair you place your legs so that you position one foot a bit in front of the other. When you raise yourself off the chair from this position, in a slightly squeezing spiral, you may find it easier for your back to participate in the task of rising. A rotating motion always allows more gradation and sensitivity than a one-dimensional frontal movement. You generate the spiral motion just as a softening preparation for the crucial moment of raising your weight off the chair. Instead of picking up the weight of both hips simultaneously, the spiral allows you to lift them gradually, one hip at a time.

Once you have safely detached yourself from the chair-seat there is no need to continue the rotation, and you may square yourself again to the front. All this deviation and counter-deviation is minimal — a sort of intimate internal ripple that can hardly be detected by an observer.

After you repeat this process several times, starting it with a right, and then a left, turn, you will be surprised that even without using the spiral, the direct forward rising also steers its course with the same ease as the rotation. It seems that it is enough to remind your intelligent brain of an efficient internal organisation which is at its disposal, so that it will immediately adapt it and become encouraged to move more freely.

In the same way you will be able to initially assist the function of getting in and out of a chair by lowering your eyes to the ground at the moment of transfer from one situation to the other. The lowering of the eyes, which triggers the reclining of the head, affects your entire back, preparing it to round out, with more flexibility, as is essential to a streamlined rising. After several such head reclinings, you will be able to get up even when your eyes are straight forward, without losing control of the horizon, and your back already knows by itself how to relate, as required, to the wave of movement.

How to Revive a Reluctant Movement
If you have a difficulty to move your head closer to the shoulder, you may bring them closer to each other from the other end of the same muscle and easily bring the shoulder to the head. When you move them around joined together as one unit, all the rest of yourself reorganises to accept their relationship. Once their proximity is registered as a feasible and safe capacity, you then gain extended freedom in the movement of your head also when it is independent.

In this way, a neck which has difficulty turning sideways will also be able to bring the head there with less difficulty if you first fasten your shoulder or arm to the cheek and mobilise them, joined together as one unit, back and forth, gently and in slight motions. The irritated muscle in the neck doesn't then work at all. However, when it is thus neutralised, your system becomes convinced that the head is able to move in space from side to side and the function is registered as safe. This is a way to build success into your self-image. After several such conjoint turns, you will find to your surprise that the neck responds, even when it is separate from the arm, and reaches with great simplicity farther than before. To know one's body is to know the clues to unravelling its entanglements.

Be creative: do it badly

There are movements that do not lend themselves to being assisted by the tactic of slowing down or prolonging them gradually, such as the momentum movements, like jumping, rocking and spinning. A fun 'break-dance'-like movement of swivelling on your buttocks can be a theme for a lesson. You sit on the ground with your legs folded, slightly lifted in the air, and you try to generate momentum for swivelling around yourself like a spinning-top. It is possible to first go through stages of preparation by swinging each arm and leg in relation to the spine, or coordinating the eyes with the rotation pivot. It is also possible to interfere intentionally with the flow of the swivel, and at times to bring it to a standstill at any given point in its trajectory. Besides the superiority of the awareness over inertia impulse, the arbitrary stops can clarify all those organisational details which are liable to remain unimproved if they are obscured by the overall flowing motion.

But it is impossible to accomplish the complete spinning movement slowly. It exists only by virtue of its own fast biodynamic frequency. How then is it also possible to improve the totality of this momentum?

Feldenkrais suggests, in this case, another point of view for approaching the circle as a whole. The challenge he presents to you is typical of his way of thinking. He tells you to perform the spinning badly — to be inventive in as many ways as you can in messing up the movement! It is unbelievable what happens to people after a few moments of trying to do it badly. When they return to the initial movement, there is not one person in the group who doesn't admit that his or her swivelling encompasses more degrees and provides greater joy.

When you experience the effect of this paradox, you cannot avoid making a projection regarding educational methods in general. Did anyone ever, all along the path of your education and attainment of skills, allow you to stop trying to succeed and instead encourage you to invent mistakes?

Refining the individual through the coherent rhythm of the herd

At other times, Feldenkrais can take advantage of the very beat of the momentum as a context for gaining refinement. His process guides an entire group to find the bio-

How to Inspire Organic Intelligence
You stimulate your nervous system to its peak vitality when you provide it with the raw material of mistakes to select from them the efficient movement. How to improve swivelling on the bottom, that is a function that does not lend itself to gradation or slowing down? You do it deliberately badly and creatively invent all kinds of deviation and failings. Your organism, on its own, then learns how to succeed and presents you with the most refined and flowing motion.

logical frequency of momentum in a certain function. For example: from the starting position of lying face-down with the hands supported by the floor, as in push-ups, swinging the bent legs one after the other to one side and then rising in a spiral to sit sideways, alternating the motion to the right and to the left. After about an hour of preparatory process, during which each person deals intimately with his or her own movement, a group of people can become synchronised and move in the same beat.

Improving by Biological Rhythm
Through the function of coming to sit from lying face-down, you develop your skill to assess the precision of investment, timing, and configuration in space. When the movement gains the momentum of sitting, once on the right and once on the left within a flowing rhythm, the coherent biological beat of the total group sweeps the individual to further refinement of his or her motion.

The collective rhythm sweeps every individual to resonance with the rest of the group, while coercing each one to polish his or her performance to precision.

It is a spectacular sight to witness the way a whole 'herd' of people can arrange themselves on their own into a coherent rhythm, moving their bodies from side to side in the same configuration, without anyone conducting their pace.

Ease is gained through ease

Perhaps the most outstanding difference between the Feldenkrais Method and other body-oriented methods lies in the quality of ease with which all the movements are carried out. In Awareness Through Movement ease is a fundamental law of learning.

Ease is more a feeling of lack of sensation than an actual sensation. When it is easy for you to move, you are more aware of all those components which are now missing from your movement. There is no difficulty; there are no barriers; there is no rhythm disorder, no pressure, no effort, no apprehension, no resistance, no ambition, no boundaries. In your space, which has been emptied of all its charges, what remains is only a silence which connects your whole self in an openness to flow in every direction and in every shape and manner.

Someone at one of the Olympics once said that movement is ideal when every one of its parts is equally unimportant.

When do you know that you have improved a movement? When the impossible becomes possible for you; when the possible becomes more comfortable, simple, flowing and easy, and when the ease becomes elegant, giving you aesthetic satisfaction.

How do you go about attaining this? Do you start from an attempt to convert the impossible to the possible? The process of Awareness Through Movement directs you to begin from the other end of the scale — from the edge of your own aesthetic satisfaction. Trying to convert the impossible to the possible is to collide with the highest resistance. The ATM process seeks the path of least resistance through a policy of easing the ease. You explore a movement and locate the range in which it is easy for you. Even if you have an opinion that this movement is difficult for you, if you examine it sincerely you will find right at the beginning several degrees or several centimetres which come to you with readiness, before their quality is altered into effort. Feldenkrais tells you to remain within the boundaries of this readiness, and to repeat only that same initial segment, slowly, again and again — as if time does not count. Give yourself permission to enjoy the quality of this little bit that you can do in your own personal style, with the cooperation of your whole self. When you let go of criticism of quantitative achievements, you may reveal your talent for satisfaction.

You can verify this idea right now while sitting, and without any preparation. Take an ordinary movement, such as turning the head to the side. Begin to turn your head to the right so as to notice when the red light of the barrier of discomfort lights up. After this turn the head slowly to the left, so as to observe to which side it turns further before it begins to be uncomfortable. Take a minute to visualise how you begin to move the head to the easier side. Imagine just the first millimetres — almost only the setting-off point. Remain there on the side of ease, and continue to turn your head only a token part of the arc, time after time. Only when it is easy for you will you be able to observe that it is possible to loosen the shoulders from their unnecessary grip, to breathe fully all over the stomach, to allow the face to rest, to imagine the vertebrae of the neck rotating in a wringing motion. When the movement becomes simple and comfortable so that you are completely at ease with it, shift again to turn the head to the other side, where you had the difficulty. Observe where your head reaches now. Hasn't the carefree range grown? You are likely to discover that something of the difficulty of the impossible has dissolved and become more simple and possible. This is, in capsule form, a lesson in the power of delicacy, or, if you wish, the wisdom to convince through ease. Clarifying the model of ease at the comfortable edge informs the brain how to expand the feasible boundaries at the edge of the difficulty.

Permission for gracefulness: a supportive climate for learning

This approach is not easily accepted by civilised people who have been raised to believe in conflict, effort and sacrifice. Going the easy way is the part of the method that is the most difficult to grasp. It is difficult for people to relinquish the mentality of doing to the maximum when confronting a difficulty. They are convinced that the more effort and strength they invest, the more successful they will be in fulfilling their task — so much so, that their entire moral rectitude depends on their commitment to act in the fullness of their power.

It is important to note that what has been said here is about avoiding the frustration of barren and unnecessary effort, in the context of acquiring skill. It is not said here that effort is unneeded in life in general, or that human activity does not need to include phases of effort, or that the Feldenkrais Method is against effort. It is said here that in order to enhance learning it would be better if you would reduce the frustration of irrelevant effort and raise the value of the quality of gracefulness.

There are people who are so far removed from granting themselves permission to be graceful that, for them, these guidelines to go slowly and gently in a lesson of Awareness Through Movement only arouse bitter frustration. There are people for whom gentleness in movement is considered self-indulgence, which doesn't suit mature people who feel obliged to achieve in the harsher world of reality. A student once told me after a lesson, 'This is more pampering than I have allowed myself in a whole year'. We think we crave well-being and softness but are we really ready to accept them? It appears that many have need of a patient re-education, firstly in the art of granting oneself permission to feel graceful.

Mindful Spontaneity

In a group which I conducted for lecturers at Tel Aviv University, there was one professor who came faithfully summer and winter, rain and shine, to a class that took place at a quarter to seven in the morning, as suited such busy people. In one process there was an instruction to lie on the back with the knees bent up, feet on the floor, and like this to pass the knees from side to side. He did this so intensely that his movement seemed like an angry strike. Every time he thrust his knees sharply to the side it was a shock to the whole of his body, which was held tensed and stiff. I could see that in his own eyes he was fulfilling his responsibility to do his best at any cost. Had I pointed out to him that he should transfer his knees with more gentleness, with more kindness towards his body, he might have taken this as an embarrassing and frustrating criticism. How can a style be changed without attacking the person?

I began to nourish his mind with actual tasks which were within his reach. I guided the entire group to leave the knees to one side and to notice the distance of each knee from the floor there. I asked them to fixate the lower knee in its location in space and to bring only the upper knee towards the middle, back and forth several times. They needed to feel what degree they could spread out one knee without the other also being dragged from its place. In other words, this is an examination of how much freedom there is in the hip joint which enables the knee to be brought along without the cooperation of the pelvis. The aggressive performance which is oriented to external achievement gives way to observation of internal dynamics. Immediately the style of that professor softened and entered a phase of listening within. He ceased to act with the maximum of force and instead began to utilise his sensitivity. Being engaged in specific details nourished the shift from an external criterion to an internal one, and brought about the transformation.

At this stage, some of the instructions were, for instance, to locate the moment in which it is appropriate to allow the fixated knee to join the movement; to detect the rotation of the pelvis as it reaches to make more and more contact with the ground; to feel the response, at different levels of the spinal column to the turning of the pelvis, and to pay attention to the rolling of the head which completes it. Special leisure time was given to experience the moment when the lower knee starts to move; to listen whether breathing tends to cease at that moment; to pay attention that the first knee did not cease at that moment to travel along to the other side when the second joined in; to distinguish that one knee is the active one, and the other is being dragged passively; and to discover how they alternate in their roles when they come in the other direction. These were questions requiring answers which the professor, like every other participant, had to find within himself.

After a few minutes, the transfer of his knees from side to side became economical and harmonious. At that point the class was asked to revert to the initial style, where both knees lifted simultaneously and arrived simultaneously at the other side. He could sense what this movement demanded of his back and found for himself the style that was more supportive of life. Instead of critical correction, he had the freedom to choose. The screening of the movement through several of its aspects gave that professor an opportunity to be kind and gentle with himself without attempting to force the outcome.

With the taste of an experience of gracefulness in movement, something deep and profound is altered, of its own accord, in the attitude of the person to his environment. This same professor was known as an over-demanding pedagogue. I was told that some time after this class, at a social gathering of his colleagues, somebody mentioned that he had changed lately. He attributed this to the 'gymnastics' that he was doing twice a week. What is interesting is that the friend who told me this presented the story to me as an anecdote. He did not participate in the group and did not imagine that work on the body could really transform a man set in his ways, allowing him to become softer, more content and open. But I knew that a person who learns to transfer his knees from side to side with sensitivity stops being insensitive in other areas of his life as well.

An achievement in movement which comes by way of gentleness and sensitivity leaves us with the feeling that we love to move. Spoiled relations between ourselves and our movement, so typical of our culture, undergo a reconciliation and we feel renewed trust. For many people, this peace which they make with themselves — this permission to be kind to themselves — is the most profound attraction of the method.

'This is the first time since the operation two years ago that I have made peace with my body,' a thrilled woman said to me after an ATM class.

Another man put it this way: 'When I feel how light and smooth the movement is, I feel the love inside me. It is as if the love is there all the time, but I am just feeling the stiffness which covers it'.

The pleasurable experience of moving is not only positive as a desirable human value. The pleasure is essential for learning. The nervous system selects and adopts new ways according to what feels safe and enjoyable. In order for the new proposal to have a chance to be absorbed and to be registered as a viable option, it has to be pleasant. A movement pattern which involves effort, pain and sacrifice will succeed in being maintained — the way taming does — only as long as the pressure exists. As soon as a person is able to live according to his or her own free will, he or she will discontinue what has been gained by coercion.

Language that invites ease

An approach which believes in ease needs a language that is different from the conventional. Throughout hundreds of Awareness Through Movement processes, I never heard Moshe use the instruction 'Stretch your muscles!'. The Awareness Through Movement version will speak about allowing your length to be released. Instructions to stretch can be especially misleading because the organism can express activity also by means of contraction. Using the term 'stretch' in an instruction will immediately activate a contraction in some other part. If in addition to this the tone of the instruction intensifies the action, then the struggle between the stretching and the inevitable counter-stretching will also intensify and reach a painful impasse. Any attempt to stretch your back by will into a straight posture will remind you of the sensation of this internal war. Sworn exercisers know that if they exaggerate in their stretching efforts, the next day it is difficult for them to perform even what they could do at the starting point of the previous day's session. But they believe that the perpetual war against the muscles is unavoidable. The myth of stretching actually builds up their tolerance to stiffness, and each time trains their muscles to contract more efficiently.

In contrast to this, an instruction given in terms of becoming shorter — which is Nature's language of activation — invites you to relate to those parts of you which do become shorter; then you have more chance that in the corresponding parts, your length will unfold and spread itself out with no disturbance. You can only elicit unencumbered elongation in a passive manner. Even in the straightening of your posture, you can find where the shortening takes place by imagining, for instance, how the distance between your head and the sky is diminishing.

The choice of words can determine your attitude to your movement — whether you relate to it as a discipline, or a grace. You have to be sensitive to the subtle nuances of your inner dialogue: do you give yourself commands, or ask questions? The command, by its very nature, stems from giving importance to standards external to you. The question appreciates your own response, something only you can know. The question then pays respect to yourself. Whatever you derive from the movement depends not on the movement you have performed, but on the extent to which you can identify with what you did.

A description of the movement's trajectory needs to be not only precise but careful. An instruction such as lie on your back with knees standing up and allow the right knee, bent as it is, to sink sideways towards the floor, can leave room for various interpretations. Many will understand that the objective is to bring the knee to make contact with the floor, which of course is liable to emphasise the barrier of stiffness in the spinal column and the hip joint, and to produce frustration. Indeed the term 'towards the floor' is given only as an orientation to imply the direction of the movement. However, a period of patient training is needed in order to educate the ear to sort out and recognise those terms which do not necessarily refer to quantity, but to your orientation.

As Awareness Through Movement does not utilise demonstration and imitation, careful and detailed phrasing is of special importance. Phrasing which will take the knee through the movement with complete safety could perhaps be, 'Slowly move the knee in the direction of the floor, time and again, at your own pace, up to whatever point it is still comfortable for you to reach'; 'Explore how the pelvis can assist that movement'; 'How can the foot which stands on the floor behave to accommodate the movement?'; 'In what way does the head participate so that your whole self will be coordinated with the opening up of the knee to the side?'; 'What is your sensation in the groin, in the space of the throat?'; 'Do you tend to stop breathing at a certain stage of the movement?'.

You need the various aspects in order to educate your sensitivity to the differences, and you need your sensitivity to the differences, in order to clarify the aspects of movement organisation. By and by, your movement becomes more harmonious. You know then, beyond any explanation, that, as in music, harmony is not dependent upon volume. When you are willing to give up the compulsive volume, it is the beginning of a change in style.

Breath of relief: biological omen

There is a biological signal which comes on without fail and confirms to you that you have found the optimal zone of movement, the zone which your body accepts, in which acquired learning can occur. You receive that signal from your breathing.

When your movement strikes the right balance, a change takes place in your breathing. The breathing becomes orderly and quiet, soft and long. Sometimes an especially long inhalation portends the change. This is a kind of spontaneous sigh of relief of one who knows he has finally come home. This breakthrough emerges of its own accord and gives testimony to the transition from an artificial exercise to a movement which belongs to you. It is impossible to fabricate this breath of relief, but it is possible to navigate movement with sensitivity until your body discovers full breathing on its own.

In the performance of any organic act, there is no need to hold a preconception of the right way to do it. It is possible to feel your way to, and approximate, your intended movement, relying on the feedback of your own sensations. It is possible to generate a movement, extending it as it comes, and then to withdraw a little and to wait. Repeat the movement, each time withdrawing in a slightly different manner, until the movement and the zone which triggers the expansive breathing become congruent with each other. It is interesting to realise how slight a withdrawal is actually needed in order to elicit the confirming breath. Actually, a minor concession makes a major difference.

We were raised to be goal-oriented, and to be honest it is not easy to give up this approach. But it is up to us to give a different content to the concept of achievement. Instead of identifying achievement in quantitative terms of range and speed, it is possible to provide achievement with a content of sensitivity and balance.

There is no need to give up striving to be a good mover, but good is not necessarily far or fast, large in quantity, or strong and overcoming. Good can be when you breathe with the movement and feel comfortable, elegant and joyful. It is your choice to perform fewer mechanical motions and selectively search for that quality which brings the breath of relief.

Beyond any expectation, the minor movements have power to bring about change and healing. As liquids rise in the capillaries, defying the force of gravity, so a minor movement with a minimum of involvement avoids the parasitic effort of the set behavioural patterns. When the amount of movement is minimal, it takes on another essence. At this minor level of activity the movement may be hardly perceptible to the eye, but it already carries the code of operation and it is there, on this initial level, that this code is most open to change.

Teach the brain to harvest satisfaction: a reversed immune process

Is the brain designed to increase pleasure in life? When you look at a clean wall and immediately point out the one stain on it, do you take the time to appreciate the cleanliness of the background or do you concentrate on the flaw?

The way it is geared, the brain is quick to spot the irregular; it tends to disregard the satisfying background and look for the imperfections. Who of us did not grow up to realise that we received the most attention for what we did wrong? It is possible that the human brain is structured to survive in a natural environment where the swift observation of negative signals can be crucial. Are we indeed allowing the defensive brain to conduct our relatively secure life? Can you figure out how life would look if we were to listen to music in an attitude of lying in wait for the flaws of the performance, instead of enjoying it? What can be done in order to re-educate the brain to listen to pleasure?

It seems to me that the objective of human progress is to consciously make room for a more optimistic perspective. To be a developed human being is to go beyond preoccupation with wrong, to acknowledge what is gratifying and to envision potential. Arrival at a state of spiritual affluence is maturing from saying no, transcending fear, functioning from a balanced place that remembers the satisfying background as well as seeing the foreground which might endanger it.

Awareness Through Movement offers constant opportunity to see the positive, to recognise the easy and the enjoyable. Whatever may be your difficulty or trouble, the movement gives you direct access to possibilities for improvement. Gentle learning is a kind of reversed immunisation process. Instead of increasing, in small portions, your tolerance to negative influences — and becoming progressively more rigid — you learn to open up your receptivity to more pleasure. When you take the time to feel your way, to find simplicity in movement, and to appreciate its balance, when it is safe and gratifying, your brain learns to say 'yes' to life.

Ninety per cent doing non-doing

To search for ease means in many cases to do things less strongly, less quickly, less far. This may be more difficult than doing more. Try to bite your food less intensely, or to speak more slowly. You will surely agree that it is easier for you to do the maximum than to find the patience and the self-discipline to restrain the mechanical momentum of your activity. No person who respects freedom tends to accept censorship. Generations of humanity needed the higher power of religion or the authority of social taboos to compel them to restrain their impulses.

Implicit in the statement that at the most we only use 10 per cent of our brain, is the judgement that we are not doing enough. It is also possible, however, to see it another way. While 10 per cent of the brain is engaged in performing, 90 per cent of it is necessary to maintain the inhibition of the rest of the organism. Not to be swept into participation is a vital element of the organisation of action. In order to play a note with one finger, the other nine fingers must know how not to react impulsively as is natural to them, but to produce a non-doing, an inhibition which is no less complex a differentiation than that of doing.

Those same traits which bring the playing of music to the level of flowing harmonic ease are also skilled in setting the body in motion. In the preparatory stage, that same mindfulness, observation, self-investigation and search for the optimal and sensitive regulation of conditioned activity is indispensable. Your performance will be sensitive and graceful, precise and competent in identifying the degree to which it is necessary to inhibit the parasitic clumsiness clinging to it — in other words, competent in coping with varying levels of non-doing. From this perspective, when you devote your resources to how it is possible to do less, how it is possible to block the compulsive, how to leave out the redundant, then you have a more extensive hold on your personality than if you only listened to that part of you which is performing. When you begin to give your attention to that which you avoid doing, you are listening to the operation of 90 per cent of yourself.

Awareness: the gate for late learners

What is the difference between movement which is done with awareness, and an exercise done without it?

Paying attention is the alchemy that improves the quality of action, as is expressed in Feyn's book *Hallo Mister God, Here is Anna*, where the little girl says that she listens to people so that the most beautiful things will come out of their mouths. Being aware of how you do what you do is the reminder your organism needs in order to restore its striving to do its best. In awareness there is always gain for life; when you are aware of something negative it generates in you a process towards correction. When you are aware of something positive it makes it into an unaccidental asset, available for you to use.

Movement that takes place without 'listening' to the way it is being carried out is mechanical movement. It's like a flight that's locked on automatic pilot. Our routine habits are like this, serving us absentmindedly, in exactly the same manner, time after time. Fixed on the final goals such a movement is only capable of poor adaptability to what takes place in the world outside, or to the body's condition inside.

Mindful Spontaneity

The trap of mechanical movement lies in its tendency to cover up its blindness with greater speed and greater force. Its striving is expressed through acceleration and intensity. The tension wasted in it is destructive and unnecessary, and conceals the way back to economic elegance. This is a gear stuck in power rather than in sensitive searching. Feldenkrais calls it parasitic effort.

When you are trained in movement that is accompanied by awareness, as in the manual flying of a plane, you learn to read your sensory clocks, and receive the feedback about the condition of each of your parts and about the interaction between them all. From moment to moment, as you keep guiding the movement, you are alert to rectifying it without any sense of criticism. You listen to its response in order to consider how to continue the function. This alternate acting and checking merges to guide you in fulfilling your intention while you learn to be in a dialogue with life.

To be aware is to be patient to interweave listening phases throughout the fabric of your activity and to collect a lot of information about the small details of doing. Awareness expands your time into leisure time, rich in happenings. It pacifies your mechanical rush to immediately react in a habitual way, pretending to have preconceived knowledge of how to do it right. Awareness gives you permission to wait and observe until things become more clear.

Your individual outlook is sometimes the only contribution you can make to the chain of events. When you agree to leave the paved road for a moment, to step aside and observe what is happening from another point of view, where things might be perceived differently, you have already succeeded in cutting off the automatic limitation of your act. The pause for awareness gives you the freedom to become involved in the act in another, original way, which now may be more suitable for you. Someone once said that awareness is like a clutch pedal to human freedom.

Doing which is accompanied by awareness sifts out the compulsion, the mentality of inevitable tension, the chronic demands, the bitterness of frustration and the impulse to barren effort. All of these become unnecessary and drop out by themselves once you notice how you do what you do.

Awareness is like a sieve which rids you of the chaff and preserves the grain. Indeed you are left with that which acts as your support, and you receive confirmation of this through the pleasure it gives you. If you want to know whether you acted out of awareness or without it have a look at how you feel afterwards. If you are drained and exhausted you have probably mechanically reconstructed the same old exaggerated manner of action, commitment oriented, that does not leave room for pleasure. If work was hard for you possibly you considered the quota and overlooked the 'how'. When you are with the 'how', and you have more than one 'how', you end up refreshed and content.

When you accompany your movement with awareness you do not struggle to stretch reluctant muscles as if it were your serious commitment to the world, reinforcing frustration, but rather you indulge in pleasurable graceful movement, building up in your brain an image of success. You use your movement as a medium for making contact with your higher faculties. Only through your prominent brain can you convince the mother tongue of movement habits to transform itself into a newer, richer, and more accurate language.

You are unable to re-enact what was originally acquired by the innocent growing child through his or her alert senses, curiosity and endless experiments. But you are able to use the same method through which the child learned. You can consciously remind yourself that you have permission to experiment with more than the one conventional way, and give yourself time to assess the new. What comes to the child spontaneously you can acquire through awareness. Awareness is your main auxiliary tool for the reconstructed learning of the adult. It consists of reading the textbook written within yourself.

When you explore the hidden world of movement in your awareness laboratory, one detail at a time, and begin to discern differences between sixty-six shades of grey, you may discover whether you are truly doing what you think you do. You may find that a way of functioning which seems to you to be symmetrical is actually biased. For instance, you've been swimming all you life, and have assumed that both your legs work in an identical way. Going through the process on the ground, intimately exploring a specific movement in each leg separately, you begin to see differences, preferences, and the dissimilarities with which each leg carries out the function. Possibly one knee is more willing to open and turn sideways, one ankle flexes somewhat more easily than the other, one leg is quicker than the other, more skilled at moving separately while the other leg seems confused when it has to move independently. You never noticed this until the systematic process gave you the opportunity to notice and evaluate the net capacity of each side separately. Such discernment by itself begins a process of narrowing the gap between the two sides.

Or you may, perhaps, reach the realisation that the investment of effort which you considered to be relevant isn't actually necessary. Take, for example, a movement like lifting your head with the help of your hands from a position of lying down on your back. You may be used to doing this in a sit-up-like manner, straining your stomach and stretching your nape, tightening your jaw, holding your breath and hardening the look in your eyes. During a process of Awareness Through Movement that reviews the various aspects of this functional topic, you begin to notice your tendencies and learn through your own experience that you can carry out the function without all those penalties. You may reach a way of coordination in which it becomes feasible for you to lean the weight of your head on your arms and not strain the muscles of the neck. You learn to draw the power needed for raising the weight of the head by thrusting your spine towards the floor, and expanding your stomach while breathing, thus allowing the neck to remain loose and the eyes to be soft. You realise that a routine reaction of overstraining the neck and the stomach muscles, which you accepted as unavoidable, can actually be replaced by a less coercive and damaging organisation. Even a pace which seemed to be the only appropriate one for you becomes open to a game of slowing down or acceleration. When you're ready for the idea that anything can be done in a number of different ways, you not only improve the specific performance but also gain a tune-up of your senses for designing your personal style of moving in general. In re-adjusting your judgemental faculties you have a better tuned instrument for playing your song of life.

This personal song is perhaps the deepest mission of each of us. Feldenkrais always emphasised the relationship between his method and the assignment of putting your own unique imprint on your life. As he repeatedly said, 'When you know what you do you can do what you want'.

You don't find through awareness a ready map for an ideal movement. The ideal you have to gain yourself through an autonomous exploration in which awareness is the compass. Your observations along the way nourish your movement intelligence and inspire you to be resourceful. Improvement is a conclusion produced by your organic system itself when you shed light on the given conditions. Awareness is the human juncture between subconscious vitality and cognitive wisdom. In this meeting you can transform your doing into learning to improve.

When you make awareness a way of life you profit beyond solving problems at a level that a minimal accidental existence requires. You begin to like the process of looking for solutions and you are ready to enjoy the expanded game of development. This is a choice of growth and not holding on to something, out of fear, that somehow manages to survive.

Movement as mirror

Beyond those advantages, perhaps, awareness has a value of its own. Our need for feedback, for receiving the reflection of our personality through the reactions of the people around us, is a fundamental, deep and constant yearning for awareness. We are pulled towards knowing and confirming again and again who we are, how we're responded to, what our limits are, and what kind of imprint we leave on our surroundings. We need a mirror until we mature to form our self-perception by ourselves.

In the processes of Awareness Through Movement, you receive an abundance of ideas that satisfy this bottomless thirst to know yourself. You also receive the message that your self-image is open to growth and change. On the floor you repeat your movements time after time, as if you were imitating what you do in order to have a better view of yourself. You do in order to observe, and you observe in order to improve what you do. Your activity constructs within you the perception you hold of yourself.

When you rest from moving you learn how to make the floor into a mirror, and it reflects back to you your topographic structure. According to the sensation of pressure, you become aware where there is a protrusion or depression, where you are capable of leaning, and where you are trapped in tension. You read in this versatile map of pressures on the floor the changes you have undergone in the course of the lesson. You realise how precisely your organism responds to the manner in which you put it to work. You wonder not only at the physical results but also at your skill in observing all those subtleties revealed to you. Your sensitivity can become so refined that you can detect subtleties of differences that you wouldn't have believed to exist. You never imagined that you could know so much about yourself.

You make your breath into a mirror that tells you about your condition, about your investment of effort and the permission you give yourself to live your life fully. You learn to make all your movements into a multi-dimensional mirror that reflects back to you your personality, your body, your style, your attitude towards yourself, your beliefs, your drives, your total self.

This mirror of awareness is one of the things that attracts people to this method. They soon feel that here there is a living source that corresponds to a thirst they didn't even know about. Beyond the improvement of the movement, this generosity of taking a full hour to be enchanted with yourself and with the metamorphosis you undergo, discovering who you are, is permission for unconditional acceptance, a pure self-loving.

You carry your enriched self-image beyond the lesson. Your presence is perhaps the sum total of awareness you had devoted to your way of functioning.

Touch for touch's sake: nourishment for self-knowledge

One way of learning movement options is through the language of touch, the most faithful of all mirrors. By one touch you can know a whole world about another person. Through the same touch you can also communicate explicitly to the other person what it's hard for words to say, and be certain that he or she understands what you've conveyed in exactly the way you mean it.

When you touch the person that's with you and feel him, that's the moment in which the person also feels himself. He then knows how he is feeling, what's going on inside him, what he's like — a kind of knowledge that precedes thought. This is a mirror of touch that not only tells but also listens, a touch that does not come to manipulate, but to converse and await the reply, a touch not meant to give or to take, but to join, to be together and learn together — a pure, acknowledging touch of which we've probably never had enough, and which remains the most deprived need in our culture. The need for touch is so deprived at times that it misleads us into believing that we need sex, in the hope that it will give us the touch we need. This hope isn't always fulfilled.

In the animal world, when a cub is just born, the very first thing its mother does is to lick it all over. With the touch of her tongue she imbeds within the cub's brain its initial image of its total self. In addition, if there are several newborn siblings who constantly rub up against each other throughout the improvisations of their training games, every part of their body absorbs further knowledge of how it is and how it functions, and reinforces the construction of the self-image in its entirety. In contrast, when looking at a human baby that is born without siblings, placed distant and lonely in a crib, isolated by a screen of diapers and clothes that allow only a poor play of touch, we can begin to understand why it's so difficult for a person to dare be fully himself or herself, why it's hard to feel at home in one's own body. When the little baby cries for help and yearns for a touch that will bring it back from the alienating space to a sense of itself, the parent suspects that the baby will become spoiled and manipulative. How many babies have the privilege of being touched for the sake of touch per se, and not for another purpose — not by way of changing a diaper or being fed?

A need that wasn't fulfilled at the time tends to bind us in the frustration of pursuit, until our receptivity becomes impaired and we are no longer capable of absorbing the benefits when that which we sought is given to us. We resign ourselves to society's taboo on touching, and even recoil from it.

Touch that bestows awareness gives immediate support. The message of support is transmitted with such clarity that no person can avoid responding to it, beginning to melt down his or her hard and defensive core. The Feldenkrais Method offers a rich path, which runs parallel to Awareness Through Movement, called Functional Integration: this is taught, hands on, individually, for special problems. In these one-to-one sessions, the teacher lends the sensitivity of the hands and his or her level of awareness to the student, assisting the student to explore and expand options. This is a profound and immensely broad realm in its own right, an art form developed from a school of thought and the wisdom of hands which may take years of direct apprenticeship to acquire. I don't intend to describe it in this book.

Those who have not been privileged to receive a private lesson in the Feldenkrais Method of Functional Integration through touch can nevertheless learn to receive its message through the group sessions of Awareness Through Movement. The guided movement sessions are actually a translation of the private lessons. In the more programmed group session, the student, following suggestions, explores those same functional possibilities, and applies the same intelligence of awareness, the same orientation towards competence improvement, the same appreciation for reciprocal relationships between parts through the same passive style; it's as if the student were guided to give the treatment process to him or herself, in the same atmosphere, with the same attentiveness. The unintentional learning which takes place in the nervous system when you are passive in a Functional Integration lesson is then enriched by the intentional conscious mastery which occurs when you are active in an Awareness Through Movement lesson.

Learning in the presence of a witness

I am not a teacher, Moshe often used to say. People can learn, but no-one can teach. Is it possible, then, to give up the teacher?

Organic Learning — Learning Through Options

I was present once when Moshe sat with a small child who was born brain-damaged; she came from abroad for a full month each year to work with him. After the developmental stages of crawling, walking and even jumping were achieved, the next problem was reading. Moshe sat with her, applying the fundamentals of his method to the issue of reading. The lesson went like this: she read several words which she knew and at the instant that she stopped at a word where she had difficulty, he read that word instead of her. After that he let her continue with what she herself knew. This arrangement was repeated all down the page. The teacher actually did not give her a chance to establish a state of frustration, and quickly pulled her up before she had time to formulate a negative opinion about her reading ability. At the same time he was careful to avoid interfering with that part which she could manage on her own. It is important to note here that even when the teacher is not directly assisting, he is still there and giving support by his presence.

Primal learning in Nature is so designed that it occurs in the presence of the parents. The pupil learns better when there is a caring witness to observe and give a feeling of support if necessary. A vulnerable and innocent creature is not meant to begin to learn alone. In order for the child to dare to experiment and make mistakes, he or she needs to feel secure, to know that someone is watching who has the power to put things back to rights.

Such a witness is not meant to give advice. The most important virtue of the witness is to control the temptation to instruct how to do things correctly. The best thing the witness can do for you is to not interfere, just to watch you making your mistakes, as long as they are not doing any harm, knowing that you need to make them in order to become stronger and more independent. Such a witness can line up an area of experimentation for you and welcome with enthusiasm your process of experiments. At most, once in a while, the teacher will provide a tactful hint to help you over an obstacle.

This patience to allow someone the time to ripen from within is a virtue that academic learning in our culture has perhaps missed. Supreme sensitivity to the degree of readiness in another is perhaps not always possible as a rule of life, but it is a biological necessity for a learning situation in its beginning stages. Its reward is the fuller independence which the pupil will gain in the future. For instance, in Japan people grow up to behave with remarkable discipline and to faithfully accept their commitments to the community. But this is not the prevailing atmosphere during the period of growth. Children in Japan are treated with an amazing lack of constraints. It is the custom that until the age of three one does not say 'No' to the child. I have seen an eighteen-month-old baby holding a toy and beating her mother in the face with it. The Japanese mother did not forbid, did not preach, did not project a judgement on the baby, nor take the toy out of her hand — but only kept on repeating the word 'gently, gently'. I was amazed at her resourcefulness in treating the act in positive terms. The quality of the child's movements was immediately transformed.

How is all this reflected when you come as an adult to reconstruct your movement habits in positive terms? When you experience the process of Awareness Through Movement you are your own witness. This is the advantage of awareness. When you act out of consciousness, you are simultaneously both the doer and the patient observer, whose presence gives support while standing on the side. It is as if you duplicate yourself and have a source of encouragement both balanced and perceptive, without disturbing your experiment. When you act without your awareness reporting back to you about your actions, you feel lonely and solitary without feedback, dependent upon others.

When you are in a group ATM lesson with a teacher, you are the main witness of yourself. The teacher of an Awareness Through Movement lesson is not engaged in personal correction of the students. If the teacher sees that you are confused, that you do not understand the instructions or are surpassing your border of safety, your name will not be mentioned in front of the others, and you will not be corrected in private; instead, the teacher will repeat the instructions to the whole group, outlining more and more aspects and images, until you catch on and correct yourself, so that what you do will be congruent with what you think you are doing. When the teacher doesn't rob you of your trust in yourself, you progress at a higher level than that of a correction of movement alone.

There is a virtue in the fact that the teacher does not deal with you personally. Even a comment in a gentle tone is liable to uproot you from your inner process and revert you to the school syndrome, in which you perhaps felt frustrated whenever you faced criticism or thought that you were supposed to hit the target of the teacher's expectations — even if the whole matter was not clear to you. A good supervisor does not, for the sake of a short-term solution, deny students the process of establishing their own judgement mechanism, does not suggest that one is supposed to grasp 100 per cent of the lesson, but rather appreciates their coping with it and knows that if they are left to their own search they will pull out the best solution possible for them at present. One of the signs that you are a healthy person is when you are immersed in your learning process and someone attempts to help: you resist and reject it. Just like a child of three who stands up for his or her rights time and again saying 'I'll do it myself!'. This is before the child has submitted and is put into the framework of assignments which deprive him of the joy of learning for the rest of his life.

If you have not received the generous support of a witness — if the witness has interfered to short-cut the process by directly correcting you — you may still be stuck in a stage where you do not trust yourself and have difficulty in sorting out your process by yourself. You still have the need for approval by others. In Awareness Through Movement you have an opportunity to wean yourself from the need to excel in the eyes of others. When you move with awareness your movement is not like reciting by heart a piece that has to please others, but your movement has rather the tone of a conversation between friends, with listenings and silences between you and yourself. When you search for a way to find more ease for yourself, it becomes clear that you will discover it only through your internal feeling. You begin to excel for your own sake, not for the sake of others.

In Awareness Through Movement you learn again to bring out, from within, your independent guide. You are given encouragement to become friendly with the confusion of ignorance which is characteristic of learning. After all, you are in a strange land, in the territory of the unknown. Even that which is already known is reconsidered, reopened to examination, and feels alien to you. The hardest thing to learn is something which you think you already know. The process induces within you a climate of learning without fear, without the penalty of being considered a failure in the eyes of others, and you learn to learn by yourself, through your own awareness.

Even a teacher needs a teacher

Self-examination is not easy, and few of us are able to do this sincerely. Teachers are especially in danger of ceasing to examine themselves, and are liable to remain stuck in one place. A teacher, having verified that the information to be transmitted to the students is valid and useful, may feel no need to continue to ponder upon and re-examine it. The teacher may have a tendency to file it away as a closed subject which can be passed on to others as it is, over and over again. This is arrested growth, in which some teachers who have succeeded in teaching are especially liable to be trapped. Not knowledge, but the striving to apply it, searching for more and more ways to put it to use, is what makes the difference in life. This striving inspired all of us at the beginning of our lives, when it was implanted in the presence of a witness. We all need the humility to admit that at every stage of our progress we still need that witness. It is a privilege indeed to find the proper witness, whether it be another person or the observer within oneself.

Change: the dynamics of improvement

What is actual improvement and how is it achieved? In the following pages you will find an example of the procedure involved in building towards improvement — one of the classical demonstrations of the Feldenkrais Method.

Sit on the front of a chair, without leaning on the chair-back. Take a moment to assess how comfortable sitting is for you. Bring the right arm forward, bent slightly at the elbow, with the hand and fingers hanging downward. Place the left hand on the seat beside you, and begin to gently lead the right arm to the left, around your body. Repeat this a number of times. Note the point on the wall to which your nose points when you reach the limit of the turn, without

trying to extend it by excessive effort. Make a note of this point as the base-line of your ability to rotate your body around itself. Put your hand down and rest.

How can this movement be improved? Is the extension of the range of the movement the only component that can be considered an improvement?

The functional approach is interested in the degree of ease with which you can experience that range of movement, in the level of harmony between all the parts of the body coordinated in the action, in the attitude which accompanies the activity so that movement will not be perceived as a coercion of arbitrary exercise but rather as a natural gesture. All these are qualities which can only be distinguished subjectively and which certainly do not improve as a result of mechanical repetitions straining to achieve a greater range, quantitatively measured.

Once again raise your right arm in front of your chest, bent at the elbow, with the hand suspended down. Let your eyes close and imagine for a moment that your forearm is resting on a table or a shelf which is slightly lower than your shoulder, and allow the adjustment in your organisation to occur accordingly from within.

Open your eyes, and this time slowly lead your right arm to the right and return again to the centre, following your hand with your eyes. Be aware of what happens behind you in your back. Sense how with every movement to the right side, the right shoulder-blade alternately tightens and loosens its contact with the spine. After a few times, put down your arm and rest.

This is actually an exploration of a variation of the original movement — a sort of intentional mistake. Instead of attempting to improve by repeating the movement of the hand to the left, you go in the opposite direction.

Once again raise your right arm in front of your chest; lead your arm to the right as before, this time turning your head and eyes to the left. The arm moves right and your head moves left. Feel if this contradiction entails a moment of confusion. See if you can be kind to yourself, taking the time you need for reaching clarity. Can you breathe while in this challenging condition? Repeat gently a number of times, then rest.

Again raise your right arm and lead it, as in the beginning, around your body to the left. This time, turn your head and your eyes to the right. Be aware of your chest bone and invite it to take part in the movement. Listen to where

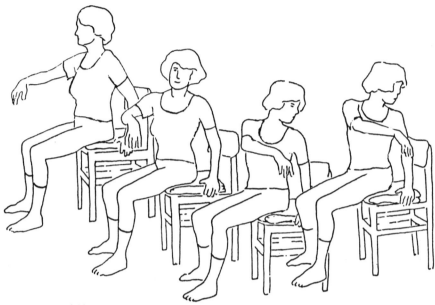

The Dynamics of Change
Twisting the trunk around one's longitudinal axis is an exclusive human skill and is utilised here as a medium for the prospect of updating movement habits. What determines the boundaries of capacity — the muscles, the structure, or the operation plan in the brain? When you experience the non-habitual options of movement you begin to discover your potential.

the chest chooses to go. Does it turn with the hand to the left? Or perhaps it is possible to turn the chest, with the head, ever so slightly, in a hint of a gesture to the right? Leave everything and rest fully by leaning on the back of the chair.

When you are ready to reap the harvest of what may have appeared to be senseless experiments, return to sitting on the front part of the chair and test again the original movement, with the right hand travelling to the left around your body. Notice now the point on the wall to which your nose can reach.

Assess whether the range of movement has progressed, and estimate how many degrees were added to your twist. More importantly, pay attention to the feeling which now accompanies the movement. Does it now come somewhat more naturally and willingly?

Perhaps you are curious to know how this works? How, in a few moments have you succeeded in making the performance of your action better and more pleasant? How do you have more vital mobility in rotation at your disposal without having to strain, without having to stretch muscles, without activating

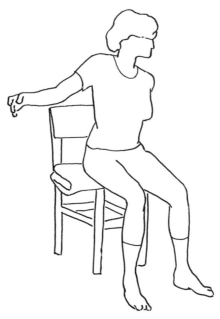

Disassociating Old Ties
Differentiating the movement of the hand from the direction of the eyes interferes with the tendency to be stuck in the conditioned relationship between them. When you realise even though in learning 'hot house conditions' that such a differentiation is possible, without threat, a surprising freedom of movement opens up for you.

your willpower, without having done all those things which people generally think they have to do in order to improve?

You succeeded because you probably did something your nervous system is built to do. You systematically supplied it with a range of deviations from the original assignment — 'intentional mistakes', from which it can choose that which is most suitable. During this independent process of filtering the raw materials and sensing their differing challenges, your system accesses its intelligence and improves its performance.

For example when you are guided, in the process, to lead your hand in one direction and your head in the other, this significantly undermines a deeply entrenched pattern. In life, the eyes are accustomed to accompanying the movement of the hand to such an extent that this becomes a conditioned relationship, in which one member dares not perform without the other. Possibly this process was the first time in years that your system experienced such a clear differentiation between the hand and eye. Since this was done pleasantly, without competition, with patience for personal pace, this differentiation succeeded in being registered in the brain as a possibility. Immediately afterwards, as you once again led your hand through the original intention, the head and the hand had already shaken off their limiting relationship and each could act to its full independent capacity. You realised that the range of the movement had been extended, and the resistance to it had been reduced.

You went through additional variations when you led your chest in an unconventional manner. This uncommon context magnified your discovery of its independent ability. All of these are clues which set the condition for a renewed decision in the brain to refine the quality of action. This, in a nutshell, is the dynamics of organic improvement from within, improvement which has no fixed limit. The more you continue to apply this principle, the more progress you will harvest.

If you are prepared to explore some more, sit again on the edge of the chair. Turn your trunk to the left, this time supporting yourself with both hands on the left of the seat of the chair. Holding this twisted position, estimate the distance of the right buttock from the seat of the chair. With tiny movements, move the right buttock alternately closer to and further from the seat of the chair, keeping your head and shoulders in their original location in space.

After a number of times, turn yourself to the front and check again the scope of the movement of your right arm turning around you to the left. Are there signs of further ease?

In the same way, lean with both hands to the left while you gently twist the torso to the left. Leave it there and straighten only the shoulders to the front, the right shoulder pulling back and the left pushing forward in tiny, slow movements. Keep the head turned to the left.

Once again, notice how the differentiation of the function of the shoulders from the rest of the body contributes to the rotational movement. Check again the result in your arm movement relative to the original twist. Pay particular attention to improvements in the quality of the movement. Do you experience greater willingness and ease as you turn around? Does the movement become smoother and more simple?

Once again, lean your two hands on the seat of the chair to the left. Twist comfortably as far as you can to the left, and this time return only your head to the front. This actually is the most habitual pattern in everyday life. The trunk is held frozen and the movement is done only by the neck.

Continue to turn your head gently, slowing down the movement so that you can release excess tensions in the rest of yourself. Then, each time you turn the head to the front, leave your eyes looking to the left. Let your eyes attach themselves to the left corner of each eye while your head continues to turn gently to the right. Take the time necessary to organise this differentiation. The most impressive result you obtain may be perhaps from the isolation of the smallest movement. This movement is tiny — only a turn of the eyeball within its socket — but its significance is not measured according to size but according to innovation. See if it is possible to breathe while dealing with a new situation.

Leave everything. Rest and listen to the physical sensation within your skull as a result of the unconventional use of the eyes. You may interpret this as a sign of awakening from routine.

Once again check the movement of the original turn. At this stage, as still more degrees are added to the turn, some people cannot hide their amazement at the removal of even more barriers. The original marking point on the wall is left far behind. This amazement is not only for the present accomplishment, but for the prospect that there is indeed no limit to improvement.

You will experience another encouraging perception when you apply the whole procedure to the other side. First make your initial check, leading your left arm in front of you around to the right, slightly lower than shoulder height. Notice the point on the wall to which your nose is pointing. It is a common observation that the initial point on the second side is considerably better than the initial point on the first side. This once again illustrates that learning takes place in the brain's command post, even if the specific muscles on the second side have not yet undergone the preparatory procedure.

Feldenkrais suggests that the work on the second side be done in the imagination. Imagine bringing your left hand forward, at a height requiring the least amount of effort, and only in your imagination rehearse the movement of the hand travelling to the left, and the movement of the head to the right. You may be surprised at your ability to know precisely what is taking place between the shoulder-blades and the spine, where the obstinate vertebra in your spine is, and what is entailed in turning your chest with your head or with your hand — all in your imagination only.

In the same way, organise yourself into the starting position for each of the other stages, and perform each action only in your imagination. Listen within, and in this quiet place gather information as to how the movement takes place.

Finally, perform the original test and actually lead your left hand to the right. Realise what grew out of a few moments spent in the imagination. You may find you have attained a more sophisticated and elegant result, and in less time.

This is the advantage that the organic brain has over the material world. In the material world, in order to repair two car tyres you have to take care of each one of them. In the nervous system, it is enough to deal with one of them, and the second will borrow the knowledge from the functional archives of the brain.

Improvement: unpredictable change

'I climbed all the stairs without becoming short of breath.'

'That was the only hour during this entire year since my husband died that I forgot my sorrow.'

'Every time I get into the car after a class, I have to readjust the mirror; it's too low.'

'I teach sports, and to my surprise I discovered many places in my body that I knew nothing about . . . all kinds of new and interesting muscles hitherto unnoticed in my profession.'

'Throughout high school I was ashamed of my body. I hated gym class. Now I see that I can feel good about my movement in front of people.'

'I barely made it to the session, I was so tired and impatient. Now I am totally refreshed.'

It is exciting to see people surprised when their own bodies change for the better. At the end of a session you get up off the floor, stand on your feet, and can assess the change against your familiar criterion of standing in the gravitational field. This is a moment in which the essence of a new message, condensed from a whole hour of Awareness Through Movement process, comes from within. As you stand quietly, you slowly become aware of an internal reorientation which leads you, part by part, to find your new place. It is as if the lesson unwinds in an epilogue of calmness, and then you are able to see the change it has created within you.

The outcome of the process might be that you feel lighter, as though floating and weightless. Yet, at the same time, you realise that your weight is fully present and your feet are planted on the ground with an extraordinary sense of security. You might have the distinct sensation of lack of tension, your total self connected through a smooth and airy alignment, without intensified sensitivity in your susceptible areas. You may also feel somewhat taller, without trying to stand straighter. You are amazed at the surprising uprightness and at your ability to change. The new self-respect beginning to grow in you puts you in touch with the well-being that Creation intended for you. You stand in such accurate balance that you can't imagine ever wanting to move away from that poise, and at the same time you feel both fresh and alert.

On the other hand, sometimes at the end of a lesson you may stand and feel as though you are going to fall backwards. This is perhaps how you interpret your new uprightness. Or it seems that one shoulder is lower than the other, or that your knees are failing, as though made of butter. You have no idea how it is possible to take a single step forward from this position. You could also find yourself so softened and open that you feel vulnerable and exposed, without your customary defences or your usual pretensions. It may even seem to you that you are standing more bent than usual.

Common to all these states is the lack of coercion or pretence. The sensations with which you are bestowed at the end of the session come to you of their own accord. Your organism presents you with its own unanticipated conclusion, and gives you a glimpse of what it feels is logical and correct for you at the present moment. Your nervous system precedes consciousness and decides for itself its new choice. However, your consciousness might be so confused by the strangeness of the new Gestalt that you may not always find it easy to see through it the benefits of this new arrangement for your well-being.

Every change is initially perceived as a dissonance, and you tend to reject it altogether. Some people impatiently shake their shoulders and neck, or hurry to do their compulsive head circles. Of course, by so doing they are simply re-establishing the previous pattern of faulty distribution of labour, with an under-used back and an over-used neck. Or people sway from one leg to another trying to re-establish in their feet the distribution of weight as recorded in the old familiar distortion. There are others who feel disorientation when they come to write a cheque after the session. Suddenly it is as though the hand hesitates, and has trouble coordinating its movement with the usual flow. The characteristic handwriting regresses to a beginner's stage of infantile ineptitude. This is definitely a feeling of confusion.

We all want to change. But are we really prepared to lose the automatic facility of our familiar style? Can change be so organised that it does not entail a loss of identity? The risk of loss of identity demands a process effective in proceeding carefully and gradually. Feldenkrais frequently mentioned his reservations about the desire to evoke dramatic changes. He emphasised repeatedly the virtue of maintaining a sense of proportion, of changing neither too much nor too fast, and progressing with gentleness and sensitivity so that the gap of strangeness does not become a new problem which precludes improvement.

When you stand at the end of a lesson, and do not recognise the person standing within you, it takes great humility to bear the dissonance without hurrying to correct it, without doing anything about it except to listen and feel what that change is doing to you. This is the lesson's harvest, reaped by means of your observation alone. When you watch in a silence of non-doing you slowly begin to perceive the image of your new state. This is a moment of grace, in which the innovation is revealed to you in full light. You have within yourself a model for a different way of organisation, and you can become acquainted with it.

You pay attention to those changes which impinge on your awareness, and you appreciate their qualities. You follow the new design of your alignment, its directions, angles and distances. You look for sensations of comfort within the new strangeness. You attempt to decipher the mood which the new posture evokes. Observation is a slow task. You need time to consciously survey the details which your nervous system has unconsciously voted for ahead of you. You need time to take note, evaluate, acknowledge, identify with and digest.

You are curious to see how this organisation of posture will stand the test of performing a dynamic function. The simplest thing is to take your new self for a walk. You don't push yourself to walk in the way you are used to doing all your life. You wait and allow an unknown walking to emerge from within. This walking, that arises from within you, is also your criterion for evaluating your actual outcome from the session.

Equals without trying to be equals

In the workshop an extraordinary thing happens. As in any group, people are very different from one another — not only in their uniqueness of personal body structures, but also in their individual level of movement skills. There are those who arrive at the session already flexible, to whom every movement in the process comes easily. There are others who arrive with limitations, for whom every movement is a struggle with their entire history. There are intense people, with an impulse to do everything fast, strong and far; and there are others who test each moment carefully. Some stand at the beginning of the session with arms turned outside so that their palms face the front and their elbows press against the body. For others, in their usual posture, the arms hang loosely so that the forearms touch the body but the elbows are a distance away from it — some more, some less. Some stand with over-straight knees until the legs are stretched in a backward arch, others with knees that knock into one another with the feet turning inwards or outwards, or any asymmetrical combination with infinite variations from person to person.

When participants begin to walk at the end of the process, everyone's walk looks similar. Walking is then in the same style, the same atmosphere, the same tone, the same rhythm which allows the same quiet breathing. In this walk the feet meet the ground with greater softness, and flow onward without the usual punctuating emphasis. A large majority have their arms suspended loosely in close contact with the body, turned so that from the front one can see the back of the hands. There is no excessive movement in the arms; even the alternate waving of rapid walking becomes unnecessary now as the walking is slow, and both arms resonate simultaneously in a passive swing to the beat of the step. People's spines seem less rigid, with fewer separate sections to conflict with one another. There are fewer angles in the contour. The back radiates a feeling of fluid continuity and coordination.

There is no-one for whom something has not melted, leaving behind the frozen, stuffed animal-like way of holding the body; everyone seems a little warmer, reconciled and humane. For everyone some of the sharp edge of nervous everyday living has been dulled. Ordinary movements which had forgotten the taste of enjoyment are now suffused with the grace of pleasure. The faces, perhaps more than any other part, reflect the degree to which people are experiencing the best of themselves. Many faces now shine with a subtle wonder, like that seen in children with their expression of carefree curiosity and modest satisfaction in the vital experience they have had.

The phenomena of such a diverse group of people now moving in the same style is particularly astonishing, since during the entire hour of the process there was no demonstration to be imitated, no standard was set, and there was no room for comparison between one person and another. Each individual dealt with his or her own movements, sometimes even with eyes closed. How then did everyone approximate the same common denominator of quality?

It seems that people become more equal to one another not because they tried to achieve a uniform outcome but by virtue of that same sincerity which guided their search for the personal optimum. As people tune themselves to function in a way which is more faithful to organic logic, they are bound to arrive at a place in which there are fewer individual deviations. This organic honesty cannot be learned by imitating a final product, an ideal movement. Organic honesty is not the movement but the quality in the self-motivated quest to find it. The Feldenkrais process which nurtures your personal search brings you, at its conclusion, to a way of standing and walking which is closer to the ideal not only from your own point of view but also that of the collective.

Integration of the change

To what extent does this taste of the ideal remain in life, after the process? What can be done so that it will always stay like this? In every group there is someone who asks this kind of question.

There are changes which, of their own accord, are directly applied for use in life, like riding a bicycle: once you learn how to ride you don't have to practice — riding becomes your asset forever. Similarly, following the process of Awareness Through Movement, when a new possibility is registered in the nervous system as beneficial, you don't need to remember the lesson. It is reflected in your actions with that same spontaneity which bypasses the consciousness through which you arrived at it.

Thus a woman who all her life walked with her feet facing outwards, got up from the session and walked forward, with her toes wasting no more time and effort in deviations to the side. Unlike her habitual way, the alignment of her feet was now congruent with her direction of walking. She needed to do nothing more in order to continue this straightening tendency in her day to day life. The process gave her the clue to the habit. It had within it a magnified view of the moment of choosing how to raise her foot off the floor for the next step, while the heel began its detachment from the ground. In the greenhouse environment of the lesson, lying on her back with knees bent and her back relaxed, she could observe several times the way the heel lifts from the ground. She experimented with the possibility of raising the foot so that the outer edge would be last to break contact with the floor. She also experienced the reverse possibility, and noticed which of these options she identified with more. She explored various relationships between the direction of the foot and the plane of the lower leg, thigh and spine. She distinguished where her heel tended to pull at the moment it broke contact with the floor and became free in space. She could feel how her ankle strove to escape inwards, which of course led to throwing the toes outwards. Locating the sensation in the crucial moment was enough to restore her intentional control over an action which had, until that day, been automatic. Like a flash of enlightenment, once she identified how she was caught in it, she never again returned to the habitual behaviour.

There was another case of a young man who suffered pains in his elbow in the midst of his military training, which could not be avoided. In the session, it became clear to him how, each time he tried to mobilise the elbow, his shoulder-blade on the same side recoiled and pressed on the spine in an impulse of self-defence. The options provided in the lesson acquainted him with a reversed arrangement, which enabled him to neutralise the recoiling response of his shoulder-blade. The new arrangement even allowed him to increase the space between his shoulder-blade and his spine. He realised that in this manner, the movement of his elbow could be performed safely. His system immediately adopted the principle of spacing out the shoulder-blade to spare the elbow from the threat of pain, and he was able to continue in his training without suffering or damage.

Nonetheless, in many cases the fresh model of the lesson fades away, and after a while its sensation is forgotten and lost. However, the next time a reminder much briefer than the original process will be sufficient to recapture the same accomplishment. The accomplishment will then have a better chance of lasting longer. Thus through repetition, retreating one step and advancing two, gradually, and in zig-zag, the transformation will come about.

The more that is less

You will achieve the greatest effect if, to the change which took place in the hidden layers of the nervous system on the organic level, you add your conscious perceptions on the human level. You thereby make use of the awareness which accompanied the movement and clarified for you its internal dynamics.

You also need to use your consciousness in order to find the patience not to waste the accomplishment, in case you are tempted to immediately put it to a test which is too difficult. Sometimes people are so thrilled with the new freedom which has been restored to them that they hurry to perform, right away, all those things that they had been unable to do for a long time. With this exaggeration they risk withdrawal.

One girl left the first day of a weekend workshop delighted that a neck pain that had bothered her for months had disappeared. The following day she arrived for the continuation of the workshop in pain, all contracted and disappointed. From her story it turned out that she had taken her new freedom to a disco, and danced with complete abandon until two in the morning. This is a story which repeats itself with many variations. One must take into consideration that the Feldenkrais process plunges you into a new state which is not yet familiar to you. You still cannot read its red lights and your whole judgment system is still not adjusted to it. To use deep change without a process of adaptation is like exposing yourself to a blinding light. Any task which pushes you then to produce results in reality, without being sensitive to the feedback which is crucial in dealing with anything new, exposes you to injury.

One athlete got up from a session and commented with satisfaction that he had significant relief in a knee which had been bothering him for years. He immediately took his recuperating knee to a game of tennis. His penalty was less severe than that of the disco dancer. He said that indeed the knee did not hurt him — it was the game he lost! It was as though he had forgotten how to play. It is not simple to see that the change, which may appear, by ordinary standards, as mere clumsiness, is actually a release from the dictates of habit and the opportunity for re-education in a new coordination. Of course this has to be done with patience, gradually, in a training period of repetition, as education requires.

There were people who said that after a Feldenkrais lesson they preferred to go home on foot. They felt so good and so much more capable that they happily gave up the bus. With all of their joy in walking, however natural the function of walking is, the necessity to complete the distance home put them after a while under a certain amount of stress — the external achievement became more important than the subtle signals from within. When you are under stress your nervous system is bound to return to rely on those patterns it has been accustomed to rely on for years. The delicate suggestion of the lesson is then set aside, dismissed from the agenda. When those people arrived home, nothing remained of the airy sensation which had permeated them at the end of the process.

Please do not jump to the conclusion that walking after a session is harmful. As always, the *how* is important. One woman reported that she left the session and continued to walk all the way home in the same style that emerged for her at the end of the session. She went the whole way without hurrying, without investing more effort, accepting the new, foreign and unconventional movements and listening to them. She said that this was for her a learning experience she will never forget. It is true that she had been a student of Awareness Through Movement for a long time, and the culture of inner listening had already become a part of her.

The session does not end with the process on the floor. Your opportunity for integration is only just beginning. This is the time to take advantage of the new situation in order to cleanse your movements of the parasitical aftergrowths of inefficient tension. This is the blessed time of unconditional openness, when you can start from the beginning to fashion anew your movement style. The confusion of the loss of coordination can be a chance to choose more pleasurable ways of utilising yourself, provided you are willing then not to hurry and not to anticipate a familiar outcome. In order that the moment of grace should not be a mere passing episode, but rather that you derive from it ongoing advantage, you need to invest in it something of yourself, your own conscious observation, for which there is no substitute.

From the standpoint of the new change, you can refine your handwriting, smooth over your stride, find your authentic rhythm, extend your height, and encourage proportional distribution of labour between all parts of your body, allowing the vulnerable parts to recover, letting the organic honesty from within express the person you always wanted to be.

In order to enhance the integration of the change you can initiate alternating motion between losing the accomplishment and reacquiring it. In a tiny range barely detectable by the eye, in doses of miniature movements, with a slowness that knows how to wait, you wander back and forth between the new and old you, until your personal key to improvement becomes clear. For example, at the end of a session you are standing in total comfort with your rib-cage fully experiencing each breath, your head carried high with a feeling that you are on top of your life, your weight feeling like a source of power to you. You like yourself this way. Try then to recall how you usually stand. Within your new stance, try to imagine yourself making a phone call, driving or walking in the street, when you are hurrying to meet all your obligations. In your imagination then you can clearly distinguish the penalty you pay, in the currency of your well-being, for your involvement in civilised life. Pay attention to what begins to alter, where you lose what you gained in the session, in terms of your way of standing, your attitude of mind. A hint of loss is enough. Return again with your entire self to the manner of organisation, the sensation and the feeling which filled you at the end of the session. Continue like this, back and forth, and practise how to bring yourself back to your best from all kinds of situations.

The contrast which is then emphasised between the ideal state and your daily demeanour can awaken your awareness to what happens to you when you are among people. For example, if you have reached a state of well-being at the end of a Feldenkrais session, bring up an image of a confrontation with a certain person in your life. You may then realise, perhaps for the first time, what you are doing to yourself in his or her presence. Do you soften and breathe more fully, or do you tighten your throat, your face, shoulders, stomach, legs, or all of them together? Experiment with shifting your imagination to a different person and you are likely to discover that you organise yourself differently again for each different person. Take the time to return to the memory of the positive model from the end of the session. In your imagination you can play with varying distances of safety to see how far away each person must be in order that your serenity remain undisturbed. You can invite the person to gradually come closer, or go farther away, training yourself to maintain your well-being intact.

This exercise was developed by Ron Kurtz, founder of the Hakomi Method, who recognised the value of the Feldenkrais Method and knew how to utilise the end of the session as a point of departure for cultivating body language consistent with psychological freedom.

3

Family Therapy for the Community of the Vertebrae

Uniform flexibility or discriminative flexibility

Imagine that you had to sign your name with a pen, the handle of which is made up of joints, some of which are linked to each other tightly while others are pliable and loose. How could you control your writing? What sort of a signature would you get? And what would happen to the pen itself at those soft and pliable sections that are the only joints that yield to the pressure and repeatedly articulate at the same point?

It is the same with the spine. Once the double standard in the distribution of labour along the spine is observed, one begins to understand the nature of the back's problem. Have you ever given a thought to how you cope with carrying the weight of your head and holding the solid weight of your shoulder girdle upright, on top of a chain of vertebrae that do not function in uniform flexibility? See if you can sense how your spine sustains the weight of your body in those sections that are tightly joined together; and how the compression of your weight affects the more articulate sections which sustain the pressure while being bent.

What are the consequences of this bending that is always done in the same way, that favours the same direction sideways or inwards to the body, a flexion that is formed with every step, in the same curving pattern? What is involved in righting the posture towards a vertical alignment that assures you reduced curve in the lower back and greater symmetry between one side and another? What are your chances of producing smooth movements that flow with ease, with no fear of injury, when a section of your back behaves like a solid block and only the articulated parts perform the task of bending, and even then prefer the same specific joint to flex?

Are you aware of your back's features; do you feel its unique channels of use? Just as there is not one face in the whole world exactly like yours, so there is no other back that is structured exactly like yours and functions exactly like yours. Your ability to be attentive to your uniqueness can enable you to learn how to improve your habitual patterns. You may perhaps still be expecting salvation to come by means of borrowed and conventional formulas, but no formula can fit the thousand-and-one complex combinations that your exclusive life has created. Even a most longed-for quality such as flexibility, when closely examined, may reveal that it is not the cure-all for back troubles, as is sometimes assumed.

The fixture in between the flexible sections

Who is considered flexible? Is it the person who can pass that common test of bending down to touch the floor with knees straight? Even if we don't relate to the aspect of imposed movement in this test and explore the aspect of the quality of the flexion itself, the questions still are: does the forward bend from the groin and waistline area guarantee that all along the spine, at the level of the shoulder-blades as well, articulation and differentiation are taking place between each vertebra relative to its neighbour?

Is the limit to bending only a physical one, in the bones and tissues? Does the program in one's brain contain the option to move each vertebra separately and one may simply choose not to use it, or is this option denied in principle, even in the realm of one's imagination?

Is the backward curving of the back, into the much-admired bridge, a more reliable testimony to flexibility? Is the deep arch in the lower back a guarantee that in the upper spine the vertebrae can mobilise to open the spaces between one another?

We were brought up to admire flexibility in the waist-line where we can see the movement outlined in space, but in fact when the waist is flexed we may not be aware that the section of the spine at the shoulder-blade level is being pulled along as a single block, fused together with no relative inner articulation.

Apparently, increased flexibility in one area does not indicate a similar quality throughout the rest of the organism. Indeed the contrary may be more accurate. Localised flexibility testifies that this organism always utilises the same section for all bending and twining where it is easier to loosen up and to flex in its own characteristic pattern. At the same time the organism will avoid activating the stiff, unyielding parts. When imbalance is struck in the division of labour, then the organic logic, as sure as the law of gravity, will once and again find the least resistant channel of functioning, and the imbalance will only receive confirmation and become established in its own pattern.

Should we conclude then that the excessive flexibility in the preferred zones is what causes us the harm, or should we first examine the other end of this discrimination in the division of labour, and observe the stiffness of the shoulder-blades?

Sideways undulation of the rib-cage in water

Is the roundness of the upper back, at the juncture of the spine and shoulder-blades, stiff by virtue of its structure? Has it always been like that?

A glance at human functioning from the perspective of evolution sheds light on what can be expected from the structure of the back. Let your imagination carry you back several million years to the dawn of life on this planet, before humans had started to invent modes of functioning that were not perhaps the intention of Creation. Possibly the earliest of these inventions was Man's discovery that he could stand on his two hind legs and free his arms for a variety of new forms of functioning, bringing him not only increased control over living conditions, but also inspiring his talent for creativity.

What then, at the dawn of evolution, in the original plan, was the function of the shoulder-blade area in the ocean waters? Call up within your body the memory of a primal swim, rowing forward with fins, undulating smoothly in a continuing motion from side to side as you propel yourself in the water with your belly facing the centre of the earth.

With the sideways undulating movement, the rib fans were opened and closed alternately, and the serpentine motion from side to side rippled the spine in sinuous loops that progressed along its total length, stroking every vertebra in its turn with a round brushing motion. In this snake-like movement, the vertebrae were engaged in a sideways plane flexion. While one side expanded and spread out, the other side contracted and closed upon itself — a movement we do not have much use for in contemporary civilisation. The ribs as well, in the early stage designed to alternate and open each fan, one side at a time, no longer make full use of their potential when functioning in the human fashion of activating both sides simultaneously. Likewise the movement of the shoulders that formerly tended to be pulled closer to and away from the head when moving in water, remains without much utilisation in our lives.

The alternating dance of pressure on solid ground

During the phase when life migrated onto solid ground, the spine was suspended like a hammock, supported by the four springy legs interacting with the earth. To the flowing from side to side was also added the dimension of the frontal wave movement with all its various modulations of forward and backward folds. The vertebrae of the horizontal back were involved in movement only, and were not called upon to sustain the pressure of the body's weight as well. Furthermore, they were free of the concern to continually balance the upright posture in a vertical alignment.

In four-legged creatures, what were the dynamics in the shoulder-blades area of the horizontal back? Imagine what the experience of your upper back was like when your arms served as front legs. Kinesthetically relive in your mind a cross-crawl wherein each arm follows its opposite foot. Visualise how stepping on the right foot activates, after a slight delay, the extension of the left arm, and thus, stepping on the left foot raises the right arm for the next step. Tune yourself to the rhythm of this fundamental pattern of locomotion. Can you detect the echoes of this movement in your shoulder-blade in walking? Can you figure out the endless times the shoulder-

Mindful Spontaneity

blades slide over the ribs in their alternating dance? Can you imagine the feeling in the upper back vertebrae as they receive this ever-repeated massage with every striding movement?

The Ping-Pong of Cross-Crawling
The force streaming from the back paw to the opposite front paw is then recoiling from the front paw to the back paw on the identical side, thus propelling locomotion. The interaction of the hand with the solid ground elicits the counter-pressure from the earth to transmit throughout the arm-shoulder-shoulder blade-spine, and works to revitalise the upper thoracic vertebrae with every step.

Can you reconstruct the sensation of the front paw pressing on solid ground, producing counter-pressure that straightened the elbow, passed through the upper arm and shoulder to the juncture of the upper back, where it pushed the vertebrae one by one, assisting the undulating motion forward, while at the same time refreshing and awakening the entire organism? Can you make contact with the phenomenon of being passive while the counter-pressure of your front paw-hand-foot stepping on the ground flows through you, and propels your back in a soft way that no wilful movement of yours in space could produce for you? This very pressure of the shoulder-blade on the upper back juncture stimulates the vertebrae to a certain backward recoil which is transmitted through the spine to the opposite rear leg. This leg uses it as a momentum with which it will once more propel the body forward, and thus move across the earth in counter strides.

Shoulder-blades — storage for unexpressed emotions

This entire game of arm and shoulder pressures interacting with the spine, this ping-pong-like tilting of the weight from the front legs backward to the rear legs and forward again, is lost to us. We need to produce steps in a body that no longer has the safe and steady base of four supports, but is also denied the gentle, backward, withdrawing motion. We are left to generate our forward lunge by our own power without the benefit of the economic and rhythmic back-and-forth pulsating motion that walking on all fours brings.

The vertebrae at the juncture of the shoulder-blades, which according to the 'master plan' were involved in the quadro-pedal stride achieving full mobility, are still cued to participate, but in bipedal standing the arms are suspended in the air and retain only a faint echo of their original assignment. Thus the shoulder-blades are left to accumulate tensions from barren readiness for action, and lend their immobile state as a storage bin for all those emotions that have not been accessed. The shoulder-blades having long ago forgotten how to cope with varying situations, will preserve the expression of defensiveness or pretense, apprehensiveness of bursting into anger or lamenting on life's burden, and the shoulder-blades then become the archive of the person's struggles.

The instinctive response to threat

Initially, the back was so constructed that it could be recruited in moments of danger to curl up like a hedgehog. This curling-up positions the body's strongest armour, the backbone, to withstand the blow, to face the world, while protecting those soft, vulnerable parts, like the throat and the belly, which contain life's vital processes.

Fearful of hurting one's head in a fall, fearful of falling prey to a violent attack, every living creature will curl up in this way, obeying a deep and primal instinct of passive defence, in order to suffer the least possible damage.

This inclination is imprinted in our human behaviour as well. Without even being aware of it, we respond to every pain and every injury by curling up, with the intention of turning inward, in a contraction moving from the periphery to the centre. In a four-legged creature the vulnerable parts are already concealed from the surrounding world, and the back can easily complete the curling up movement and fixate in a position of defence; skilled in full motion, it can just as easily recover its carefree, fanned-out form when the danger passes. The last remnants of fear and tension are shaken away by striding on.

Distorted defence

How does the back of the human being, standing on two legs, actually deal with this threat reflex? Where does the curling-up recoil take place? When the lower back, inherently designed with an incurve, receives the emergency signal it increases the curve in the direction in which it is already being held. It pulls the shoulders back and exposes the chest. In the upright stance, self-defence confronts the environment with increased vulnerability, both back and front.

The human back, triggered by the emergency mechanism, will mobilise itself to respond in this way in situations less severe than any physical threat to survival. The lumbar tends to deepen its incurve when dealing with the daily challenges and stress presented by civilised life. The threats of civilised life do not come from unexpected directions in space; most daily challenges engage humanity from the front. The front becomes so dominant in our world perception that the chest may take wholly upon itself the rounding out, protective task of the back. In this reversal of roles, the chest becomes more and more rigid and is pushed out in a statement of its capability to withstand any dangers lurking on the human path. On the other side, the lower back, stripped of its original role, becomes weaker and weaker with the erosion of the compressed vertebrae in the lumbar curve, and the memory of its original protective function fades away, even from the imagination.

The rounded, defensive, hedgehog-like stance at the rear when standing on two feet can only be carried out at the level of the shoulder-blades. The upper ribs behind also volunteer to round out at every threat and will excurve into a hunch at every instance of helplessness and frustration. Lacking full expression of movement as in crawling, there is nothing to shake the shoulder-blades or ribs back to their neutral state and they remain stuck in their defensive hunched posture.

This rounding of the vertebrae and of the ribs attached to them may become solidified in the bones if the need for self-defence is acute and frequent, especially during the growth period. The registration of hard feelings overshadows the feelings of contentment in life; the defensiveness leaves a deeper impact and can distort the body's self-organisation.

And so civilised human beings incline to a crooked back, with the upper half fixated into self-defence, rounding out, and the lower half exhausted in a hollowed, compressed curvature of false defence.

A back that is ceaselessly engaged in the pattern of self-defence is no longer capable of providing protection: chronically overworked muscles that become knotted like hard ropes, to a degree of being painful, are no longer capable of contracting or stretching, and are therefore no longer effective. This very fact that the back is imprisoned in its own pattern might be the source of its trouble. Exchanging one mould for another will not bring about the rehabilitation of the back's ability to manoeuvre for defence, nor give it the capacity to let go of it when defensiveness is no longer needed. In order to rehabilitate the back's intelligent and accurate response to life, the organism needs a way of moving that will be equivalent in its effect to what crawling on all fours does for animals, or to what movement in natural environments does for people in primitive cultures. In order to release the back from its tension-charged posture, it needs to be reminded how to activate its full range of possibilities, including the skill to return each time anew, from any situation, to the grace of a neutral state.

Victims of lazy convexity

People know where they feel pain but they might not know where the disturbance is that causes it. The disturbance which impairs a full movement is not necessarily located in the area in which the pain is felt. The most rigid vertebrae that are reluctant to move in any way are usually those of the upper back around the juncture of the shoulder-blades with the spine. Since the vertebrae in this section are large and strong, and are held fast by the ribs and protected by all the sinews and ligaments binding them together, as in a plaster cast, they can remain in their fixated convexity without arousing any protest or causing any pain.

The penalty will be paid by the areas where the vertebrae are more willing to move. This willingness to be pliant leads to vulnerability and imbalanced exaggeration. The two chains of vertebrae — one in the lumbar curve and one in the cervical curve — the movements of which are not constrained by linkage with the ribs, are the victims of the lazy rigid curve between them. In their diligence they take on themselves the transference from four to two-legged walking, serving as a faithful gyroscope, striving ceaselessly to maintain the vertical alignment of the neck and the lumbar vertebrae, and extending themselves to this task even if the thoracic vertebrae will not cooperate; they take upon themselves extra effort to make up for what is lacking. The waist and the neck will have to absorb the shock of clumsy movement that's sharply cut off in the rigid area — while in addition to all this they sustain compression from the weight of the head and body.

The spine's double standard

Are you willing to devote a moment to estimate how difficult a task it is to operate a back that has different standards of behaviour, with some of its vertebrae constantly summoned for hyperactivity, being compressed under the body weight and becoming chronically defensive from over-strain, while other vertebrae are joined together into one rigid block, becoming more and more frozen in their fixation, passing through all the functions as a single unit, until it is hard to imagine that isolated articulated movement between them is possible at all?

Understanding this adherence to the habit of repeatedly using the back in the same uneven manner can be one of the clues to unravelling its troubles. To succeed in manoeuvring various and efficient motions through such a back, without accumulating tensions or getting hurt, is a mission requiring skill and sensitivity — no less than one needs to drive stallions with worn-out reins, as the wise and ancient Chinese defined skill.

Can you feel through your unique body to what degree your back behaves according to this discriminating pattern? Can you locate those vertebrae that immediately go into action when you bend or get up, or lift something? Does your walking always elicit a response in the same area of your back? Does keeping your head raised in order to be fully in control while driving always create pressure on the same specific point in your neck? Are you familiar with the vulnerable parts of your back?

Are you also aware of the other vertebrae upon which you do not play? Can you identify the non-moving areas of your back and feel how stiff they are? Are you familiar with the lazy partner supported by the one who works overtime? Are you capable of knowing what you are not doing?

A two-way communication channel

If you are willing to take an inner voyage to explore yourself and to observe every part of your back from the perspective of the whole of you, sit comfortably and let your breathing lead you into tranquility. Begin your journey by visualising your head. Imagine your skull as a well-sealed box, guarding the most sophisticated tissues of organic life, your brain. Can you locate the areas of the brain?

When you are ready, transfer your attention to the pelvis. Visualise your large pelvic bone as a huge bowl holding the organs that constantly generate the vital processes of metabolism and sex. Seek a sensation that bears witness to this inner process.

See how these two spheres are connected by the flexible spine, made up of many joints, transmitting and receiving messages from one to the other. The head is equipped with the senses and teleceptors for receiving information from the environment and processing it, and arriving at decisions to be executed by the pelvis. The pelvis is the power station: from its elevated, central position it can easily manoeuvre every part of the body.

The flexible spine, with its multi-purpose functioning, serves the intentional movement, while sustaining the body mass, as well as the unintentional movement of returning the body from whatever position to an upright posture. Thus the spine transmits two-way messages between the head and the pelvis — the command and the execution, the intention and feedback — supporting a dialogue with the ever-changing reality of the environment.

Direct your attention to visualising your entire spine. Can you discern various qualities of flexibility, and feel differences in your readiness for movement? Where are your most petrified vertebrae located? If you are attentive to the rear of your pelvis, you may visualise those vertebrae that are forever attached to the pelvic bone. This is the part of the whip most tightly fused to the handle.

Have you any sensations relating to the character of your tail — its size, and the direction in which it points? Can you imagine an ancient time when you had a long and active propelling tail? Can you imagine how much easier it was for the entire spine to sway and move forward when the tail conducted the movement from behind with its figure-of-eight dance, lending it the power of its weight and length as well? Evolution has long since erased from the movement catalogue these parts of the spine in the pelvis and the tail. What remains mobile is the linkage connecting the two spheres, the head and the pelvis.

The intermediate bead of the rib-cage

In order to better discern the less mobile vertebrae, begin marking a third sphere in your anatomy, the sphere which encases the ribs. Suspended like a bead in the middle of the spine, it is detached from the head and the pelvis. Not a well-locked sphere like the head, nor a solidly formed sphere like the pelvis, it is also a box made of bones designed to safeguard the respiratory system and the heart that beats within it.

Can you, through sensation, identify that part of the spine running through the rib-cage? Can you feel which vertebrae belong to this third sphere and are attached to the ribs? Take a moment to mentally mark the two borders between which it extends. These vertebrae branching to the ribs, more limited in their movement, may be perceived as a single connected block. Can these vertebrae still move and articulate separately, as they once did, in that undulating wave that moved every living creature from the dawn of Creation? Do they still remember how to respond generously, even to the constant act of breathing? This section may feel so fixated that it might occur to you that, likewise, your personality is also fixated.

Flexibility and vulnerability

Finally, seek those vertebrae that aren't connected to any bones, the vertebrae that are able to manoeuvre a bend or a turn. Concentrate on the chain of vertebrae in the lower back, from the pelvic bone to the rib-cage. What alignment does this chain follow? What can these vertebrae do? What load of expectations and apprehensions do you carry there?

When you are ready, pass on to the second chain, between the roof of the rib-cage and the head, and sense the vertebrae of your neck. What's their pathway? Where do you feel their over-used bending axis?

Can you sense simultaneously the chains of both the lumbar and the cervical vertebrae, feel their pliability? Do you realise they are the only vertebrae in the entire back capable of articulating with ease? It is this pliability which makes them more vulnerable, more overworked and more irritated. As long as the mid-spine, along with the rib-cage, is held rigid, the task of mobilising the body falls on the only vertebrae that still remember to move: the vertebrae at the two extremities — the lower back and the neck.

Must you, therefore, stop using the remnants of movement still left in the over-sensitive flexible areas, in order to protect them from harm? It seems that some people make this concession. They avoid extra movement and are careful to keep the activity of the lower back and neck to a minimum, so that their entire torso behaves as a single stiff unit. Civilised life makes it possible for them to get away with such a small amount of mobility. It works, until one day they are called upon to act beyond their habitual range. And then, especially if their action is also accompanied by emotional charge, their usually inactive body takes it a lot harder, and in their despair these people wish only to stop the pain; they do not realise that it is a matter of re-educating the functional integrity of the whole system.

The holistic approach

One of the ways to rehabilitate your tired lower back and ease your afflicted neck is to view them in the context of the activity of the whole back. Ask yourself what can be done to alter the division of labour? Move your attention away from your irritated lower back, and look for a way to reverse the process of fixation in the rib-cage. Relief from the extra burden on the sensitive and flexible vertebrae at the extremities will come of its own accord as the fixed vertebrae in the middle spine in between become more open to participation.

This is a holistic approach — family therapy for the entire community of the spine, that aims to help the stiff members to soften up so that the sensitive, suffering ones can stop being victims of rigidity and begin to be what they were meant to be by their nature.

How can you bring the stiff vertebrae to your awareness and sense how rigid they really are? How can you give them the experience of a different mode of organisation, a permission to revitalise through mobility, and perhaps even to accept that with enjoyment?

An example can be taken from the movement of your torso while driving in reverse, when you must see what's happening behind you, glancing over your shoulder. Isn't this act being carried out for you mostly by your neck, demanding from it an effort that borders on pain? Are you aware that the rest of the vertebrae of your spine and the two shoulders held stiffly create a joined unit that continues to face the front? If, in addition, you also hold your breath and are determined not to give up leaning back against the seat, then turning your head to see what is behind you will be difficult and painful.

Do you feel the extent to which the effort at rotation focuses on the soft and flexible cervical vertebrae that are compelled to rotate the neck against the resistance of the torso? In this confrontation between the torso and the neck the friction always aggravates those same vertebrae which do all the work, the same sore joint at the curve of the neck.

Trying to twist your back when your pelvis sits fully on its seat and does not cooperate with the turn, demands increased participation from the lumbar vertebrae as well. The pelvis doesn't take part in the twist, not because it's incapable of moving or changing position, but because the idea does not occur to you. In a climate of poor mobility you begin to think in static terms. A pelvis that gets used to being glued to the seat of a chair begins to develop dependency on sitting. A pelvis that has been spoiled by the comforts of a chair and that has been spared the challenge of lifting the body's weight from a natural sitting on the ground to standing up will also find it difficult to rise from the elevated position of a chair. Organic logic tends to erase from its movement vocabulary those modes of functioning that are no longer in use, and the entire system becomes impoverished — not only in this function, but also in its resourcefulness for initiating this function.

The functional distribution of labour

Imagine that when driving in reverse, you could distribute the labour differently and develop the function in reverse order. You could let the large and strong pelvis initiate the movement and first of all shift the base of sitting, so that it will generate the major act of the turning around. When the entire back shares in the rotation, the lumbar area does not reach exaggerated compression. When the upper back vertebrae at the shoulder-blade level give up their leaning back against the seat and allow some loosening-up between the joints, the wave of the twisting movement initiated by the pelvis will flow all the way through, assisted also by the readiness of the ribs to open like fans, one opposite the other. The shoulders also have to let go of their alignment towards the front and, each moving separately, one shoulder moving forward, the other drawing backward, to find their appropriate level in the spiral. Thus the neck finds itself freely perched to observe without being torn by extra effort. In this method of organisation, the neck has only to complete the shift in direction, finding the precise point where the eyes are free to softly scan about, no longer bound even by the direction of the face.

Can you see that this was Nature's intention when it designed the magnificent complex structure of vertebrates? We were given a large and stable pelvis easily able to manoeuvre the body from any posture. A slight gesture in the pelvis is sufficient to signal the entire spine to guide the head, the periscope of the senses, in such a way that the back does most of the preparatory work, the rough part of the twist, whereas the neck remains only with the delicate task of the final refinement of homing the eyes and the olfactory sensors to the target.

Can you see that the distress of the organism comes as a consequence of ignoring Nature's intentions, and as a penalty paid for utilising the body in a wasteful and clumsy way? A culture of chairs generates a stiff upper back and a sedate and lazy pelvis, so that the waist becomes frustrated and sore carrying out the mobilisation tasks without the upper back or pelvis' cooperation. The neck, caught in chronic tension from rough physical work not meant for it — moving the head without help from the torso — loses the delicacy and fineness of precision it needs in order to serve the senses. No wonder that with such distortion the neck not only reacts to every movement with reluctance, but also the senses that it is meant to serve — sight, hearing, taste and smell — become dull and may eventually deteriorate.

Restoring inner wisdom

What can you do when you are sitting in your car and want to drive it in reverse, so that the beneficial way of organising yourself will be performed pleasantly in an atmosphere of grace, with balanced, uninterrupted breathing? How can you learn the easy way, not out of discipline, trying to remember what you were told was the right way, artificially imposing it upon yourself, but rather relying on the inner wisdom of your organism which knows how to find a solution from moment to moment. The healing process is not just a matter of changing the proportions of labour between the vertebrae in one way or another. Healing is the rehabilitation of the primal intelligence for movement that, in every situation, knows how to find for itself the efficient and graceful way of dealing with reality — that inner wisdom without which no organism could survive.

There is a classic process of Feldenkrais that demonstrates how this method works. As a medium for this process Feldenkrais uses the function of twisting the torso to see over the shoulder. This movement of the body rotating around its own axis is a skill characteristic of bipedal man — not because he uses it when driving a vehicle in reverse but because he stands erect. When four-legged animals look over their shoulders, or chase after their own tails, they are carrying out a sideways movement and not a movement around their own longitudinal axis.

Since movement around a vertical axis is an exclusively human skill, there have been religious sects that regarded it as one of the ways to reach spiritual development, such as the well-known spinning of the Whirling Dervishes.

Improvement in this exclusively human function will also significantly project the principles of human learning, as you may find in the full description of the process in Chapter 2, in the section titled 'Change: the dynamics of improvement'.

Integration of function, structure and state of mind

The rolled-up blanket process presented below is a powerful process in re-education towards a new division of labour in the organism on several different levels. The roller process integrates your reconciliation with gravity, re-patterning your structure into a more upright alignment, your surrender to the rhythmic vibrations that emerge from the primal wave of life's pulsation, and the bodily organisation that allows you to believe that you are being loved.

This is one of Dr Feldenkrais' inventions for the achievement of Functional Integration, brilliant in its profound simplicity, and used in his private lessons. I have found a way of guiding groups of people to administer this treat to themselves and I am always amazed anew by the powerful effect this device of a roller produces. Indeed it is this process that motivated me to write this book, and pass on this information. In my workshops, when I arrive at the rolled blanket process, I tell the participants that this is going to be the gift they will take home with them. The rolled blanket can be a faithful friend giving comfort to a tired back, easing its pain, leading it gently without effort to reach a more upright alignment that is organically anchored in changing the proportions of the distribution of labour.

The Magic Roller

Preparatory stage: the primal wave vibration

To go through this process, all you need is a single blanket, made of wool or some other substance with a similar texture, a space on the floor, and the willingness to be kind to yourself. The first time you may need two to three hours to learn it thoroughly. Later you may reach the stage of gaining further improvement within several minutes.

Get down on the rug; lie flat on your back with your legs extended. If this way of lying is hard on your back, you're better off bending your knees straight up or supporting them with a pillow.

Spend a few moments being attentive to the manner in which your body makes contact with the floor. Mentally go over each and every part of your self and locate those protrusions which are significantly pressed against the floor. Acknowledge those areas which don't reach to make contact with the ground. Imagine your entire body as a structure that's reclining upon a few stilts, while all the rest of yourself is held off the ground. Feel the tension of the work invested in preventing the body's weight from settling down flat on the ground.

Extend your legs and join them together to their full length, without pressing them tight. Very slowly, begin flexing your feet, pointing them upwards in the direction of your head. Your heels dig into the floor and your ankles bend at a right angle. Release the feet and let them return to the original position, still touching each other. Repeat that movement slowly several times.

Coordinate the movement with your breathing, so that each time you flex your ankles, you allow the air in and inhale. As the air leaves your lungs, let the exhalation lead your body back to its usual position. Be aware of how the movement of the ankles affects your entire body. Sense how with each flexing of the ankles into a sharper bend, the entire body is pushed towards the head and becomes more flat on the floor.

Each time you release the ankles from the effort of holding them flexed, and they return to their neutral position, the entire body also returns to its habitual way of lying, in which possibly there is a greater gap between the lower back and the floor. Slowly carry out the movement for several long moments. Assess the contribution of the ankles to your posture, when they are bent the way they are designed to be in a real state of standing.

Let go of everything and rest. Let your feet draw apart at a comfortable distance from each other, and be attentive to the changes in your contact with the floor.

With your feet still apart from each other, at a comfortable span, repeat the same movement of bending your ankles at a right angle, and then releasing them both. Flex and release them back and forth, but this time do the movement at a quick, rhythmic pace. Develop a light wagging motion of the feet, slightly deviating them from their usual angle, moving up in the direction of the head and back down again. Allow the movement of the ankles to rock your entire body with soft vibrations. The ankles do all the work, and the rest of the body responds passively. This is no longer a slow, calculated movement that can be halted at any given point. These are rhythmic, vibrating minor motions that are swept up in your personal frequency, similar to the rhythm with which a baby rocks himself back and forth.

Some people will require more time and practice till they're able to surrender to the spontaneous rocking. You have to be willing to relinquish the mentality of control in order to allow your inner wisdom to lead the alternating movements in a fast rhythm that is suitable and comfortable for you.

Find the rhythm that requires the least investment of power from the ankles, a rhythm that rounds out the vibrations and connects them one to another without any sharp emphases. Soften the rest of your body, inviting yourself to enjoy the cradle-like gentle swinging. If the rest of your body is truly free to respond passively, then your chin will also move up and down with the ankles' beat. You may also loosen your jaw and let your mouth fall slightly open while you are oscillating.

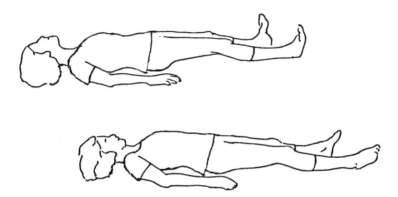

Let everything go, and rest. Feel which areas have now found their way to lean more fully on the ground.

A roller along one side: a lesson in adjustability

Now you come to the roller. Take your blanket, fold it once on its width and once on its length, creating a rectangle that is one quarter of the original size. Roll up the length of the rectangle, forming a tight roller approximately 12 cm in diameter, the length of which is the length of the rectangle (at least 1 metre).

Lie on the rolled-up blanket in such a way that the right side of your body will lie on top of the roller, and the left side will lean on the floor. Be sure that the entire right half of your pelvis and the right shoulder-blade will fully rest on the roller. Let your head roll towards the left onto the floor.

Extend your legs to their full length and observe the sensation of lying in this lopsided position. With closed eyes, invite the weight of your body to find its way towards the depth and to settle there in comfort, despite the uneven surface.

Imagine that you can be like a tender infant who is able to fall asleep in any position. Soften yourself from the inside and reduce the resistance to the asymmetrical surface, so that you can slowly organise yourself to suit the mould.

Mindful Spontaneity

Take a moment to feel in your mind the rhythm of the oscillations. Gradually, let the ankles develop the actual motion. Allow your entire body to rock back and forth as you lie slanted on the roller. Let the vibrations find the lightest rocking motion, until you feel that no effort is being invested in the movement.

After a while, stop the motion and continue to stay with half your body still lying on top of the roller and the other half resting on the floor. Observe whether your posture seems a little less strange now. See whether your organism has learned to adjust itself to the distorted conditions.

Roll slightly to the left. Remove the roller and once again spread out your entire back on the bare floor.

Listen to the new sensation. Observe the difference between one side and the other. This is an opportunity to appreciate how different is the organism's response on that side which received the support of the roller, where it filled its depressions and absorbed its protrusions, compared to the side that was exposed to the hard floor.

Give this lesson to the left side as well.

A roller along the spine: medial line in crawling

Lie on the roller, leaning your central axis on it, along the full length of your spine, from the coccyx to the top of your head. Remain this way for a while, to savour the sensation of your middle line. Locate those vertebrae which in this way gain the experience of being touched and supported, contrary to their usual state.

Begin flexing and extending your ankles alternately, developing a rhythmic rocking motion that spreads throughout your entire self with gentle, back-and-forth vibrations. Stop and feel the broadening of your chest on the roller, the drop of the shoulders, the volume of your breath.

Bend your knees perpendicularly, with your feet standing on the ground. Slowly slip the right hip slightly off the roller in the direction of the floor. Feel how the chest accommodates the diagonal twist as demanded by the slant of the pelvis. Let the head turn somewhat to the left, as a completion to that twist.

Family Therapy for the Community of the Vertebrae

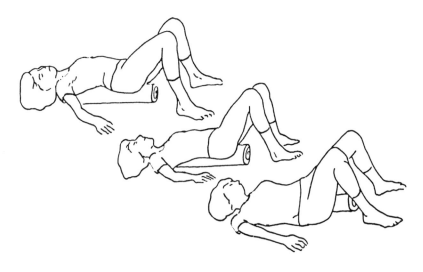

Roller Along the Spine
Lying along a rolled up blanket grants each vertebra of the spine with the rare experience of making
contact while leaning. The gentle vibrations from the ankles train the rib cage to soften in its set design
and blur the traces of personal history struggles.

Stay like this for a while, breathing through the new configuration. Reduce the tension of inner holding and see if you can arrange yourself even more comfortably in this position. Remember, it isn't the movement itself that is important, but rather the response of your organism to it. Take your time to adjust to the motion. If you find the movement difficult, there is no need to slide the hip all the way to the floor. Find the range that allows you to make peace with the movement.

In order to return to the position of lying on top of the roller along your middle line, you may help yourself by pushing your right foot gently to the floor. Repeat this movement of sliding your hip towards the floor several more times.

Lower your left hip towards the floor as well, a few times.

Slide your pelvis from side to side, turning your head in the opposite direction to the sinking hip.

Raise your arms above your head, in a continuous line with your body along the floor, or in the air if they don't reach to touch the floor. Slide, as before, your right hip to the right, your head facing to the left, and this time slightly bend your left elbow and drag it a little along the floor, in the direction of the feet, all the while keeping the fingers pointed upwards, towards your head. Extend your right arm even further above your head and sense how your right side spreads out more of its length, from the hip to the palm of the hand, while your left side becomes short.

Alternately, slide down from side to side, as your hands and legs simulate a diagonal cross-crawl pattern of walking while your spine experiences the twisting manoeuvre, first to the right and then to the left, as it fully leans upon the reliable and sensitively fitting support of the blanket.

Rest upon the roller with outstretched legs.

Again flex your ankles in gentle, rhythmic vibrations several more times, with your hands resting comfortably down along the sides of your body.

Let everything cease, and rest. Notice your ability to find comfort now, despite the roller underneath your back.

Turn gently to one side, remove the roller from under you, and once again lie down flat on your back on the bare floor. Give yourself time to listen to the new experience. There's no need to verbally decipher the strange sensation. Sometimes it may feel as if there were a hole in the floor. Perhaps the brain isn't familiar with a spine that knows how to make contact with the ground when lying flat. Now that the spine has come closer to the floor it seems to the brain as if the back were even protruding out. Hence the interpretation that a furrow has been opened along the floor to accommodate that protrusion. Take a moment to wonder at how misleading the subjective perception can be.

Slowly rise and stand up on your feet, and savour the new uprightness that has been bestowed upon you now. Walk around and acknowledge your independent ability to find within yourself the more ideal arrangement for you.

A roller at the neck: supporting your own mould

Spread out on your back and take a few moments to feel the focuses of pressure of your body upon the floor. Pinpoint the zones that avoid contact with the ground. Listen especially to the curve of the neck and locate the area that doesn't reach the floor at all. Visualise the outline of the neck's vertebrae. Listen to the sensation there.

Family Therapy for the Community of the Vertebrae

Fold a regular blanket once on its width and once on its length. Roll it up on the short side of the rectangle, forming a tight roller with a diameter of approximately 12 cm.

Lie on your back with the roller supporting the curve of the neck across its width. Take some time to adjust the thickness of the roller to the individual structure of your neck. Set the roller so that it will congruently fill out the entire gap from your shoulders up to your skull. Your face is then parallel to the ceiling and the back of your head can be slightly lifted off the floor. Trust your common sense in adjusting the support till it provides you with a sense of satisfaction.

Consider the possibility of sleeping in this way, as indeed has been the custom in several other cultures. Feel how the vertebrae of your neck find, on top of the roller, the comfort of a sensitive support that meets them precisely at their individual mould. The roller provides you with a chance to eliminate the tension invested in holding the neck in the air, as often happens when sleeping on a pillow that supports the head alone.

With your legs spread out, invite your feet to develop rhythmic oscillations back and forth, reaching every part of your body. Each time the feet are flexed towards the head, the entire spine responds and is pushed upward towards your head, so that the chin is slightly lifted off the throat.

Feel how your neck increases its rotation around the roller and appreciate the sense of security that comes from its leaning upon the support underneath.

Roller Supports the Neck Arch
You support your neck with a roller of a texture firm enough to give reliable support and soft enough to take its shape. Your organism resonates to the sensitive support and gives over its weight. Your tired neck learns to return to neutral innocence.

Bend your right knee and place your foot flat on the floor. With your right palm on your forehead, slowly roll your head to the left; remain there a little while; breathe through this position, and then pull your head back to the centre.

Repeat this several times.

Allow your neck to remain passive, and invite your hand to guide it.

Visualise how the neck vertebrae alter their alignment and re-arrange themselves according to the roller's shape, as the head turns sideways.

Remain with your head facing to the left and, like this, let your ankles oscillate your body with the rhythmic motions, back and forth.

Sense how the left side of your neck is learning to grant its full heaviness to the roller as it resonates with the motions. Continue these oscillations for a few moments, ever so lightly, with small minor movements that resemble spontaneous vibrations more than intentional hard work.

Bring the head back to the centre, slide your leg down, and rest.

Feel the difference between the two sides. Notice the sensation in the side that went through the movements while being supported, as compared to the side that moved without support.

Go over that pattern of movements on the other side as well.

Continue to create oscillations with both your legs stretched out for a while.

Then bend your knees and place your feet flat on the floor. Slowly turn both your knees to the right, one after another, letting them sink down by means of their own weight. Extend your left knee further away from your head. Feel how the entire spine is being pulled down until the vertebrae of the neck become slightly stretched on top of the roller. Breathe comfortably through this diagonal elongation.

When you're ready, repeat the same movement on the other side. After several slow movements from side to side, that allow you the leisure to breathe and to sense each configuration, slide your legs down.

Rock your body back and forth some more along the head-to-toe axis, until the pulsating motion flows softly and smoothly, connecting your entire body to respond to it without resistance.

Let the movement come to an end, and take a rest for a while.

Find a way to remove the roller without activating your neck. You may use one hand to lift your head while the other hand pulls the roller out. Carefully escort your head back to the floor and sense the change in your neck.

Do you feel the neck is now aligned differently in relation to the spine? Take in the serene atmosphere that permeates the neck in its new alignment.

Roll onto your side and slowly and gently stand up on your feet. Observe the change in your posture. Notice whether the neck is now less giving under the weight of the head, and is not as compressed at its permanently bending hinge. Note whether you have a feeling that the neck is now more willing to float upward and find for itself a line more consistent with a continuation of the spine, with the angle between them reduced.

Start walking around and look at the level at which your eyes now are meeting the world. Feel the mood that such a carriage of the head elicits.

The roller across the shoulder-blade: an uplift of the back

Lie down on your back. Take your time and observe how your body gradually becomes passive through giving over its weight. Locate the focus of pressure where your right shoulder-blade protrudes upon the floor, then locate the left one. Notice the distance at which each shoulder is held from the floor.'

Prepare a tight roller from a folded blanket, with a diameter of about 12 cm and at least 60 cm in length.

Lie across the roller at the level of your armpits, so that the crest of your shoulder-blades from right to left is leaning on top of the roller. Locate where the roller supports the most protruding section of your back.

If you find it difficult to place your head on the floor, you can use a pillow.

Feel the provocation of the roller upon the back's structure. Acknowledge the inner resistance to this direct confrontation with the spine's most rigid section. See if nevertheless it is possible to breathe in this position. Gradually invite the chest, the ribs and the back to give up their resistance, to surrender and allow their weight to find rest upon the roller, even in this unusual arrangement. Be in touch with your capacity to soften up from within and to re-organise yourself for greater comfort.

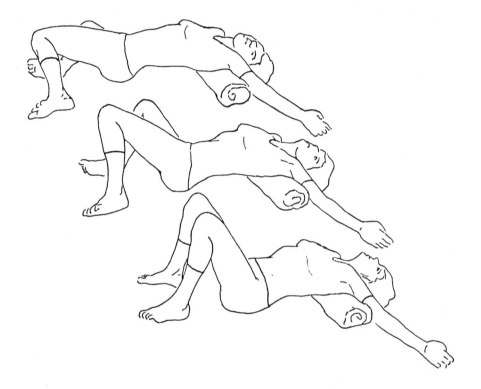

The Roller Across the Shoulder Blade Crest
Like a finger on a string, the roller directs the slow motion of the knees from side to side to produce articulation at the most rigid section of the spine.

With legs extended, begin to generate the gentle vibrating movements. Give your rib-cage permission to stop behaving as unified, rigid armour. Imagine that each rib can respond separately to the vibrations and resonate in its own way.

Bend both knees upward. Turn your knees to sink ever so slowly to the right, and then to the left. Allow time for the rib-cage and the pelvis to adjust to this diagonal outspreading and find a way to organise yourself comfortably in it, so that you can take a breath in this position. Repeat several times, slowly.

Again generate the vibrations with your legs extended. Perhaps at this stage your chest is more prepared to be jiggled lightly like jelly.

Cease all movement, and feel whether your inner resistance to the roller has been reduced, if it is less troublesome to you than at the beginning. Take a moment to appreciate the organism's ability to adjust its internal organisation to the external circumstances.

Bend your knees and bring them to a vertical position, with your feet flat on the floor. Interlace your fingers behind your head and let your hands carry the head's weight, raising it slightly from the floor. Raise it as much as you can without straining your stomach. Bring your elbows forward and let your stomach remain soft and breathing.

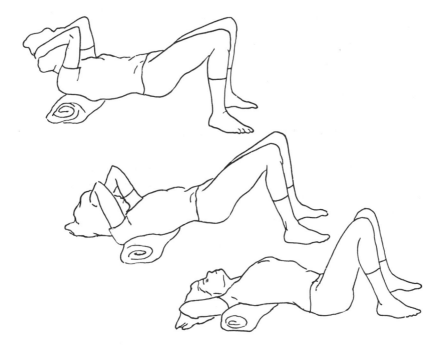

Altering Structure Through Selective Function
You anchor certain vertebrae on top of the roller and manoeuvre the rest of your torso in relation to them. Like an animal that rubs its back to a trunk of a tree, you succeed in influencing that section of the spine which is most difficult to reach while standing.

Ever so slowly, cradle your head back to the floor while moving the elbows apart. Repeat this movement several times. Sense how lowering the head invites the most rounded and rigid section of the back to begin straightening backward. This is a differentiated activation of a specific area which, in a habitual standing position, is very difficult to elicit intentionally.

Raise the pelvis at the same time as you raise your head, and bring both of them down simultaneously to the floor, very slowly. Repeat this movement several times and remember not to force the raising of the head to its utmost capacity. The benefit of this movement is derived from the phase of returning to the floor.

Remain with your pelvis and your head, supported by your hands, lifted up off the floor, and organise yourself so that your shoulder-blades' crest at the utmost protrusion is actually leaning on the roller. In this situation, find the equilibrium that enables you to stay in it for while and breathe.

Begin rubbing your back across the roller, back and forth, moving yourself along the head-to-toe axis, parallel to the floor. The feet anchored on the floor set the oscillations in motion. Imagine yourself to be an animal scratching its back on a tree trunk. See if you can welcome the massage that the roller gives you at the most stubborn area of your back, which is so hard for you to reach with your own hand.

Let go of it all, extend your legs, and rest.

If you wish, rock your entire body some more with your ankles, flexing and extending them alternately, to complete the back's acceptance of the roller's challenge. Take a rest, and feel if indeed you now have more willingness to rest in this way, despite the roller underneath your back.

When you are ready to explore the results of this process, slowly roll over to the side, and remove the roller with the least possible agitation. Once again lie flat on your back on the bare floor and listen to your experience. What has happened to the shoulders' pressure points now?

See if you can interpret this more uniform flattening out of your back as a success in convincing the nervous system to reverse the chronic tensions that distort your alignment.

Sense your more innocent back as being testimony to the fact that there's hope to alter and improve the body's structure no matter what your personal condition or your age might be.

Take your new back to a standing position and let it introduce itself to you. How old do you feel now? Acknowledge the absence of any struggle in being upright. Begin to walk and feel how your personal history has been erased from your back. Take a moment to contemplate how you can benefit your well-being if you agree to grant this process to yourself frequently.

The roller across the width of the pelvis — reconciliation of the lower back curve

Prepare a tight roller from a folded blanket, with a diameter of up to 15 cm, and a length of at least 60 cm.

Lie on your back. Locate those areas of the lower back that don't come in contact with the floor. Define the borders of the gap between your lower back and the ground. Be aware of the emotional charge you carry there.

Lie on your back with your knees bent. Raise your pelvis and place the roller between the pelvis and the floor, then lie on top of it so that the roller supports the lower half of your pelvis from right to left at the level of the sacrum and coccyx.

You may shift the roller higher or lower until you find, according to your own sensation, the place that feels most acceptable to you. Feel the relief of the lower back vertebrae that are now suspended like a hammock and are spaced apart by the force of gravity.

Slide your right leg down to its full length. Your left leg remains standing with the knee bent. Let your feet create the oscillations that rock you gently back and forth. Your right foot outlines its movements in the air while your left leg assists by interacting with the floor. Be aware of the expanded rotation of the pelvis around the roller and note how the curve of the lower back becomes more convex and concave alternately.

After you have experienced the movement with the legs reversed, bend both knees, and turn them slightly to the right; breathe, remain in this lopsid-ed arrangement and look for a way to anchor your heels and the sides of your feet onto the ground; then in this position push against the floor and rock your-self back and forth from head to feet.

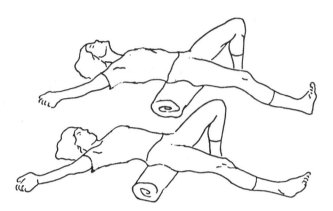

Rocking the Pelvis
The roller in the sacrum alternately magnifies the in-curve and out-curve of the lower back. The cyclic motion of the ankle coaches the pelvis to transfer easily and smoothly from one position to another. The adjustability of your back begins to heal.

Do the same again with your knees sinking towards the left.

Extend your legs out along the floor, flex and release your ankles in rhythmic motions. Let the pelvic undulations happen passively, the work being done by your heels and ankles. Allow the wave that swings the pelvis to go on through the entire rib-cage and rock the back of the neck and head as well.

Bend your knees. Raise your pelvis slightly into the air, and shift the roller a little higher, then lie on it so that it supports the upper half of the pelvis, from the waistline downwards, but not actually at the waist.

Bring your right knee, bent as it is, to your chest, and hold it there with your hands interlaced. Press the knee ever so gently against your chest and stay like this for a short while. Take a breath and roll your head ever so slightly from side to side. Repeat this gently several times, then switch knees.

Now bring both knees close to the chest, hold them with your hands, and remain lying like that. Feel how in this position the roller's support helps to bend the pelvis towards the chest to the utmost flexion possible between them. See if you can find comfort in this rounding for your lower back, and rest like this for as long as it's comfortable.

Slowly return your feet one by one to stand on the floor with knees bent.

Raise your pelvis slightly in order to shift the roller back to the lower half of the pelvis, and as before, stretch out both your legs, and once again wave your ankles, letting your entire body respond to the rocking, until the motion uniformly reaches all parts of yourself, connecting all of them in rhythmic pulsations.

Rest with your knees bent.

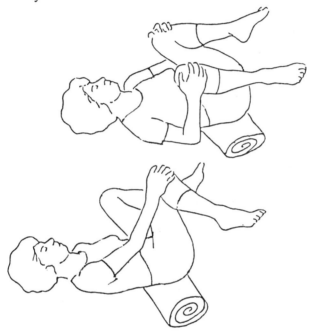

Resting in Roundness
Supporting the upper half of your pelvis with a roller and bringing the knees towards your chest, your lower back simulates the most roundness possible. You use the knee as a handle to align each vertebra into a place of forgotten comfort.

In order to remove the roller from underneath you, raise your pelvis ever so slightly, just enough to pull away the roller, and continue breathing all the way through. It's important to keep your knees bent as your pelvis descends to rest on the bare floor. Sense how the floor receives your body. Can you recall a time when your lower back could ever descend and flatten out like this on the floor's surface?

Take your time to become familiar with this unique sensation. See if you're willing to interpret this experience of the tranquil resting of the lower back on the ground as testimony to your organism's intelligence, which under appropriate conditions is capable of unlearning old patterns of superfluous tension and begin responding to life with healthier logic. When you feel ready, slowly roll to your side, get up and stand on your feet.

With eyes closed, feel what has been changed. Be attentive to the sensation in your lower back. You may now feel a smoother continuity between the back and the pelvis. The pelvis now tends to suspend downwards of its own weight and the freed back allows it to sink. It's as if the chronic, emphasised compression of their encounter has suddenly been dissolved.

Feel the new organisation your feet now find for themselves. Observe what kind of knees go with this kind of an eased back.

Start walking. Be attuned to the lightness of your walk, the tranquility of an aired stability, your reconciliation with what's good for you.

This is a moment of grace from which you can clearly learn how the changes in the quality of your function and the new choices of your alignment are reflected in your attitudes towards people around you. If there is someone with whom you would like to share a hug, hug him or her and let this hug reveal to you how open you are now to being close to another person and to believing that you are being loved and accepted.

Figure eight: the faithful expression of organic movement

The roller can be a source for an endless variety of manoeuvres. One especially effective variation is the figure-eight movement. The figure-eight configuration is the most characteristic of organic self-mobilisation. It reflects the alternating wave between convexity and concavity, coinciding with the undulating to the right and then to the left, that propel living creatures in their locomotion in space.

At any level at which the roller is placed, whether it's the neck, the shoulderblades, the pelvis or the length of the entire spine, you can swing your arms more or less parallel to each other, while your hands outline the figure eight on the ceiling. Allow your head to respond and to nod in the opposite direction of the hands.

When the roller is placed to support the neck or the pelvis, you may trace the figure eight with your knees as well as with your hands. Raise your bent knees into the air, and alternately swing them in a clockwise loop to the right and then in a counter-clockwise loop to the left, in opposite directions to the hands.

Your body will tell you when it identifies within this coordination a profound cyclic harmony that has in fact been known to you from the dawn of life.

A lesson in standing while lying down

A few insights are presented here to shed light on the process ideas. The process begins with an innocent movement, lying on the floor. You flex your ankles at a right angle, pointing your toes in the direction of your head, while you dig your heels into the floor, pushing them away from you. You feel how the planet's counter-pressure gently pushes your body in the opposite direction, up towards your head, while at the same time your back finds a way of spreading out on the floor that is different from the usual way.

If you allow the movement to be carried out slowly, pacing it with your breathing, with each inhalation you sense how more and more parts of your back are reaching a more intimate contact with the floor. Each subsiding wave of exhalation takes you back to your starting position.

The function of flexing the ankle and thrusting the heel is registered and filed in the brain as a state associated with erect standing on solid ground, and it stimulates the entire system to organise itself into the posture and tone programmed for actual standing. This innocent movement serves as a training in the more ideal options of posture which the comfort of lying down makes possible. The floor beneath is like a wall behind you, that gives clear feedback as to how you organise your structure in relation to an objective, upright standing line. You read the topographical map of your body's protrusions as reflected from the floor, and you can sense how arranging your ankles according to the pattern of standing mobilises you, with the assistance aof the floor's surface, to re-organise your total self toward more uprightness.

This is a profound lesson that you can apply in your life. In day-to-day living, even while in a sitting position, any hint of gently pressing your foot to the earth is enough to activate the hidden force which raises you to a more ideal upright posture. Singers know very well that the quality of their voice depends on the way their feet interact with the ground. You may experiment and find out how differently people hear you when your feet know where the centre of the planet is. Lying on the floor, when your weight contributes to straighten your alignment, while leaving your ankles free to move, you can cultivate this lost dimension of uprightness through the aspect of ankle organisation.

The support reflex

In addition to your back flattening out on the floor following the flexing of ankles, you now add a rolled-up blanket, which you shape into a cylinder.

Place this rolled-up blanket across the back of your neck so that it supports the curve in the gap between the vertebrae and the floor; the roller serves as an extension of the ground which meets your neck in its own unique configuration. Every one of the cervical vertebrae experiences the sensation of being touched and supported.

This is a rare situation for the neck. Most of the time the neck's vertebrae are mobile in space without being supported. At any moment the neck is called upon to make decisions as to which direction to set the periscope of the head in order to absorb the environment, while, at the same time, it needs to adjust the vertical alignment of the entire body and compensate for any deviations in the limbs.

The blanket reminds the neck what it feels like to lean and rest. The most profound teacher for relinquishing your weight is the actual state of being supported. When you provide the organism with what it needs, even if in hothouse conditions so that it can taste the change, it learns to respond differently than is its habit. This is a way of teaching which bypasses frustration — teaching which does not pretend to correct the body's posture by command, but rather through exposing it to a positive experience. The logic of the nervous system registers the sensation of the neck being supported by the blanket and responds to it by relinquishing its weight. This is a primal reflex whereby a supportive touch unravels within us the need to protect ourselves and inspires us to trust, which in body language is expressed by transmitting the weight to the support.

When the neck rests on the roller, which sensitively fills in the gap according to the individual structure of the neck, the brain interprets the sensation of full contact, which every vertebra is receiving, as a signal that the neck is now not only secure but also flat. The brain perceives this by analogy from the early experience of being a baby when a flattened structure was associated with the sensation of every point receiving equal contact from the support beneath.

After removing the roller, you may note that the neck tends to continue to remain there in a flattened-out manner, settling closer to the ground than usual, in a more continuous line with the spine. It succeeded in learning by itself, with ease, what it was not ready to learn through a direct, intentional instruction to flatten out. Even movements and manipulations — if they are not done with awareness and at a pace that patiently awaits the organism's response — will tend to become mechanical and bear the prejudice of the habitual self-image, so that in the long run nothing changes.

Reconciliation with gravity

The roller creates contact with the fundamental organic characteristic of relating to gravity. The specific way in which you sustain your weight is so habitual and permanent that it is difficult for you to imagine that you have any choice in the way that it happens. The roller forms a cradle of learning which accentuates the confrontation of each part of you with the force of gravity and awakens your ability to give over your full weight. The yielding texture of the roller, with both its softness and reliability, provides the over-pressured protrusions and the neglected depressions with a support which is congruent with your mould, until you may feel as if you're floating on water. With your inner tonus regulated to more uniformity and innocence, you reach a feeling of healing the relationship between you and the earth.

This training in allowing the weight of every fibre and tissue to find unhindered passage to the ground nourishes your talent for creating effortless posture.

With your refined adjustability, you stand without fighting your weight or collapsing with it, and you feel weightless.

This experience of being weightless is your reference model for recovering your neutral state, as getting rid of pent-up tensions in life is only possible through your own accurate sensory appreciation.

Confronting the convexity of your back

When you transfer the roller to the back, lying on it so that it supports the crest of your shoulder-blades, this creates a kind of provocation that you cannot fail to sense sharply. The roller in this position provokes the most protruding and rounded part of the back to give up its arching. You become aware of your resistance and you learn the patient art of surrendering. You may moderate the thickness of the roller so that it will still present a challenge to your structure, but not beyond a point where your resistance engages all your resources and you become incapable of learning anything except how to increase your resistance. Since your body is more supported, the system feels secure enough to dare to attempt opening the spaces at this level of the spine.

Placing the roller as a challenge at a certain point in the back is like placing a finger on the string of a musical instrument to elicit a certain sound. The roller confines the stubborn vertebrae of the rib-cage into an arrangement which, in the context of habitual standing, they would not have known how to achieve by themselves. When you start to bring about a change in the upper back vertebrae and shake them out of their established fixated behaviour, then you are on the road to touching the root of the disturbance of your entire back's function. In this sense it is a family therapy for the body.

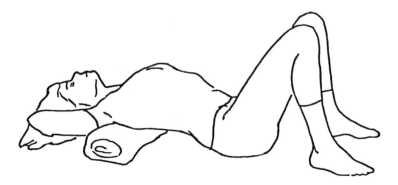

Suspending the lower back like a hammock

When you place the rolled-up blanket across the width of your pelvis, lying on it flat on your back with your knees bent, it invites your entire body to a re-orientation. The chain of sensitive vertebrae in the lower back has the opportunity to be suspended contrarily to its habitual way. The vertebrae are now hanging from the raised pelvis down to the lowered chest in a gentle and gradual slope — a slope which you can adjust to suit your comfort by altering the diameter of the roller. Your back rests on the floor and your buttocks lie on top of the roller, while the small of your back between is suspended in the air upside down. Whereas in an upright position the vertebrae of the lower back have to continually sustain the body's compression, they are now spaced out in the opposite direction by the force of gravity alone.

The second chain of sensitive vertebrae of the neck finds itself spread out towards the ground in a unique experience of contact. Just to lie like this for a while brings meaningful relief.

Surrender to primal undulations

At each of these stages you can shift the flexing and releasing of your ankles from a breathing rhythm into a quick rhythm of oscillating. The rhythmic vibrations flowing through the challenge of lying on the roller reinforce even more the effectiveness of this arrangement. You allow the quick motion of your ankles to sway you like a baby rocking, till you're ready to give yourself over to the vibrating motions.

Not only does your back receive a rubbing massage from the floor, monitored precisely to your personal frequency, but you also begin to receive a master lesson in the organic motion of primal propelling undulations, as Nature meant it to be. On the ground you experience the method of locomotion which is echoed in each of your steps. Your undulating motion is not the primal sideways pattern, but a frontal one. In this undulation every vertebra passes on the subsiding wave in softness and harmony, allowing your weight to sink to the ground, accumulating momentum for the ascending wave that pushes against the ground and bounces you from it, giving you the power to move forward.

On the roller you experience this dimension of a frontal-moving wave, forward and backward, which is relevant to human vertical movement in space. The more the many parts of your body recognise their involvement in this primal undulating movement, even if only through the process on the floor, the more your walking will later be well coordinated, smooth, springy, and full of liveliness. The more the many parts of your body forget the taste of the undulating wave and exclude themselves from its dynamic alternating game, the more you assume an imaginary plaster cast and become rigid. The organism will then be left to move in its old exhausting way, with every step requiring a new investment of effort against a structure that has lost its momentum and won't cooperate.

This is the same rhythmic cradling that enables a baby with soft and unorganised muscles to reach and break through to new possibilities that cannot be discovered from a static position. This same type of rocking can be seen in retarded children whose development was arrested at a primitive stage. This is the same tilting with which we sway, seeking comfort when disaster strikes. This is the same fundamental undulation without which there could be no procreation, and in which the enjoyment of sex increases in direct proportion to the body's willingness to surrender to it. This is the swaying movement of prayer that brings humankind back to its source.

In former generations people had a deep appreciation for rocking movements. Babies were raised in swinging cradles, and adults sat for hours in rocking chairs. They let the generous force of the pendulum flow through every part of the body and disperse the points of tension, until the level of involvement became the same all over, giving a sensation of being drowned in a trance.

Is it possible that part of the civilised world's characteristic impatience may be due to having discarded the use of cradles, hammocks and rocking chairs? Gone with them are their balancing, soothing, meditative rocking motions that gently stroked again and again every joint, fibre and tissue in the body, making each of them equally unimportant.

Releasing movement from control

Some people need more time to reach the essence of the rocking motions. In adult life it is not generally acceptable to shake oneself rhythmically. It takes a degree of willingness to let go of being preoccupied with what others will think and to surrender oneself to a primal animal-like frequency from within. The rocking motions release movement from social criticisms and return you to yourself. When you reduce the tension and superfluous involvement and arrive at soft, round, vibrating motions that come without any effort at all, and your entire body is resonating with them, you realise that there is something within you that knows how to guide you in a rhythm that is authentically yours, tapping into a frequency that carries you. You discover how minute is the investment required to produce an organic movement which is self-perpetuating. It is as if only the willingness, only the intention, only the imagination alone is sufficient. Even though you are in a trance-like state, you are capable of moderating and directing it, like any conscious movement. You are guided by the wisdom of undulation itself, which is the method of every flow of force in Nature, until you cease being a body and become the movement.

A climate of openness to change

In this climate of undulating letting-go the habitual ways in which your body is held and your image of them become open to change. While experiencing the gentle rocking, you feel how the curve of your lower back can gradually, and with no resistance, reach beyond its routine barrier, both in forward and backward motion, and each time it pulls along with it more of the upper back vertebrae, teaching them too how to play the game. Magnified by the lever of the roller, the in-curve turns into an out-curve with a round, connected flow which does not tighten your stomach muscles or cause you to hold your breath.

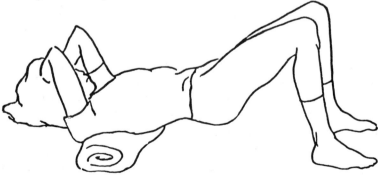

Family Therapy for the Community of the Vertebrae

When your shoulder-blades lean against the roller, you move your back like an animal scratching itself against the trunk of a tree. This fixated area between the shoulder-blades, stubborn in its tension, hard for you to reach by touch, and in which it's difficult to produce any movement, now receives a massage from the ground's extension by means of the roller. These vertebrae become ready to open towards straightening up backwards. The large protrusion in the back begins to behave more like a plain.

To isolate erect uprightness in the upper back without summoning up the vertebrae of the lower back to increase their in-curve is a desired change that is very difficult to achieve through willpower when standing independently in space. Here the change comes to you in small portions by itself. You can feel how, from moment to moment, with each vibrating motion, your resistance fades away. Your back is more willing to adjust and organise itself to fit the mould of the roller, and you feel more natural with that assignment.

The minute vibrating motions are the levers for change, as they reach your system below the radar of defensiveness. They are so tiny and subtle that they talk to the cells and fibres and not to the large muscles that carry their old prejudiced patterns. The reluctant vertebrae in the stiff region of your spine spontaneously begin to take part in the more integrated functioning of the back, and you find yourself able to adopt this as a simple part of life.

The change in your back and your belief that it can change

When you remove the roller from underneath your shoulder-blades and return again to lie flat on the bare floor, a surprising sensation is waiting for you. You may feel as if something is missing, as if your shoulder-blades have disappeared. You have a sensation of contact with the ground in places that you did not know were capable of such a feeling.

Your surprise may double. Not only has your back changed its topography, but your belief that there is a chance for you to change revives. You realise that the structure of your back is not a mould cast in concrete; there is a way for communication between you and your organism, through which it seems willing to listen to your offer, and to change. When you acknowledge a style of communication that bears beneficial results, you get the message that in order to bring about change in your body organisation, you need gentleness and not force, subtlety and not striving.

When you address your movements to the level of the muscles, seeing them as responsible for the way your body is organised, you may be trying to produce a posture for which they are not ready; thus you enter into a confrontation with them, and as in every confrontation of two powers, the result is a stimulation of greater resistance. Every muscle forced to stretch will react with an intense contraction. The more the exertion, the more the organism will be drawn to do the opposite.

However, when you recognise the innate wisdom of the organism to coordinate its muscles so that they manifest subconscious intentions, then you address your movement to that subtle mechanism that makes those decisions — the nervous system. It is the sensitivity and awareness that you invest in the movement which can take you into a dialogue with the brain. Your brain is capable of detachment from the habitual program, and can follow a new suggestion, consider it, and possibly change its route — indeed the brain may consider the new suggestion when you communicate with it on its own terms, for example, when you move at a pace that allows you to assess your sensations, when you make enough repetitions to clarify distinctions, when you utilise challenging enquiry within the boundaries of relative safety and comfort, or when you use a self-reference for comparison and listen to your body's response. In such a climate the brain can disengage itself from its involvement with survival and become free to view new possibilities. When the noise of aggression subsides the solutions of the brain are more relevant to reality.

When you respect your brain's resourcefulness you don't need force or pain in order to undergo change. This is an insight concerning the power of gentleness. It is such a profound transformation in our attitude towards learning, that some people find it hard to accept. They are not ready to trust the accomplishments they have attained in this way, since suffering and toil have not been invested to achieve them, as they had been taught to anticipate.

The silence that cries out in discovery

The moment people remove the roller from under their hips and sense how the floor receives their body, is often a moment of overwhelming stillness. It is a silence that cries out in discovery. The back finds itself flat and relaxed. Some people are moved to tears. They would never have believed that such relief in the spine is possible. It is like shutting off a constant background noise. Now the lower back shows that it remembers how it used to be, before it adopted the permanent defensive posture. It stops working against the force of gravity, ceases to take responsibility for bridging the other curvatures of the spine, and also removes itself from the effect of the angle that the pelvis forms with the legs. At this moment, the lower back can be innocently itself, spreading out its true weight into a flat contact with the ground. This is a moment of grace, of healing.

Healing the response

People are amazed that the in-curve of the lower back has flattened out. They are glad for the wrong reason, however. The important thing is not that the back became flat on the floor, but that it now responds to the floor with a healthy organic logic. As a result of its actualising more of its movement potential, as Nature intended, experiencing its ability in concave and convex undulation, it finds how to return to its neutral innocence. This neutral place is inseparable from the full potential of its function. The back has ceased being stuck in a certain pattern of holding, and now allows the force of gravity to find for it a more logical position — a position which the back can accept and rest in. Through the pelvis' extended rotation over the roller, the back re-learned not only how to become more convex and more concave, but more essentially, how to alternate and shift easily from one polarity to the other.

The goal is not the flattening of the back, but the intelligence that fertilises it. This is not a static alignment; it is a dynamic alignment that is resting in the middle of the movement range, and it is adopted by virtue of the ease of the movement.

Accepting the new posture

When people stand up at the completion of this process, they listen to the new posture that emerged of its own accord. They may experience what it feels like to float upwards, out of an inner conclusion that came beyond conscious pathways.

Someone once said at the end of a session: 'It's as if another person is standing inside me'. Someone else thought the new posture seemed too arrogant. One woman felt like a little girl free of the need to appear smart.

Standing straighter is not just a change in the back. There is a profound moment of change in all your beliefs regarding upright posture. All the old tapes in your head that play the same old tune about your having to make an effort in order to stand up straight, all the nagging and advice you got to straighten your back, all your opinions about slouching because you lack self-discipline and are too lazy to obey and correct — all these are no longer viable. You are now standing straighter than you ever did, without trying to be straight, and you feel it has come from an unknown source.

Slowly something deep inside you comes to recognise that this new situation with which you have just become acquainted is like finally coming home.

The shoulders are suspended differently, perhaps not according to the conventional Western concept of imposed good posture. They are now reminiscent of monkeys, or of Neanderthal Man. You taste the sensation of arms hanging softly, resting heavily, ready to perform any task without prior mobilisation.

The neck seems to know where it should be, and in its new place there is no struggle. The eyes are soft and, without even trying, can absorb more from the edge of vision.

Reciprocal re-organisation

Many feel the change in their knees and are astonished for, after all, they did not do any work with their knees. This is the virtue of a natural movement; it coordinates and affects all parts of the system and not only the part involved in generating local movement. While the pelvis, the back, the neck and the ankles learned to refine their inter-connection and their relationship to the force of gravity in moving, room has been created for the other partners who make up the postural chain to renew their organisation and to come closer to more sensible functioning. For example, if in day-to-day habits the knees are not ready to soften to a spring-like bend, and they are locked while standing in a super-straight hold, the pelvis will be pushed to form an exaggerated backward arch where it joins the spine, thus absorbing the extra height from the straightened, elongated legs. This will happen especially if the curve in the lower back is already deep, and cannot transmit through it the elastic forces from the earth. All this takes place within the complex context of preserving the body's vertical alignment intact. The process of movement on the ground that brings about the change in the pelvis and irons out the in-curve of the lower back also involves the knees, reminding them of another optional organisation that is congruent with changes in the pelvis. All changes in the positioning of the pelvis are expressed through re-organisation of all the rest of the organism.

In this same reciprocal manner, the knees also find a new way to bend as a result of cultivating the flexibility of the ankles through the repeated flexing motions on the floor. Bringing the ankles to flex generously during the process is reflected later in standing, in the removal of those limitations that the rigid ankles inflict upon the knees. In this re-organisation of standing that integrates all the parts into one whole pattern which you did not program, you notice that your knees are more pliable. Of their own accord, they have found a new position — namely, unlocked knees — and they are comfortable with it. This is the basic stance in all the martial arts of the East, such as judo, akido and karate, where standing with knees slightly bent is a guarantee of one's availability to move easily in any direction. When you admit how much easier it is to embark upon an activity, such as leaping forward, from a position of softness rather than rigidity, you begin to wonder about the validity of the West's ideas on erect posture.

At the end of the process you may feel as if dams have been opened in the knees. The muscles along the thighs, too, might become less tight: the leg's tissues reduced their tone and the body weight is sustained by the bones. In this state of springiness the knees don't block the descending body weight from seeking support in the ground; they transmit without waste the ascending counter-pressure from the ground upwards into the skeleton, as if surging forth to spontaneous uprightness. The feet, too, might feel different. Possibly the soles of the feet are more full of life; they are more alert and more sensitive to the dialogue with the earth.

The wonderful feeling of balance is reminiscent of a tree reaching upward, softly resonating with the breeze. It may take a long time, with many repetitions of the process, until you are able to reconstruct such a way of standing with just a flicker of intention. Meanwhile you can rely on the process that will guide you every time to attune yourself to the organic compass that has the capacity to repair itself.

A back which is less subject to personal history

The major change is in the lumbar region. People say that they no longer feel a fragmentation in the lower back; the pelvis is aligned in a more consistent continuation of the spine, suspended from the back, and in the buttocks there is a sensation of their full weight. One person defined his feeling as being as if something were missing there. In the waist there is now a feeling of emptiness, of strange tranquility; it has ceased its constant exertion to hold on to the pelvis, trying to bear its weight. Now the lower back is willing to let the pelvis glide to wherever its weight pulls it, while the lumbar spine itself becomes comfortably elongated and remains at ease.

At the emotional level it is like erasing from the back the expression of the lessons learned in dealing with survival, reminding a person once again how to be innocent. Now you stand less bent under the load of your personal history, with lessened traces of anxiety in the shoulders, lessened responsibility in the neck, less anger locked in the upper back, less defensiveness in the lower back, and less need to show off in the chest. Now you can feel how your back can be relieved of the armour of struggle.

In this delicate comfort you have the feeling of starting a clean slate that will allow you to choose from the beginning what you would like to be. This beginning point can retrieve for you an early time, a time prior to your adoption of defensive strategies. For some people it is a feeling of tenderness accompanied by vulnerability; for others a feeling of serenity and inner truth.

Then when you begin to walk about your movement seems to sweep through your body in a wave that is more smooth and rounded than usual. The soles of the feet glide over the ground without sound. Some people clearly sense that now their walking is not being blocked sharply in the same spot of the waist. This is a feeling of relief, when more parts of the back accommodate the walking instead of resisting it. The noise in the back disappears. As one young girl said: 'I'm suddenly walking from my legs and not from my back'. The back is on vacation and the legs have awakened to do what they were meant to do. The distribution of labour is beginning to balance and the spine is beginning to recover.

Zig-zag of steady progress

Walking around slowly, you engage yourself in listening to what your own body tells you about your manner of walking. This is the time to gather in the harvest of the process.

Some people walk carefully, worried that their achievement may fade away. Sometimes someone will ask, perhaps not quite seriously, how can I make it last forever? This, of course, reveals that it is the possession that is more important than the talent for obtaining it.

It may be that the result which emerged spontaneously out of the process was the discovery of the choice of the organic judgement faculty, which at the deep level of the nervous system became convinced to let go a certain habit for a while, agreeing to exchange it for a more attractive proposition. The organic system, of its own accord, is interested in applying this to life, and will continue to assess its impressions and test how it works. This is still a very young and fragile suggestion which needs a supportive climate, and leisure time for appropriate rhythm, repetitions, reinforcements and observation. Your daily habits, which were dominant for all these years, will overshadow the new suggestion sooner or later, and return you to your habitual patterns, especially if you rush back to a daily schedule of pressures and obligations. The more pressure to produce immediate results in the world out there, the quicker your organism will return to using its habitual methods, which it was accustomed to trusting in all its struggles. Devoting your attention to learning the feeling which the process inspired, projecting it upon your kinesthetic self-image, linking it to a term you make up for it, and continuing to observe it, will give it more chance to be reflected in your everyday life. The process allows you a glimpse into what you could have been. The integration of the new capacity into your life, as with every educational process, requires motivation and awareness.

I have not been describing miracles. I call the process the Magic Roller because of the revolutionary breakthrough into a close-to-ideal experience. The advantage here is that you can do it by yourself, and you can trust that each time you go through the process again it will take you to another level of improvement, according to your condition and your receptivity. Whether your achievement is major or minor, you can see that heading in this direction holds a blessing and offers you hope. At the beginning, the results may recede in a short time. However with each additional repetition they will stay longer, and you will need less time to re-create them. This zig-zag is a sign of steady progress.

Organic learning: an inner conclusion

What happened in the process was a thorough reshuffling of proportions in the distribution of labour throughout the organism. The adjustment is an organic transformation that did not come about through a preconceived decision based on analysis, pointing out the errors in the posture. Neither did the transformation occur through imitation, following instruction to walk in a specific manner. No-one was expected to remember and rehearse a list of items that compose an ideal posture or ideal walk.

The transformation in coordination emerged on its own, as a complete con-clu-sion of the nervous system after negotiations between the organism and every one of the challenges met along the 180-degree rotation around the roller. This is an updated choice, voted upon by all participants of the system in terms of configur-ation, inter-relationships and style, and, after experiencing the options available, assessing the receptivity of the organism to every one of them.

This is organic learning. Your inner sense of coordination generates it when you present it with all the information in such a way that it will be encouraged to try out the new instead of defending itself against it, or trying hard to overcome it.

When presenting your nervous system with challenges that evoke varied and unusual aspects of functioning, you use your consciousness only to check that you are actually doing what you think you are doing. You can only listen and observe how your organism copes with each challenge. You trust the inner wisdom of your vitality to obtain from this encounter what is needed for your well-being. You can only witness and read the solution which it came up with for you today. The solution in movement organisation you can sense throughout your total self, and you are the one to know whether this is what you wish to see materialise again in your life.

4

Movement for Life,
Movement for Love

Multi-functional by Nature

Isn't it characteristic of Nature that every one of its phenomena serves more than one single purpose? In its supreme wisdom, Creation engineered the structures of living creatures with perfection and economy, so that often one organ can be used for several functions at the same time.

The liver, for instance, carries out many functions that are not only different but are also contradictory. It converts surplus sugar to glycogen and stores it, until such time when, according to the body's needs, it converts it back to sugar. The liver is also capable of producing sugar from proteins and fats. It breaks down nutrients which reach it, removing the superfluous and toxic elements into the excretion channels of the body. It regulates the hormonal balance in the entire organism; and produces red corpuscles in the blood. Not without reason is the liver considered the computer-brain of the internal organs.

In the domain of human movement, the tongue is perhaps the most intelligent organ of the human body, by virtue of its rich variety of functions. The possibilities for utilising the tongue for different nuances of sound in pronunciation — unique to each and every person — are at least as numerous as the number of all the languages in the world multiplied by their consonants. This is in addition to the tongue's basic skill of stirring and selecting chewed food and transferring it on to be swallowed in the throat. A less acknowledged function of the tongue — though no less essential — is that of acting as a concealed steering wheel which directs the entire spine during its manoeuvres in space.

When you tune yourself in to the multiple purposes of many natural phenomena, you begin to understand the blessing of Nature's message of integration.

Multi-purpose methods of natural healing

Similarly, there are multi-purpose remedies that bring about healing even where you don't expect it. You improve one component of your vitality, and you receive a generous response on several other levels. When you assist that which is supportive of the whole of life, rather than stimulating only one individual response from one specific direction, it is then that specific local problem areas begin to clear up on their own. It's just like communication between people. Instead of trying to change another person's specific disturbing way of reacting to you, it might be better to work on cultivating good relations between you, as Bilha BenDavid says at her workshops in Jerusalem.

On the organic plain, a holistic approach seeking to restore the overall climate can also have a positive effect on various conditions, even when they contradict one another. For instance, dealing with the issue of weight gain from the wider perspective of the efficiency of the digestive system will not depend on calories of one type of food or another, but on the development of the person's own sensitivity to what promotes the well-being of the entire metabolism. This approach, in which we learn to heed inner warnings, to recognise what is supportive, to identify internal signals of satisfaction as well as of hunger, may well thin down the overweight person and fatten up the underweight.

The same is true with fresh air which works to refresh the weary, and induces the over-tense and overactive person to feel sleepy. That's how love works too: if you give sympathetic attention to an aggressive person he might begin to give up his stiffness and soften up. If you give sympathetic attention to a shy person, he'll most likely dare to bring out more of his power and more of his presence.

The same also applies to organic coordination in movement: the exhausted will perk up and become more dynamic, while the nervous and over-stressed will find, through the same movement, more tranquility. Nature strives for a balance which benefits the harmony of all things, and even its manifestations of violence have a sense of overall accountability. When you're oriented to reaching a balance and not just achieving a single arbitrary result, you begin speaking the multi-purpose, momentum-filled language of Nature.

The multi-purpose nature of the Magic Roller process

The process on the roller also works as a multi-functional balancer. By now you are already familiar with using the roller to rock yourself in rhythmic vibrations authentic to your own frequency, opening more freedom between the articulations along your spine as you resonate with the pattern of the primal wave — the archetype of all crawling and self-locomotion. The roller's intentional protrusion confronts you with the force of gravity in a non-habitual manner and provokes your organism to make a new decision about its alignment.

These changes are reflected in your emotional state, as well. The way you carry your body induces a state of mind of surrrender, in which you are receptive and open, and feel that you are accepted as you are, unconditionally. On top of all that, there is one more dimension which the roller process inspires.

The bonus of the Magic Roller for sex

I was privileged to learn about the further bonus one gets from the workout with the roller from one of my students.

Several days after a workshop in which I guided the process of the roller, one of the participants came to me for a private session. She told me something I hadn't thought about in quite this way before. She said that when she returned home from the workshop, she found her boyfriend suffering from backache. So she gladly showed him what she referred to as the trick with the blanket roller. Later, not only was his pain gone, but also the quality of movement in their love-making was improved beyond anything they had previously experienced.

I wondered how a process meant to remove extra tensions and curves from the body's posture could make a significant contribution to the most vigorous of all functions, to the undulating dance of love.

The story evoked a rush of insights in my mind. A host of evidence came together, completing the full picture, in which the connection between the lesson and life became clearer. I could see how the movement on the roller has the capacity to bring relief to the back, not just because it opens each vertebra to convexity and concavity, but also because it activates a primal function, related to the deepest meaning of existence. It sets in motion those same rocking movements with which two people who are drawn to each other resonate spontaneously with the dominant vitality of the sexual urge.

Primal undulations that bear the excitations of love

Your rocking to and fro on the rolled-up blanket pulsates in you the original undulation, the primordial wave that Nature adopted for movement in space.

This is the movement from which all the fundamental functions in life spring. This is the same wave of contraction and expansion, beating from the centre out to the periphery and back, that carries life to every single organic cell; it is the same pulsation of the blood that's pumped forward, on and on, in the veins; the same breath that's continuing, through ebb that matures to flow and flow that matures to ebb, over and over again; the same wave-like motion of walking that alternately loops between a forward thrust and a pause. The same wave that repeats its own undulations also carries with it the excitation of the bond between two people.

The wave that heals the back

The vibrating movements on the roller remind your organism — each part separately as well as the totality of them together — how to adapt movement to the rhythm of cyclic flow. Through your body you manifest the method Nature uses for expressing life.

In the privacy of the movement lesson, with the comfort of lying on the floor, you observe and learn again, in detail, the motion which in daily life you recognise as a spontaneous phenomenon complete in itself. The close observation perfects and enriches it. On the roller you become aware how the wave pushes your entire spine upward, towards the head, as the pelvis thrusts the pubic bone forward. You notice how your chest is willing to respond and to broaden to make room for the wave to pass through it to the head. When your rib-cage softens and your ribs loosen one from the other, your emotions also have more space in which to be expressed.

You trace the movement of your back as it creeps upward, pushing the neck all the way up until your chin lifts and your head is thrown back, exposing your throat in a gesture which, in Nature's language, means surrender.

The sensitive small-of-the-back has the opportunity to round out and protrude backward until it finds support on the floor. The roller reminds you how to simulate this position without straining your stomach, so that it can continue breathing, granting you full vitality and safety. You experience the forward thrust of the pubis, not through straining the stomach, the buttocks, or leg muscles, but through the safety of cancelling the curvature of the lower back. The forward movement of the pubis comes as a passive response to the movement of withdrawing the lower back, as the vulnerable curve is eliminated. In this way, the pelvis can continue its movement, not only without tiring and endangering the problematic area of the lower back, but even healing it.

Respecting the ebb as well as the flow

The motion on the roller pulls you back downward, in a reverse course that knows its own way back home — the place of comfort. You experience the in-curve as completing the back's undulation, which comes about with no effort and without contraction. The section of your lower back that is being supported between the roller and the floor is forming an elongated arch which reminds your pelvis of its permission to experiment with the expanded potential of rotation backward as well as forward. This safe and comfortable movement shows you that you can respect the ebb as well as the flow, until you are ready to respond to the repetitive ongoing motion between them, and let it lead you. The light, rhythmic repetitions compel you to clear your passages and let the primal wave pass through your entire body.

Locally emphasised movement during sex

In a culture of chairs, in a life overloaded with tensions and obligations, underactive in bodily movement, our talent to arrange ourselves comfortably is declining. We regard every bodily movement as an impoverishment of our energy reservoir. We'd rather exhaust our nervous, overloaded intellect with all kinds of manoeuvres and devices to find a parking space nearby, just so that we can spare our leg muscles the activity of walking. Movement is considered legitimate in a gym class, or while jogging dressed in tracksuits, but in a social setting we usually refrain from extra mobility and may even feel ashamed of the need to stretch, as if that were some embarrassing grimace. Movement is regarded as penalty and we try to move as little as possible, using as few parts of our body as we can manage. While driving, if we need to turn the head to look backward we do so without the help of rotating the shoulders and pelvis. We pick an object up off the floor without taking advantage of the springiness of our knees, and we don't even notice how we are hurting ourselves.

With such a tradition of dull movement, people easily accept the concept that the movement involved in lovemaking is limited to the sexual organs only. If, in addition, the only style we know is the style of effort, then the intensity of the pelvis' movement during sexual activity, which makes a critical demand on the back, is sharply blocked at that very same vertebra of the lower back that gets caught in a compression and hinders the transmission of the pelvic movement on to the rest of the body. All this takes place at a high level of emotional involvement which, if it is further burdened by anxiety, a need to prove oneself, or hidden reservations, or any other considerations that don't belong to the present sensation, will carry the person far from the safe ground of self-care. Sexual movement, if its style is limited to local emphasis, can become a trap for back pains.

How to pass your back safely through the wave

The blanket roller relates directly to this particular vulnerability. From the simple roller you can learn how to take that sensitive area of the lower back safely through the vigorous movement that repeatedly bends it.

The effect of the roller on pelvic movement works to integrate this movement with the rest of the body. You learn from it to experience your pelvis at the height of its activity, while at the same time you remember your entire self and feel the connections from the tip of your toes to the roots of your hair. The provocation of the roller reaches and awakens each part of your back, also inviting mobilisation between the vertebrae of the upper back that aren't accustomed to articulate and to move in relation to one another. The flexion between the pelvis and the back is then distributed along more vertebrae higher up in the spine, and spares the waistline from focused wear and tear in its set groove.

Lovemaking in the context of the interaction between the pelvis and the body

Lovemaking is unique from the standpoint of the pelvis moving in relation to the rest of the body — in daily life it is the body that moves in relation to the pelvis. For instance, if while dancing you give the pelvis the initiative, you broadcast that you have entered into the territory of sex.

In lovemaking, the nature of cooperation between the pelvis and the rest of the body is of primary importance. The same movement that, for example, forms an angle between the thigh and the belly is carried out this time with a change of roles. Instead of the legs coming towards the pelvis, the pelvis moves towards the legs. To the extent that, in daily life, communication between them is coordinated without unnecessary waste on restricting blocks, then also in the dance of lovemaking the interaction between the pelvis and the legs will unfold in an organic flow. But if a person goes through the day with little activity, with just a vague sense of the pelvis in the self-image, or if every step taken strikes a sharp blow of the hip-joint against a resisting pelvis, then the lovemaking relationship would not be the most suitable context for beginning to learn how to improve interaction between the pelvis and the legs.

Similarly, the interaction of the pelvis–back movement will magnify, during lovemaking, the problems of the sensitive encounter at the area of the lower back. It is important to note that the vulnerability of the lower back is especially increased for the partner on top. Any position of lying on the stomach with legs extended straight makes the lower back susceptible to tension, and makes movement difficult, in the way that standing on locked knees stiffens the back. In the regular prone position it is possible to create relief in the knees by placing a supporting pillow under the ankles. But in sexual relations if one attempts to mobilise the pelvis while holding the knees straight it is impossible to avoid back vulnerability.

A clear reciprocal connection between the pelvis and the spine, or the thighs, the knees and the ankles' organisation, or the set of the jaw, the ribs' manner of behaviour, or the quality of the look in the eyes, is essential to the flow of the primal wave of moving.

A wave isn't a position or a structure, or any other static condition. A wave has living space when it flows back and forth, and you take part in it in your entirety through fluid adaptation, clearing a path for it to continue flowing and renewing itself. Any focus of effort will obstruct it, and force the wave to stop, and waste itself in a self-defeating struggle. You seek a way to generate repetitive vibrations without straining the back, without stressing the use of the deep gut muscles, without stiffening the thigh muscles, without locking your jaw, without impeding your breathing.

From where do you derive the power to generate the wave?

From the roller you learn where you can derive the power to generate the wave: you discover the mobilising force outside of yourself, and learn to draw it from the ground; you realise that when your feet are anchored on solid ground, just a hint of pushing them towards the earth, away from yourself, is sufficient for the earth to respond in counter-pressure that will float you upwards, in a smooth, continuous wave from toe to head without hindrance.

This is the same dynamics of efficiently coordinated organic walking. The body's weight is innocently transmitted from one joint to another, through every muscle and bone, down to the stepping foot, and from it on to the ground, thus evoking the response of spontaneous uplifting of the posture, climbing from the ground upward in height, threading the entire skeleton to align accordingly while striding forward in space.

When a well-organised organic complex is in movement, every part of it is sensitive to the task of readjusting to the two-way flow between the authentic weight and the counter-force coming from the ground. The roller sharpens your system's response to this organic logic. You begin to re-organise the distribution of labour all along the chain which makes up posture. Your legs are doing the work for you, and your back is secure and relaxed. Without investing any effort, your back finds itself in the full movement of the primal wave.

Instead of lazy ankles, compressed knees, thigh muscles that are held in unnecessary tension and a back that pays the penalty for this, you have legs that awaken to do their job and a back that is free to dance with ease.

When you function in organic coordination instead of being blocked by dams and vulnerable points, you unite your total self in effective cooperation. The sensation of harmony in the organic coordination convinces you beyond any explanations. You feel that this movement is supportive for you. You recognise that something inside you knew it all along. A new willingness opens you up to reducing effort — to reducing unneeded involvement — and with lightness you perceive new qualities of pleasure.

Coordinating your total self: a source of sexual energy

When you broaden your concept of movement in sex, understanding that this is a global movement of your total self and not a local performance of the sexual organs alone, a dam of sexual energy is opened for you as well.

Both men and women recognise the paradox that directly investing more effort, more ambitious motions, and placing more demands on the sexually located movement does not guarantee greater arousal. Perhaps even to the contrary, this effort undermines it. If you express your desire to encourage Nature by making every possible effort, then the flowing wave doesn't have a chance to endure.

What can pass through legs that summon up their stiffness as strongly as they can? What can pass through a rib-cage that is fossilised in stressing its willpower, doing all it can to demonstrate its pride and to prove itself? What can pass through hands that hurry to fasten their grasp, revealing the fear that if they don't hold tight, the opportunity will be lost?

With a mentality that believes in the most and the strongest, people are driven to use the language of ever-increasing force. At the critical moment, when their involuntary system doesn't support their sexual intentions, they deal with it by investing more physical effort, more tension, more rigidity; and here lies the trap.

The greater the effort in all other parts of the body, the more blocked will be the fragile wave of sex — wasted in colliding with stiffness. Renewing the wave's flow requires a body that won't interfere as it passes through. It requires a body that's moving with coordination, with an inner readiness which is congruent with the production of the movement outlet.

When the inner summoning-up towards mobilisation is great and the production of an outlet is locked in misplaced efforts, the tension is not only unnecessary, insensitive, ungraceful and unpleasant to the partner, but it also neutralises sex. You think you're stepping on the gas, but actually you are hitting the brakes. If then the sex still succeeds in regenerating, in spite of a body that puts obstacles in its way, the sensation accompanying it is that of having struggled to overcome a difficulty.

In the rhythmic pulsation of the vibrating waves, alternating from action to repose, contraction takes place during the active phase. The nature of muscular work is such that letting go of the contraction and expanding to the periphery is a passive reaction, a time span in preparation for the next contraction. If you invest force, your nervous system, impressed by your vigorous activity, will relate to it as to the phase of contraction and prevent any possibility of expansion. Expansion can only be encouraged by allowing it to occur within a space of passivity. The wisdom of sexual energy is not what to do but how not to disturb.

Perhaps the actual encounter of lovemaking is not the appropriate time to learn about a new attitude — trying not to try. During the workout on the floor those who are training in Awareness Through Movement practice again and again the relinquishing of success. They know that when the movement is difficult and frustrating, it is best to repeat it with reduced effort, with decreased range. It's as if they were illustrating only a trace of the idea, with a minimum of actual movement.

The modesty of a moderate attitude bears true fruit. On the floor you learn not only the secrets of movement, but also how you behave towards yourself when facing difficulties and frustration. Do you torment yourself by trying to compete with greater willpower, more compulsiveness, and increasing bitterness, or are you kind, tolerant and supportive of yourself as you would be if your child were having difficulties?

At the level of refining movement, it helps to shift achievement to another course, by feeding the need for achievement with new substance. Instead of depending upon physical strength, invest more in the wisdom of coordination. Instead of expecting a lot, immediately, look for pleasure and ease. Instead of focusing cerebral criticism upon the sexual organs, take time to absorb the sensation of the rest of your body and relate to its movement. Instead of a one-way effort, observe the ongoing interaction that connects all your parts in a sweeping flow. To worry about lack of energy is to deal with something intangible; it does not exist, and it is therefore frustrating to search for it. To become aware of all the rest of the organism, to detect where excess energy is stored and to reduce it, is an actual task that can be done.

When the space of thought is filled with consciousness of failure, the organism responding will manifest the failure in reality. In order to engage the mind with positive thinking, it would be better to let sex remain on a back shelf of the mind, and innocently address the thought resources to other areas in which success is more simply assured. Movement is always available — an actual and lively reality. You can always pay attention to how the wave — carried throughout the entire body in effortless vibration — becomes more flowing and harmonious until it forms a mode of expression in its own right and has its own value.

Passivity that inspires vitality

Soft micro-motions have the ability to melt hard cores, to smooth out and equalise inner patterns of holding, and to bring about a 'swooning' atmosphere that allows a letting go of control, ceasing interference in the unprogrammed dance. The wave that derives its inspiration from its interaction with the ground thrusts the sexual organs forward, as a passive byproduct. They reach forward with ease, free to receive the river of support flowing throughout the entire body. The sensation in the feet is like the sensation in the face, in the belly, in the chest; all passages are open and alike, and each part equally enables the energy to pass onward through it, encouraging the vitality.

Until you dare to give up your ambitious involvement, you'll have no way of knowing what part sex could have played by itself, and what part is up to your intentional responsibility to lead. When you can apply one style as well as another, when you are able to control, to strive, to push yourself to do your best, and can also relinquish this control and passively surrender to be carried away by the flow, only then will you be able to act out of free choice.

A mystical urge of the universe flowing through you

In this atmosphere of surrender you have leisure to breathe, time to feel your own feelings, and to listen to those of your partner. You are ready then to wonder whether sexual energy is a need beyond the individual intention of your solitary ego, that tends to believe it must manipulate its way through an alien world. You are more ready to accept that sexual energy flows through you and needs you — a child of Creation — to manifest the mystical urge of the universe. When you entrust yourself to the hands of a greater power, you remove the sting from your anxiety and you are willing to let Nature take its own course unhindered. This is a revolution in the way you relate to life that goes beyond the plane of movement coordination.

Shifting gears to emergency respiration : the pelvis that chokes with effort

You may come to a special observation in the realm of breathing. While slowing down the pace of movements, in the hothouse conditions of experimentation on the floor during a lesson, while your full weight leans upon the support beneath you, you are free to listen, and decipher the correlation between breathing and pelvic movement. By means of the roller, you take certain positions to their extreme, where you can observe connections that, in your daily life, you might never find yourself experiencing. While your brain is being trained in the openness of initiating new patterns of functioning, you can draw your conclusions about the ties between breathing and the way your organism behaves in lovemaking.

There are many different and unusual combinations in the dynamics of mobilising the lower pelvis in relation to breathing. You can bring the pubic bone forward, by working the inner thigh muscles close to the pelvis, contracting the buttocks, recruiting your stomach muscles and your inner organs, tightening your jaw and your chest, your hands and face. You're engaged in a struggle, and your breathing is patterned according to a state of emergency. It's arrested and held with every accent on the forward thrust of the pelvic bottom.

This is perhaps the most common pattern of breathing, the focused effort that cuts off the breath. The pelvis chokes in its own efforts.

Exhalation plus a forward movement of the pubic bone

You can also design another combination. When you aren't engaged in a struggle, but rather allowing an atmosphere of surrender while leaning your full weight, with your feet pushing against solid ground, your pubic bone is carried forth on the returning wave that counter-bounces from the ground without any effort. This way is conducive to breathing. You can breathe without any association with the pelvic movement. You can inhale with every forward movement and exhale with every withdrawal. Or you can coordinate your breathing in a less conventional way, so that with every forward movement of the pubic bone, the air leaves the lungs and you breathe it out.

Exhalation, in the language of the organism, usually signifies a letting-go, a relaxation. This is an opportunity to experience the meaningful movement of the pelvis, in a context of comfort, of succumbing to trust, and the leisure of passivity.

Air fills your lungs when the pubic bone recedes again and moves backward. The inhaled oxygen magnifies your sensory capacities and your sensitivity becomes more focused in the present and attuned, so that while the wave recedes at the phase of withdrawal, you are at a level of arousal that is no less than when thrusting forward at its crest. For many people this is a profound revelation about the way they relate to the dynamics of sex. The retreating of the pelvis takes place in its own right, and has a pleasure of its own, and isn't just a hasty preparatory phase for the next thrust. The withdrawing motion is no longer a sharp act; at the same time the deepening of the curve of the lower back is done with more softness and with less chance of being hurt.

When you learn the agile back-and-forth motion on the roller, you also attain a separation of your respiration pace from the timing of the pelvic movement. Your breathing can be chaotic, sometimes fractional, or flowing smoothly, without any apparent pattern. It awakens and enlivens every muscle, bone and tissue in your entire body, as it guides your unscored song. With a movement vocabulary that is further enriched with a variety of breathing patterns, you return to your life with a more intelligent body, with a chance for more congruent resourcefulness that will continue bringing you closer towards the limits of your true potential.

A pelvis that rolls with laughter

In trance dances amongst cultures living close to Nature, people reach rapid vibrating motions of their hips without any effort, and can continue this fluttering movement for many moments on end, even hours ,without tiring or harming themselves. This is the same sort of vibration that people experience spontaneously in *kundalini*, or at times under the influence of drugs, or just in free dance. This movement is both light and vigorous, forceful in its fineness and in its perfect frequency. If one tried to produce this kind of vibration through the intentional investment of effort, which recognises only the large muscles, the quick rhythm would become clumsy and the back, to some degree or another, would become sore and worn out.

It seems that this vibrating movement comes from a place of primal knowledge in Nature. It isn't acquired through a gradual learning process. When the vibration appears, it is alive in its complete perfection, resonating with a certain frequency, the source of which is often the beat of drums.

At times, the skill of vibrating is acquired in a different way. In Bali, during the initiation of a young dancer into her first ritual trance, she touches with her hand a taut rope which is being vibrated by two adults. When she resonates with its vibration she enters into a perfect trance, and she will know how to recreate it by herself. The vibratory movement guides the pelvis in a very specific way which makes it totally safe for the back. Those who have experienced this vibration of a trance while lying on their backs testify to its being an experience quite different from the ordinary, in the way the back comes to touch the ground. The hollow in the back is flattened and touches the floor with a feeling that this is what was always missing. It is as if the inner wisdom that generates this vibration also knows what the back needs to soothe its fatigue and the vulnerability at its hollow, and teaches it over and over again the way to the safe and right path.

In the trance movement the rhythm reaches a self-renewing momentum, and the level of the body's involvement with the movement is precisely adjusted to what's required, in order to keep the unique frequency intact. At this rhythm, with perfect lightness, the lower back knows how to cancel its curvature. The waistline at the back jumps backward, so that the forward movement of the pubic bone takes place in complete passivity. It is also done while exhaling, as if the pelvis were coughing, or better yet, were rolling with laughter.

Entrusting hegemony to your body's wisdom

On the roller you get a taste of a style of movement which you perhaps never associ-ated with the fundamental undulation of organic self-directedness. During this pro-cess on the floor you realise that you can pass the undulating wave through various shades of involvement — from intensity to gentleness, from powerful activity to subtle passivity, from light dynamics to slowed-down attentiveness, from sharp and stressed vibrations to a unified continuum of round, connected movements.

The moment comes when you can cease your involvement altogether, and entrust yourself to the hegemony of your body's movement. Enriched and perfect-ed through its exploration of many varied angles of rotation around the roller, it guides you to such a comfortable repetitive frequency that you can't tell any more if you're guiding the movement or the movement's guiding you. And when you don't resist the wave or try to accelerate it, it endows you with an experience of pleasure without struggle, flow without investment, a taste of a blessed state of trance that sweeps you away in a continuity of recurrent sensations.

The frequency is so authentic for you that it seems as if no part of you is working or held in tension. Your consciousness can witness from the side, observing what is unfolding. There is nothing to do, nothing to criticise — the movement knows how to continue by itself. Under these conditions, thought can rest, fade away and turn off the noise at the top of the head. You are now in the province of sensations, a place of no words.

A semblance of fainting while in motion

What's unique is that you're in a floating state, similar to a faint, while you are in action. Perhaps you're familiar with the sensation of near-fainting in certain passive situations where no activity is taking place, possibly during meditation, or while withdrawing into a headache when you're tired, or during the last moments before sinking into the stillness of sleep.

The oscillating motions enable you to combine an obvious action of moving with a state of mind resembling a trance. The surrender to this trance while in motion is the lesson that prepares you for lovemaking that isn't a struggle or an effort, that has no mental considerations, but rather is a spontaneous flow.

Utilising your awareness to reach a state in which you don't need it any more

The more you experience, through the hothouse conditions of the rolled-up blanket process, feelings of becoming familiar with the relaxation that coincides with move-ment, your organism restores the deep systems of vitality that are designed to guide you towards spontaneity. You utilise your awareness, your human talents to observe, evaluate and pay attention, so that you can reach a state where you no longer need them. It sounds like a paradox. You restore physical resourcefulness that was missing all along, in a life involving excessive cerebral activity and insufficient movement challenges, by using this very same intelligence which life developed at your body's expense, in order to return to and decipher mobility once again.

With patience and attentive thought, little by little, you reconstruct from the start a learning process that resembles the original process which formed the initial decisions, sifting and perfecting them till they became spontaneous. As at the dawn of the development of humankind, the kinetic sense, quicker than thought, is now the one that decides for you. Your awareness only assists you to make contact with it and learn its hidden ways.

Does your body know how to align itself so that your heart can believe you are loved?

All of us want loving relationships. Do you know how to receive love? Does your body know to align itself in such a way that your heart can believe that indeed you are loved? Does the manner in which you organise your body influence what takes place in your heart? Is there a way to enhance your readiness to accept being loved, through the style of your movement?

Working on the roller gives rise to several perceptions about the way in which you coordinate yourself, and the way this reflects upon your ability to feel that you are accepted for what you are. The movement against the roller's support invites your organism to respond with greater fidelity to the pull of the earth, to let go of your weight so that it can lean more innocently on the ground, and not rely on your muscles' effort. This is a reconciliation with the force of gravity.

Surrendering your weight and being loved unconditionally

When you cease resisting the force of gravity and allow your weight to sink into the depth, the sensation takes you back to an early time of your life, when you were very small and had no choices, when you leaned with total reliance upon a loving bosom — when you took for granted that those upon whom you leaned had your well-being in their heart, that your weight, surrendered fully, was the most precious gift in their eyes, that carrying you was a need within them. In your mind receiving unconditional love was registered in the most dominant physical aspect of your existence — the manner in which you coped with gravity.

Life is so full of the element of gravity that we forget to consider it. Letting go of weight and leaning fully is interwoven with trust. In body language, receiving love is trusting the one who holds you, being willing to lean yourself onto the earth or onto the person, with no concern that you may be a burden and with no fear of falling, which is the most primary and direct fear in life.

After the roller teaches every tissue and fibre in your body that it's alright to lean fully, you understand that your way of carrying your weight is an expression of your state of mind. As long as you continue carrying your weight all by yourself, instead of letting it take the support of the earth beneath, you aren't behaving in the way Nature intended for receiving love. You are engaged in trying to secure your survival by your own powers; you are cautious, and aren't aware that the security has already been granted to you.

When you're prepared to orient yourself towards leaning, and trust the support that carries you, you set your body in accordance with an atmosphere of being cared for. If indeed you are being cared for, you then have a better chance of recognising it, at a deep level of your being, beyond rational understanding, through the most vital of movement talents, the indispensable skill of stabilising equilibrium.

Touching the core of vulnerability through self-organisation

It's easier to train and change the body's organisation than it is to alter emotions, attitudes or opinions. When the blanket roller re-shapes the scaffolding of your body and prepares you for adapting to the support, you will also be more prepared to accept love, to believe that Life strives to bring you love in abundance, and that trust will have a better chance of fulfilment.

This is the grace of the Feldenkrais Method — that it touches upon the core of human vulnerability from the simpler and safer end, from body movement. Without re-enacting old suffering, without trying to analyse anachronistic motivations, the method guides you directly to taste the original version of yourself, before troubles begun.

On the floor, you experiment with innocent movements, rolling on a roller between you and yourself, and at the same time, of itself, a wider expanse of trust is opened for you in your relationships with others, and you become more comfortable receiving from them and feeling that you are wanted.

The living silence that you always desired

When you get up at the end of this process, and there is someone with you who also passed through this experience, you may want to share an embrace. You sense then, beyond any explanation, how much the way of holding your body has been changed and how a layer of chronic stiffness has melted away. Your body weight now more willingly lets go, deepens its leaning towards the ground, and towards the other person as well. You also notice your change of mood. Instead of any considerations, doubts, assumptions, and need for reassurance, you are left with the living tranquillity of both your presences, and you surrender to its electricity. You sense that being with a person who is comfortable within and allows himself or herself to be held, also gives you permission to lean your entire self, softening and receiving full support, as you always wanted.

Your nervous system registers you in this state of being, and will remind you when the appropriate moment comes.

A question mark concerning the necessity for aggression

Nevertheless, your thinking brain can't escape the profound lesson to be drawn from this experience. Perhaps its lesson is to put a surprised question mark to your persistent habit, your acquired second nature, of wasting aggression. If, by such a small investment in the roller process, you can bring about such a significant change in your being, you begin to wonder about the concepts and principles of operation you have had regarding the necessity for aggression. For many people, this is a turning point in style.

Too much where it isn't necessary

Aggression here denotes a way of organising a movement in which you invest more effort than is required for producing it. Feldenkrais calls such organisation 'hitting the screw with a hammer'. Aggression is that addition which deprives the act of its equilibrium and loads it with extra tension, without which it had a chance of being more effectively executed.

In lovemaking, people — in all innocence and out of caring — tend to give all they can, all the time. They may diligently create more and more action, without pausing to listen, without sensitive moderation, and they may be inclined to become carried away with exaggeration. Even if the exaggeration is done with the best of intentions, it carries the action over into aggression, characterised by a bitter striving to attain increasingly sharp, emphatic movements, which eliminate any grace.

The difference between wasted aggression and efficient dynamics is, perhaps, not large in terms of the amount of power invested or the configuration produced, but it is immense in its attitude, in its inherent message. This very fine and meaningful difference is what we wish to learn. This is the issue of today's culture: the difficulty in ceasing to use blown-up mechanisms meant for emergencies, in situations that are less than an emergency; the difficulty of responding congruently to changing needs, moment by moment; the difficulty of engaging at times in dynamic activity, but without going overboard in acceleration, which tends to become a goal in itself, no longer allowing a person to feel when it becomes unnecessary.

An outward orientation that invites excess

Few of us have been brought up to develop grace and lightness in our movement. Few of us are sensitive to the subtle differences in our internal set-up which grant movement its harmonious balance and economic elegance. We tend to give priority to confrontation with the environment. Our listening is directed outward more than inward. We find it hard to disconnect ourselves, even for a moment, from ongoing events in which we are involved, and to check what is happening to us on the inside. It's hard for us to identify our discomforts, pressures, distorted postures, and the emotions that are embodied within them. Perhaps we don't even realise that we ignore ourselves. We are concerned with our actions only in terms of the way they are projected outwardly. We've become accustomed to evaluate results according to how they are seen by others. In order that our actions have a more dramatic impact, we are swept towards investing ever-greater efforts of strength, energy and determination. This outward orientation invites exaggeration.

Giving up the habit of trying to excel

If sex for you is also a test of yourself by others, you may be prone to finding yourself exaggerating the amount of physical power you invest in it. On a deeper level, inadvertently perhaps, you have an opinion that you are not enough as you are, thinking that you must help Nature along. If so, you might be caught in the habit of chronic over-striving and over-tensing.

If you have never known the taste of unconditional acceptance, if you haven't understood that you are loved, not for what you do or how you do it, but for what you are, as you are, then you may find it difficult, particularly in sex, to relinquish your striving to excel. With time, this added striving becomes a habit, like a background noise that is no longer heard. You may no longer search out the reasons for your striving. Even though you understand rationally that you have no reason to do so, you continue acting with exaggeration because the possibility of it being otherwise has escaped you. The sexual urge has become linked for you with a response of maximum-volume activity.

Aren't you denying yourself receiving as a gift that which you try so hard to win by your efforts?

It's hard to regress from accelerated aggression to the innocence of an exploring gentleness. If you believe you've achieved what you have because of your intentional aggression, then it will seem risky to you to give it up. Eventually, however, whatever you've achieved through aggression doesn't convince you; on a deeper level of your being, you do not believe that you earned it by your own worth, that it truly belongs to you. You would rather think you achieved because you manipulated, not seeing that in Nature's way, things were meant to come to you and go of their own accord.

This is a basic difference in approach to life. Have you adopted, as a guiding principle, the attitude that you must always be ready with your full resources in order to get what you want out of life, or do you believe that your well-being is inherent in Creation and will come to you in its own wisdom, even if you don't push it?

Life, as you know, has abundant evidence for either approach. People hasten to gather the evidence which confirms their point of view, and tend to overlook alternatives. Can you see that if you behave aggressively you are denying yourself the chance of receiving as a gift that which you are trying to achieve through your efforts?

In gear for fulfilment

When you begin to identify your sexual excitement with the aggression that accompanies it, then you miss the freedom to play with a variety of changing levels of involvement including, if you wish, the option to live in peace with your sexual awakening without doing anything about it, celebrating it as a gift, and not viewing it as a frustration.

When you interpret more aggression as more pleasure, you have no way of knowing the rich world of fine pleasures that lies below the threshold of effort. Nature is organised in such a way that a sense of fulfilment does not dwell in aggression. The statement of aggression is desire for more, which also sometimes implies a fear that it won't be enough, so you must try to grab as much as possible as fast as possible.

In order to shift into gear for fulfilment and pleasure, you have to direct your attentive listening to what's already there, to that which exists in the present. Those who know how to set aside time for a pause and listen to the sensation of that which exists in the present, create a milieu in which fulfilment can be identified. This readiness to listen inside is the bridge to increasing satisfaction and pleasure.

The stressed effort that renders dissatisfaction

There will be those who claim that what brings them pleasure is the uncontrolled aggression itself, with the exhilaration of its inherent struggle. This is a direct and legitimate statement, and everyone has the right to retain the choice between having a partner who enjoys being together in sex and having a partner who enjoys being aggressive in sex.

Your straining effort reveals how far you are from fulfilment. Your partner picks up your attempts at trying hard — that unmistakable echo in his or her gut — and will eventually interpret it as a poor mark for themselves, as if your partner's presence were not enough to inspire you to feel good about yourself, for you're still trying hard to be more than you are. Isn't that what we all want, to be with someone in whose presence we'll be inspired to feel how wonderful we can truly be?

There will be those who interpret the excitement of aggression as the exhilaration of love itself. But can aggression really create a climate of mutual growth, of intimacy? When you're at a level of involvement which concerns exaggeration, you're busy with yourself and with what you're doing, and you're less ready to be attuned to someone else, especially if your partner's expression comes at a level that is more subtle than that of your own involvement. As in group singing, in order to sing and at the same time listen to how others are singing, you have to reduce your attempts at making yourself heard at the highest volume.

Some people won't be able to sing when your aggressive volume overpowers them. Even with their best intentions, if their organism picks up the dissonance of deviation from harmony it will respond by withdrawing. You may classify them as reserved, and not have any idea how capable they may have been of flowering at another level of sensitivity, with another rhythm.

Sex — suggestive context for imprinting its atmosphere on daily life

Clumsy, over-tensed movements during lovemaking leave their imprint on you for hours afterwards. Energy applied to a system works to reinforce the establishment of the specific pattern by which that system was organised at the time of operation. In this way the act of brushing your teeth, if done too forcefully, can have a crucial effect on fixating the curve of your neck, especially if you are in the habit of looking in the mirror while brushing. Similarly, a strenuous morning run can determine the tonus of your muscles throughout the day. Even the facial expression adopted in running can stay with you for hours afterwards.

The intensity of lovemaking that sweeps in its wake all the vital systems, involving them to their utmost, is one of the most forceful manifestations of movement energy. More than the movements of other basic functions, like eating or walking, it acts as a suggestive context that reinforces the characteristics which coloured you at the time, and establishes that same style for future use. The style that gives the tone in lovemaking projects its impact over your personality patterns in everyday life.

Your state of mind during sex, which tones your facial and bodily expressions, imprints within you an accentuated route to which your movements will tend to return, even outside the context of sex. You've surely noticed that if you want to know the nature of your sexual experience, you may look into how you felt the following morning. The style of your movement during lovemaking will determine if you'll be drained and ill-tempered, or refreshed and feeling good towards the world. If, during sex, your facial expressions show more suffering than trance, more bitterness of struggle than softness of surrender, that's what will be reinforced in you. If your movements during sex are sharp, hasty and forceful, you'll find it harder later on to find within yourself the rhythm of softness and grace that perhaps you wished for.

The beliefs which lie behind your movements also tend to acquire permanence. If your manner of movement is drawn from a hidden anxiety that perhaps there isn't enough sex for you in this world, there's a chance that this anxiety will continue to influence you later, even more strongly, without any relevance to reality. Similarly, when you accept the experience as a confirmation of the abundance available to you in this world, and your movements are congruent with this belief, it won't be easily impaired.

Do you urge yourself to want what you don't want?

Perhaps what really motivates you is the suspicion that if you leave aggression alone and simply be yourself, you may discover that you doubt whether you are at all interested in sex, or in the person that's with you. Do you need the exaggeration to help you want what you don't really want? Do you need the noise of aggression because it helps you to not listen to what disturbs you, your true voice from within?

Of all creatures only humans separated mating periods from the seasons. The persistent, sexually oriented advertisements around you never mention your permission to desire sex on your own terms.

Or perhaps you prefer to be aggressively geared because you can't entrust yourself to someone else's hands when you're not in your stance of control, and moreover, when you're swept away by your sensations. The category of being in control also includes remaining soberly reserved, which is the other polarity of that exaggeration.

I won't presume to explain the social motives behind the manipulations and traps, the games and penalties in which people become engaged in order to deal with their disappointments. In civilised humankind, the search for love passes through a maze that winds through deep vulnerability — and this is perhaps the most unsolved riddle of life. Here I'm relating to the possibility of learning — through the medium of the body's movement alone — how not to inhibit the love-making encounter from being organically authentic.

Mutual conditioning on each other's responses

Sex is a mutual encounter. Your behaviour is influenced, if not conditioned, by your partner's reactions. People expect their partner to provide the inspiration to bring out the very best in themselves. Both men and women expect that their partner will know how to lead them into refinement, or they expect the partner to allow them to run loose without it seeming in poor taste. People find it especially difficult to come to terms with their self-image when it includes being impulsively aggressive in sex, for this aggression deviates from any other aspect of their daily lives with which they can identify. When people are torn within themselves between a double standard, then a distortion occurs in their attitude towards the witness present at the time that this other side of them is revealed.

The ignorance of non-pleasure

Many religions, through various periods in history, gained control by playing upon this conflict caused by the sin of aggressive passion in one's self-image. Many people were convinced that the best way of solving this problem was by avoiding it, and took upon themselves a regime of puritanical abstinence. Whether they gained a sense of moral superiority when they succeeded in abiding by such discipline, or felt guilty if they failed, the option of having pleasure in sex was denied them. In contrast, other people who were undaunted by religious awe reached a level of cynicism that turned permissive aggression into their own private religious dictate. Both types of people remained equally ignorant of the human capacity to enjoy dynamic sex that is free of tension and full of a tenderness that doesn't signify any omission.

Sex as meditation : an unintentional way of moving

The schools of thought of the Far Eastern religions, which place high value on the harmonious integration of all Creation, reserve a special place for sex. At certain historic periods, sex was clearly perceived as a state of consciousness of non-verbal exaltation, and was related to as a form of meditation. Sex was considered to be one of the paths leading to the source of intuition and the hidden world. Whole societies used eroticism to inspire spirituality, and its many images were carved into the stone of their temples.

The method of Tantra gives detailed instructions as to how one can reach a spiritual experience through sex, by remaining passive throughout. This doesn't mean sex without movement, but that the movement inherent in sex is what moves the person, and not vice versa.

Through continuous education in the expansive traditions that encourage values of individual refinement, people learned to be together in sexual intercourse without generating any wilful movement. This means having the patience to maintain a serene and alive togetherness, in which the level of stimulation is fully present, and subtleties don't pass unnoticed. At times the couple moves in response to an organic urge that stirs them, without any intended investment on their part. The rhythm of this movement is unpredictable, and is far removed from any set mechanical beat. This movement has a swooning quality to it, a submissiveness, a vibrating pleasure that any purposeful act will only disturb.

Not interfering with Nature

In the passive attitude, the gift you give to your partner is your trust in him or her, putting yourself in the other's hands in the vulnerable state of non-control, without trying to beautify, without trying to embellish, without trying to impress, just drifting together with the feeling that something greater than both of you is pulling each of you through the other. You may then believe that the sexual urge is a need of Nature and doesn't belong to either one of you, and you are not really entitled to grades for the performance which, for better or for worse, finds expression through you. Can you imagine how relieved you'll feel when you know that the only credit you can get in sex is for succeeding in not having interfered with Nature?

Transforming the roar of sex into music

In ancient Chinese manuscripts the various phases of lovemaking are described in precise sequence. Like the notes of the musical scale that made order out of the wild roar and turned it into music, so does the Chinese scale coordinate the dance of love. Every phase had a name and a defined domain, its own rhythm and its appropriate level of intensity.

People were trained to discern the distinctions and read the signs in their partners, to know accordingly when to continue into the next phase. The final phase of letting themselves go in full spontaneity comes only after a thorough and lengthy preparation, ripened by a style that is both dynamic and free of coercion. In the light of these sensitive rituals, we Westerners appear ignorant, clumsy in our blindness and impatience.

'Waken not nor stir the love until it please'

The tolerant schools of the Far East were not alone in fostering refinement. Even in the Middle East, an area notorious for upheaval, fanaticism and reacting to extremes, people in ancient days knew how to be more sensitive than we are to the hidden pulse of life. They knew the art of intertwining with the flowing of the wave at precisely the right moment.

In the *Song of Songs* of the Bible, we find the same recurring motif: 'Waken not nor stir the love until it please'. This may perhaps be the Hebrew version of how to moderate aggression and trust the course of life. The hero is considered to be he who subdues his passions.

Can you figure out what virtue is required in order to compete on who will arrive last?

You can change the style as you offer yourself more pleasure

You will never be able to know how much aggressiveness you waste in sex until you experience the other polarity, and train yourself not to help Nature along. Everyone can recall a special intimacy that awakened within a tenderness that surely didn't lessen the pleasure. It is often complained that there are people who start a new relationship with refined patience, but this refinement fades away with time when the motivation to win the other person's attraction is no longer present.

The important thing to learn from this, at the level of movement quality, is that gentleness in the sexual encounter is included in the spectrum of human capacity, and is reserved for enhancing the experience.

You can change your style of moving more easily than you can reform your outlook on life or your attitude towards sex. The quality of your movement lends itself to change without frustrating criticism, without force, and without curtailing your enthusiasm, since you're offering yourself a way of movement that will endow you with more pleasure, and further inspire the deep vitality within you; movement that's as flowing and dynamic as it wishes to be, and at the same time sensitive and harmonious; movement in which you give up only the sting of surplus anxiety expressed through aggressiveness. The difference doesn't seem to be big, but the feeling and its accompanying script are entirely different.

Elevating sex to a human domain

When you transform a blindly aggressive style into a selectively sensitive style, you are at the same time disengaging sex from its primal programming for reproduction, as in Nature, and elevating it to a level of conscious human pleasure. You are then further released from the chain of stereotyped reactions which, in the animal world, urge the male to strive resolutely to insemination, and once that's done with, to immediately lose further interest. His successful copulation stimulates him to continue his conquests in the rest of the herd, while at this very point the female is oriented towards becoming more attached to his patronage.

On the human level, you are both oriented towards refinement of pleasure and surrender to each other's essence. And so you remain, after the wave of lovemaking has reached its crest and subsided.

Living relaxation in the silent aftermath

When you are sensitive to refinement, you become aware of many nuances and tones in the silent aftermath. You feel the difference between the relaxation of collapse, in which you feel yourself wiped out, and living relaxation, in which you're carried on the flowing silence to another level of relationship. Have you noticed the correspondence between the invested effort and your capacity for renewal? Doesn't the effort, interfering with the wave and trying to manipulate it, also disturb its revitalisation and its continuing on to another cycle?

The quality of relaxation is conditional upon the style of activity which preceded it. A living relaxation is an outcome of a way of moving oriented to clearing the movement of its unneeded, parasitic excess. To be in a relative relaxation while moving is the profound lesson learnt throughout the entire Feldenkrais Method. The roller just helps you to resist the temptation of non-relevant involvement and takes you to the minor relaxations between one movement and another, preparing for the major relaxation when your movement comes to an end.

5

A Straight Back
or a Wise Back?

If people would not presume to know, and would not interfere to repair according to what they know, they would not spoil what Nature herself knows how to do...

From the Tao

In the West to correct — in the East not to spoil

There is a deep difference between the East and the West in their approach to correction. In the West when you are not satisfied with your way of standing, and regard it as a shortcoming caused by sloppiness and neglect, you may be told you do not do enough in order to improve.

In the East, on the other hand — and on this issue, as in many others, Feldenkrais' way of thinking is in tune with that of the Tao — it is believed that Nature knows how to organise in the ideal manner. What spoils this is something extra which you have added to it. This is the 'more' that is 'less' — like too much food, or too great a volume in sound.

The West urges you to try, and to act. The East advises you to refine and clarify. Can you accept both approaches without contradiction? What is that extra intervention which sabotages ideal posture? Can it be reversed?

The reflection of your private ecology

The way you stand is indeed your visiting card which you carry with you everywhere, and which announces to the world who you are, your condition, and your attitude towards life. More clearly than a thousand words, your posture broadcasts your personality and your history. With one quick glance it is possible to get the message of your posture and to sense the value you attribute to yourself in the social hierarchy, from inferiority to arrogance or from humility to dignity.

It is very difficult to pretend to have a certain posture, trying to appear to be a certain personality, if it has no correspondence in your emotional reality. The body has an astounding sincerity, always projecting that which you intend to hide.

It is also difficult to construct a posture of wishful physical uprightness when there is no backing for it in your functional honesty, in the quality with which you mobilise yourself, in the level of service that your body gives you in all your daily activities. The ability of your back to be straight depends upon your ability to bend down safely when necessary, or to turn your head over the shoulder when driving in reverse, the way you breathe after jogging, how your knees react to going up stairs, and what happens in the muscles of your entire body when you brush your teeth or thread a needle. To fabricate an image of straight posture when all your daily functions are performed with poor efficiency is to reveal more than anything else your striving to pretend. Your posture is congruent to your mental and physical ecology.

Moshe Feldenkrais used to say that people can expect to be no more ideal in posture than they are ideal in social communication, in family relations, competence at work, creativity, capacity for pleasure, optimism for life, efficiency of response in all areas — not only in movement coordination. To treat only the posture without dealing with what comprises it is to deal with a facade, to constantly exhaust yourself in your conflict with life, instead of learning to change and improve your entire self.

I have heard many people complain that their posture is poor and that it is the source of all their back pains. I have not heard anyone complain that they move without grace, without joy. I have not heard anyone complain that their response is not appropriate and not efficient. I have not heard anyone complain that their movement repertoire is not rich enough in its variations. I have not heard anyone complain that their movements are not smooth, not ideal.

But many people who come to ask for help do complain about the shape of their stance as depicted in a photograph, in a frozen moment of time, divorced from the flow of life. Perhaps the generation which grows up on video will liberate its body image from the model of the still photograph and begin to appreciate its talent for movement.

Structure or the functioning style which fashions it

People who think in static terms interpret the deviations in their body structure which are apparent to them as the causes of their suffering. If only the back were less hollowed in the waist, protruded less in the shoulders, was less twisted to one side, tensions and pain would end. Those same people try to imitate a given posture according to conventional standards, and they are disappointed that their bodies are usually unwilling to use the correction — at most for only a short period of time. Taking the static structure as a guide for correction is a frustrating strategy.

Of course there is an interactive relationship between the structure and the quality of the service it provides to the organism. Perhaps aesthetic appearance and social image are relatively secondary concerns for you, like luxuries. But you may have a profound existential concern when your twisted and asymmetrical posture creates dead-end stress traps which accumulate distress and suffering, impairing your freedom of movement and diminishing your sense of ability. The question is: from which direction, and with which method, can you most efficiently arrive at recovery?

People who put the blame on structure are actually declaring that until their shape is perfect they have no chance of ridding themselves of suffering. This is bad news.

The unending correction of posture

Have you ever tried to correct your structure? You come with a number of borrowed opinions which preach to you what is right and what is worthwhile and how it should be. Each time you remember them, you hurry to correct yourself. This of course does not last long and you find that you are always in a state of mind that is self-critical. When you remember your way of standing you only look for what is wrong about it. Do you notice what happens to your relationships in life, when the essence of your state of mind is fault-finding?

You have an idea that the shoulders are not in place and you decide to pull them back, but then your chest hardens and sticks out, your jaw clenches your teeth in an expression of emergency, and full breathing in this condition is out of the question. You wish to relieve the lower back, which deviated from the vertical position: your shoulders once again round forward, your eyes freeze, your ankles tighten with extra effort, your legs tense and your pelvis locks. Each correction triggers a chain of unavoidable reactions in different areas of the body. In this condition you are unable to do anything other than be engaged with the correction, and you cannot listen or respond to the life around you.

How long can you hold out like that? You can trust your habit to rescue you and return you to your characteristic posture with the determination and fidelity of a printing mould.

It might be that if you could study about more and more parts of your body and learn about the conditioned relationships between them, you would be able to simultaneously remember the whole network of participating factors which balance one another with extraordinary sophistication — a sophistication so advanced that no computer program has yet come close to duplicating it. Even if you then succeed in arranging your posture according to a blueprint of the ideal structure with accurate control over all parts of the body, the correction would still feel forced and artificial. This is still not the spontaneous vitality within you which chooses that way of standing out of its own considerations, out of the inner sense that this is the will of life. You still have a conflict of alienation between your righteous thoughts and your organism which has its own logic.

Straight for what?

What is the organic logic of your reluctant body?

Why is it not willing to remain straight if Nature intended you to stand straight?

Allow yourself to take a small step to the side and ask from a perspective of the service of life: straight for what?

If you were the ideal straight, what could you perform from such a position? Would you be able to shift from standing straight to sitting in a chair without softening yourself first? Would you be able to break into a leap from standing straight without first reminding your ankles to set themselves in a spring-like stance? Would you be able to drive your car in reverse without first squeezing your back in a certain way? Could you, while standing ideally straight, laugh, be angry, hurry, rest, love, lift a load, wash dishes, thread a needle, or perform any of the multitude of activities that people do in life? Is ideal posture just the one position erected in the symmetrical middle with no motion? What about all the other positions which serve most of the functions in life?

Dynamic structure

Life is not static. It flows and changes continuously. The one thing you can count on to remain constant is change.

The very use of the common term 'structure' tends to bring to mind a building which is not given to change. But your structure is not a cast in concrete placed on you once and forever. Your structure is alive and dynamic and it recreates itself anew, moment by moment, in accordance with your needs, in accordance with the agreements, programs and habits in your brain, in accordance with the design of the bones and muscles which repeatedly verify those agreements with every movement. Your structure is not only inventive — it is all that participates in the cycle. Your posture, in its true nature, perhaps resembles a fountain whose characteristic configuration changes simultaneously with a change in the conditions feeding it. When you speak with the organism in its language of change you begin to search for your straight alignment in dynamic terms. You begin to appreciate the qualities that create it; you begin to understand the process which nurtures it.

To deal with the final, static product is a frustrating and exhausting mistake, an eternal struggle. To investigate the process of the formation of the organic posture which is patterned differently every moment anew, opens for you a world rich in possibilities for action.

Functional posture

In dynamic terms, your posture is a context from which you set out to act. Your posture is good when it allows you to move with the least amount of effort. Organising this position in the perspective of activity is done by an organic instinct. Your organism does not wait for you to tell it each time how it should set itself, with what angles, tonus level, shape, or power. It knows all this by itself. Each organism was created with the knowledge of how to arrange itself with the minimum investment of internal muscular tension in order to pass efficiently from state to state, and how to return each time to the neutral place from which it won't be difficult to embark once again on the next function. If your organism did not have this wisdom, your chances of guiding it by the intellect would be no greater than your ability to control your digestion consciously.

Among all the infinite postures which precede the infinite number of functions, there is one particular posture — the master posture — which serves you when you are doing nothing and don't intend to do anything. A rare state in life. Your comfortable starting position then sits in the middle or your mobility repertoire, in the symmetrical place from which you can access any movement in any direction with the same ease of investment, the same range. In this neutral place you stand at your most upright.

This functional posture is not a pattern of alignments and angles, even if it appears that way, but an expression of skill in orientation, of wisdom for self-organisation, which enables you to begin any activity in life with the least time and energy being wasted in preparatory arrangements.

If this talent of making yourself available to life has been dulled, if you have lost the sensitivity, the fitness, the versatility to create all the postures which serve your daily life, then your symmetrical master posture will also be impaired. The opportunity to sharpen the skill of adaptability occurs not when you are standing still, motionless, but in the field in which activity is taking place, where you are cultivating and refining all the peripheral movements.

Your stability is as good as your willingness to risk it

A full life calls upon you to create stability of equilibrium in thousands of configurations and temporary postures, as well as to give up stability, to deviate from it, in order to produce movement in space and again arrive at another, new, stable posture.

As you acquire more skill in achieving equilibrium in more diverse and unconventional configurations, not only will your dynamics of life become expanded and enriched, but your way of standing — the posture of doing nothing — will become more ideal.

Your stability is as good as your willingness to risk and lose it, trusting yourself to reach stability again in a different position. Your structure is good to the extent that it is easy for you to breach it and construct another in its place.

Your posture is good to the extent that you have a movement culture which strives to find for itself the easiest and most efficient path.

If you are alert to your comfort and can change and adjust yourself so that you remain comfortable in your actions despite changing conditions, you already know how to make all the adjustments required in order to regain reliable balance when your action ends and your position stops changing.

Sharpening the intrinsic gyroscope

For example, in transferring your support from leg to leg while walking, each time you transfer your weight to stand on one leg your pelvis begins to shift your weight over that same leg, while the knee seeks to place its projection over the arch of the foot. At the same time, in your spine, each vertebra signals a certain twisting inclination to the next, until the neck turns your face in the opposite direction to the supporting leg, aligning the weight of the head in a continuation of that supporting axis. The second leg can now leave its supporting role and move, as does its opposite hand. All this happens in a smooth and flowing way, with no break in the continuity of your movement in space. Even though with one leg in the air the angle of pressure between the lumbar vertebrae and the pelvis is not identical on each side, the pelvis in this asymmetrical location will respond with maximum efficiency to the force of gravity, and will suspend with a minimum of work for the muscles, as it creates with the spine a continuity without an exaggerated inward curve, which could interfere with the breathing of the ribs and abdomen.

If you do all this, without thinking, while also turning the foot in various ways (as when stepping over varying pitfalls), while turning the head in every direction with the same ease, without hardening the eyes and without calling on the shoulders to protect against the momentary loss of balance, and do all this while also performing tasks with your hands, and your mind continues to think undisturbed, then your talent for finding your equilibrium in any position is being refined. You are perfecting your wisdom of response to life in a way which is relevant, economical, elegant, simple and pleasant.

When you are not doing anything, this same talent for functioning as a gyroscope which repeatedly reorganises its vertical structure relative to the centre of the earth, takes you to your best way of standing — a standing that strives for the vertical and is supported by leaning on itself, through the bones, arranged such that one rests on top of the other, and the muscles rest from their labour. You find yourself then in the desired position, approximating ideal standing, as a bonus for your successful way of coping with the pitfalls.

Your asset in your ideal posture is the intelligence of all your movements to respond spontaneously and efficiently to the changes of life, and not merely the ability to arrange yourself on one certain given line that is, after all, appropriate only for doing nothing.

Not what you do but how your organism responds

Your organism does not stay where you intended to put it, but where you stimulated it to arrive on its own. What determines its behaviour is not what you demand that it do, but rather what your actions provoke it to do. Sometimes its response is, surprisingly, in a direction opposite to that which you intended.

It is possible, for example, to wrap yourself in a supportive girdle which will show the back how to be straight and keep it that way. The test of this straightness will be, of course, in the independent condition, without the support. When you remove the girdle you are likely to discover that the reaction of the back will be a tendency to sink into helplessness, having forgotten its independent ability to carry itself.

How does one plan an activity which will evoke a response of straightening up?

How do you awaken in the back the impulse to be upright; how do you bring about a situation in which the independent need of the body will be to draw itself upwards?

The greatness of the Feldenkrais Method is that it applies its theory in practical experiences. You can, through your independent experiments and your personal sensations, arrive at meaningful insights, conclusions and changes.

All of the practical procedures which will be described here, in an attempt to find answers to these questions, are intended to stimulate your healthy response, to train your innate talent for returning yourself to balance from any situation. They will not deal directly with the straight line of standing, and will not instruct you with formulae for ideal angles and lines. Sometimes it will seem that they are taking you away from straight uprightness, as when they deal with bending and deviating from the ideal. But the upright alignment which is feasible for you now will emerge as a result on its own.

Upright alignment is like a gift. You can never know in advance what will be the harvest of the process. For the gift to speak to your heart you cannot manipulate and initiate it: you can only receive it if the relations between the various parts of you are good. In Awareness Through Movement you work on improving the relations.

Descending to elicit ascending

Everyone knows how effective a strategy of paradox can sometimes be. If you believe that the constant tendency of your back is to sink and become crooked, take the time to study this tendency and encourage yourself to crouch over and obey the persisting need from within.

Standing up or sitting down, allow yourself to sink downwards. See where your body tries to go when you don't prevent it from collapsing. Allow the eyes to give up control of the front ahead, and lower them to the floor.

Allow your shoulders to round if that's what they want to do, and allow your chest to fold in and loosen. If you do this while standing, invite your

knees also to abandon their responsibility for uprightness and let them bend generously. Allow every fibre and bone to surrender their weight and to slide, little by little, towards the centre of the earth.

Linger at each new level and pause to arrange yourself comfortably. The purpose is not to arrive at a deep bend but to begin tuning in to what your body wants to do. Let it be a passive, unprogrammed sinking. Allow yourself to reach asymmetrical, unpredictable positions, provided you are comfortable.

Maybe this is a worrisome position for you, something you do not wish to look at. You certainly wouldn't want anyone to see you this way, bending under the burden of life without resistance. Acknowledge this concern and suspend it for a while. Continue with the experiment, inviting yourself to stay this way for as long as your body wishes, even though you might suspect that on its own it will never want to recover from the position.

You will be surprised that the moment will come when you no longer want to stay there, crouched over. With a new breath an awakening will sprout within you to return to your full height on your own. This is an important moment — a moment to remember and take note of. This is the moment in which you make contact with your own independent urge to straighten.

This is a revolution in your self-trust. You realise that there is a condition from which you straighten up out of your own need and not out of discipline. Your body signals its own interest in straightening without the pressure of your opinions. This needs to be repeated a few times, to reinforce the message. Though the bud of uprightness might be subtle and hidden at first, the more you pay attention to it, the stronger and clearer it will become.

The image of seaweed can assist you to sink down and rise in a passive way. Imagine that within you an ocean stirs. Sense the currents of water which reach slowly to every part of you with a fluid tenderness. Imagine that instead of bones you have sea vegetation — swaying at the mercy of the currents. Allow the silent dance to reach every distant place in you which has long been lost to consciousness.

Feel how the image opens in you permission to respond passively to sinking or rising. Allow the internal movement to carry your overall movement in space. When you begin to rise, especially, you will need to marshal your awareness in order to resist the temptation to help your body return to its familiar place. Give the movement the time it requires and do not tell your back where to come to and where to stop. You may be surprised to discover that the rising will continue to float you upward to a more elevated place than you anticipated.

With the feeling that the internal wandering continues when you stand, observe what kind of body carriage your internal need has devised for you. Listen to the comfort there, to the spacing out. If you are open to subtleties you can appreciate the inclination towards improvement even in its initial stages. Notice if you meet the world now from a slightly straighter stance, in an atmosphere of more serenity and acceptance.

In daily life, when you feel that your back is tired, heavy, oppressive, can't find a neutral place and has a hard time holding up, remember that it is within your capacity to let yourself surrender to the most lowly bending down you feel like doing, and to wait until your back wants to come up from there on its own. In order to restore your impulse to surge upwards, you first of all fulfil your organism's need to collapse. By surrendering to crouching over, the nervous system can rest from its constant engagement with resistance to crouching. When it takes leave of the internal conflict between the tendency to yield to collapse and the effort to inhibit it, it recovers and can once again respond as a healthy organism. It is then that you feel the upward orientation initiated from within.

At the exaggerated level of collapse, perhaps for the first time in a long time, the dormant need to rise upward becomes clear to the nervous system. From that extreme it awakens to generate movement toward the other extreme — something that does not happen from a routine partial state. On this momentum of initiating stimulus upwards, your posture takes a free ride and reaches far beyond its usual habit.

Springiness: the organism's method for vitality

Every deviation from the state of balanced standing trains the organic complex to return to create stability. With every crooked twist, the urge to straighten becomes clearer and stronger. Intentional deviations from the straight alignment are a way to train, in small portions, the righting powers, and to arouse them to straighten the posture towards the vertical line.

There is a network of springs, throughout all the joints, which works to accumulate momentum in order to take off and propel the organism onward, as well as softly absorbing the shock of landing with each return to the ground. The joints of the ankles, the knees, the balls of the feet, each vertebra in the spinal cord and the neck, are springs set up to alternate up-and-down movement in an efficient, safe manner.

This ability to shorten and lengthen is an organic intelligence, the characteristic virtue of every individual cell and of every complex system of living creatures. The breaking through into space and the return home, the extending out to instability and the withdrawal to the secure median, the bending down and straightening up, are part of a wave motion which permeates all of life.

One of the mistakes which perhaps leads to impasse and frustration on the issue of the posture is the unequivocal importance given to the vector which raises the body upward, without seeing the full organic phenomenon of an alternating play between lengthening and shortening, streaming simultaneously towards the sky and the earth in extension, and withdrawing within itself from both the earth and the sky in contraction.

Both tendencies — towards the heights and the depths — are unceasingly co-existent within you. Through the interaction between them they assist and comple-ment one another as, moment by moment, they provide you with postural balance.

Defining an organism through the aspect of gravity

To ignore the orientation of movement downward is to ignore the most dominant reality — the force of gravity, which acts upon every thing in our universe at every moment and in every situation.

There is a tremendous assortment of unique strategies by which every species obtains its food, reproduces, and protects its existence, both in terms of the individ-ual and the group. That which is common to them all — so common that one doesn't even see it — is that all the varied and discrete functions in their infinite, resourceful variations are designed to take place within the context of the earth's magnetism.

One of the characteristics which distinguishes live organic beings from non-liv-ing bodies on the planet is the fundamental difference in structure in live beings between the part which faces the earth and the part which faces the sky. There is not a single living being which is vertically symmetrical. This double orientation is the most basic aspect of the organisation of movement in life. The tissue of the muscles and bones developed to enable them to perform their work in terms of the direction of gravity.

The two poles of uprightness

In every movement, with every function, there is a fluid balance which wanders between the vectors of the sinking of the weight to be supported on the ground beneath, and the counter-pressure response from the ground which thrusts at the same rate upwards.

In order to cancel out the burden which the force of gravity imposes, your body needs to bear down on the ground with a weight equal to your body. If you are not able to allow your weight to bear down because you are busy with a movement in a different direction, then your muscles, as well as performing the movement, will have to work on carrying the weight of your moving body. You can spare your muscles the effort when you heal your relationship to the earth.

Instead of regarding the desired uprightness as an intentional striving upwards, which is a clash of power versus power (i.e. muscles versus gravity), try to let your uprightness take a free ride on the interactive movement of contraction and expansion, pressure and counter-pressure. Be mindful of the flow towards the heavens while remembering the simultaneous flow towards the earth, as well as the retreat from both these polarities. Like a cyclic wave, it alternates between lengthening and shortening.

Instead of trying to straighten yourself upwards and enter into conflict with life, think about expansion and see yourself thrusted both downwards and upwards. The thrust of your feet to the ground will assist your body to achieve uprightness effortlessly.

The axis of sitting straight

For example, if you wish to sit straighter, begin by thrusting your feet to the floor, gently and gradually, with the heaviness of their weight only, with a hint of anchoring them into the floor as a confirmation that you are aware of the centre of the planet.

Listen to the outcome. You may observe a hidden axis taking shape within you, that of itself carries you generously and decisively upward. When your feet acknowledge the ground, your head knows where the sky is too.

When you begin to think in organic terms of expansion and contraction, pressing and emptying the pressure, centre and periphery, you tap into a powerful wavelength which leads all of organic life and which carries you of its own accord.

Standing to sitting: synchronising pressure and release

When you get up from a sitting position to stand, a function you perform many times during a day, do you have any idea of the dynamic you undertake in terms of your dialogue of pressure with the ground, in dealing with the force of gravity? Most people prepare themselves for getting up by thinking of it as rising upward. They implement this by extending the chest and straining the back in an attempt to pick up their full weight and detach it from the chair.

If you are ready to try a different way, see how you get up when you think of rising as an act of expansion, which takes place in all directions, downward as well. Begin by increasing the pressure of your feet on the ground as you incline your body forward over them. You will find that a considerable uplifting power is generated for you from the ground.

In this context of rising while pushing your feet into the ground, your calves are indeed required to work harder — but this is the way to save your back from effort. This is a distribution of labour that you are perhaps not used to, but is it not the relief you are seeking for your spine? Repeat this a number of times until the detachment from the chair happens of its own and you find yourself standing.

You would think that the descent from standing to sitting would be easy, like sliding with the current. The fact is that for many people it involves difficulty, a moment of doubt struggling against a barrier which puts the movement out of phase with the intent. Most people intending to sit down think of the downward direction and then push their feet into the ground with greater intensity. The straight legs become rigid; the pelvis has a hard time overcoming this rigidity and cannot find the space which allows it to fold in. This is a trap, in which a person works against himself.

Try instead, while sitting down, to think of the orientation of withdrawing into the centre of your body, as though you are about to detach your feet from the floor, as though you can empty your legs of the pressure of your weight when your head begins to descend, and in this way try to contract into yourself. You may witness how easy and smooth sitting down on a chair can be. People are amazed when they see that all their lives they were trapped in a wearying habit and never imagined that it could be otherwise.

Evoking the anti-gravity forces

The elastic forces in this game of interaction with the ground can be evoked not only by the feet, but by any other part of the body, especially the head. This phenomenon is apparent in the classic alignment of the water carriers. The head, which responds to the weight bearing down on it by thrusting upwards, threads on its upward trend all the other joints in the chain of the posture.

You can verify this for yourself with a simple experiment.

To the weight of your body, add the weight of a load that you put on your head. You can use a pillow which will not be difficult to balance on the crown of your head. You can also do this in a sitting position.

Sit or stand like this for a few moments and identify the sensation of the pressure of the weight of the pillow which compresses you in the direction of the ground. Slowly you begin to distinguish the awakening of an inner tendency, and you feel your skeleton set itself up to counteract the pressure of the pillow. While coordinating the sensitive equilibrium for the pillow, you become aware of a determined push upward.

Notice whether or not the upward thrust tends to drag with it the lower back in a way that aggravates its hollow. You may put your hand next to your lower back, and very gradually move your spine backwards into your hand. Repeat the slight curving movement of the waist in and out, each time reducing it until you feel you have found the alignment that sustains the pressure safely.

The most important surprise takes place after you remove the pillow. Continue to stay for a while without the load and you will begin to sense the streaming upward, just as though a dam had been opened to a physical flow which carries you up.

A Straight Back or a Wise Back?

Make a note to yourself that your body, under certain conditions, knows how to initiate uprightness on its own.

Eliciting Uprightness
The weight on the head evokes the counter pressure from the earth throughout the spine upwards. Initiating the slight protruding of the lower back against the hand behind guarantees that the uprightness will be free of the common linking uprightness with the straining of the lumbar in an in-curve.

When you carry the load on your head while walking, you can use it as a faithful guide for reformed walking. The added weight will be like a magnifying glass which enlarges the outcomes, and brings them to your awareness. If, for example, you had no trouble accepting a certain crookedness in your spine, with the added weight you feel clearly how the compression is being aggravated there. The load clarifies to you precisely which vertebra is being held in a way that threatens your comfort. This accurate feedback also guides you in how to find a way of walking which will bypass the threat. You learn from your own sensations where to make the selective change, how to mobilise one vertebra in relation to the next, and how to assume a line which is safer, more comfortable and organic. The change which takes place during the actual function of walking also instructs all your other joints as to how to adjust themselves to the new arrangement, as well.

You are perhaps likely to discover that you achieve relief when your pelvis begins to sway more generously from side to side. This new way of walking may seem more alive, perhaps even exaggerated. What determines whether it is correct does not arise out of an idea that someone told you about, but from your own discovery of what can help you in your individual structure at the present moment.

You can put your conclusions to use in the future too. Whether to carry a suitcase in the hand and become crooked, or put it up on the head and straighten, is actually a question of what is socially acceptable and depends upon how much you care about what others may say.

A liquid balance between the fear of falling and stability

The innocent yielding to the sensation of gravity reminds every cell and fibre in the body of the permission to find efficient support beneath it. This orientation to search below for reliable support and to land on it peacefully is inherent in humankind, perhaps from the prehistoric era when people lived in trees which were constantly variable. The talent to find dynamic balance is a process of negotiation from which you haven't a moment's rest except while you sleep.

This is the body intelligence that is most utilised and most vulnerable. A sudden loss of stability, giving no chance to develop an appropriate response, is the most frightening of shocks. The fear of falling, the fear of the ground being pulled out from under you, is the primal and most direct fear in life. A person who is sleeping may not be woken by a noise or the increase of heat in his surroundings; even being shaken may not wake him immediately. But he will wake up fully, instantly, when the bed collapses under him.

This is a fear related to the early anxiety of falling from the mother's lap into abandonment. In the sudden emergency of a loss of balance, whether real or imagined, the fear returns and freezes the organism in terror. The mode of self-defence then is instinctive from birth; it comes in a reflex of clinging to the nearest object and curling the spine into a ball, which tries to minimise damage to the head and essential organs. That same instinct, brought into play in moderated and initiated situations, can be the guide which teaches you to find a solution of security under all conditions.

Perhaps you remember your need, as a child, to challenge your fear of falling in small doses, in the exhilaration of jumping from a high place — the fear which at once threatens and thrills.

After a proper study of Awareness Through Movement people who suffer from insecurity in elevators and aeroplanes, on escalators and street crossings, reported that in an unexpected manner, all those activities which previously caused them to panic had now become simple and comfortable.

Training in loss of stability, in small, deliberate doses under safe learning conditions, contributes to the stimulation of the talent for creating stability inestimably more effectively than any direct command to stand straight and overcome fear by willpower. Stability is not a matter of standing straight, but of being able to act like a gyroscope, knowing where the centre of the earth is and adjusting to it from any position. When you relate to the ground, and your feet find on it a stable stance from which you are not easily dislodged, then you are also in your most effective upright stance.

The rehabilitation of your internal gyroscope means, in essence, a sharpening of your sensitivity to comfort while moving, developing an inner sense of self-organisation which is gratifying for you, and maintaining a balance between investing energy and obeying gravity while the balance wanders and sways with the ever-changing variations of flowing movement.

A dynamic definition for static straightness

How can flowing movement elicit static uprightness?

How is it possible to express straight standing in terms of variant movement?

For example, in trying to describe the straightness of a young tree through its mobility, one could say that it responds to every change of the wind with the same degree of bending. If the tree can yield and bend equally in all directions with the same ease, then it can stand straight and tall when there is no wind. The condition that its movement response be equal in every direction is the guarantee of its ability to stand straight.

In human standing, too, the dynamic expression of static posture is the potential ability to bend in the same way equally to right and left, backwards and forwards. If the bending can be done with the same ease, the same uniformity, the same continuity, the same rhythm and the same range on each side, then the stationary standing posture will be straight of its own accord.

This functional definition of upright straightness opens for you a practical world of possibilities for action. Trying to force yourself to stand ideally without movement is working against life. Enhancing your ability to bend in every direction, and promoting your willingness to move to each side with the same quality, are things which you can do. You have an easy access to the dynamic activities which guarantee your straightness.

Aligning your sitting: allow the deviations to find the centre

You can begin while sitting on a chair.

Move slightly away from the back of the chair and take a moment to scan your initial sitting position as it is. What is the line of your spine?

At what level do you have more difficulty sitting straight?

Place your feet apart, flat on the floor. Put your hands in your lap, palms up, and do not try to sit as you think you should. Allow your breathing to guide you to comfort.

Imagine that a light breeze begins to blow on you from the left side. In your own time, allow your body to begin to respond, leaning ever so slightly to the right as though the wind is pushing you and you are just surrendering to it passively. Remain that way, leaning to your side, and take a free breath in this position.

With the subsiding out-breath, let yourself return to your original place. If you are open to fine distinctions, you can observe that something in you knows the way home and, as slow as it may be, it returns you to the centre of itself. This is your organism's talent for self-righting.

Repeat the same movement, on the same side, a number of times.

Each time you come to the right and breathe there, ask yourself how you could arrange yourself there even more comfortably, more faithfully to gravity. Perhaps you will find that your right shoulder is willing to loosen there and to hang a little differently. The elbow can find a different location for itself. Perhaps even the right cheek is pulled downwards in a manner different from the usual.

You do not turn your face to the right. You move in the side plane, and your right ear salutes your right shoulder. Each time you veer to the right notice how the pressure in your sitting bones increases on the right side. See if you can interpret each leaning to the right as a shortening of the right side; the ribs are pressed there one into the other, the chest is more compressed into the pelvis, while your left side releases more of its length, and the ribs open in it as in a fan.

After a few times, stop the movement and sit for a moment, still without leaning back, and listen to how you are sitting now, to the sensation that you have on each side.

Slowly suggest to yourself the image that the wind is blowing on you, this time from your right. Wait until your body is ready to respond and begins moving in the other direction. In what way is this different from the other side? Allow the return to happen slowly on its own, as though unintentionally something is leading you. If you do not help, you may experience the grace of being carried by the inner knowledge.

Continue in this way a few more times until the veering to the left becomes as acceptable to you as to the right.

Take a rest and compare the sensations on the two sides.

If you like you can lean back fully for a while on the back of the chair. When you are ready to continue without support for your back, move forward and sit on the front part of the seat.

This time you may imagine that a tuft of hair on your skull is being pulled upward, growing longer and longer until it is tied to a hook on the ceiling. Imagine how the pulling up of your hair picks you up along your central axis higher and higher, at the same time as you remain comfortable and heavy, allowing the full weight of your pelvis to rest on the seat of the chair, with the full weight of the chest on the pelvis, the full weight of the shoulders on the rib-cage, and the full weight of the head on the spine. Something outside of you is responsible for your straightening and pulls you upward. You accept passively both the pulling upward and the suspension of your heaviness downward.

Imagine that the suspension from the ceiling, on the long cord of your hair, allows a slight movement left and right, and begin to sway with it from side to side.

Gradually extend the swaying , observing the movement on one side relative to the other, and gently invite the right side to imitate the deviation of the left side. Do not try to equalise the distance, just the feeling, the form and the rhythm. After a number of times, exchange roles.

Slowly begin to reduce the movements. Each time go slightly less than the previous sway. You may discover that it is not simple to do a little less than your capacity. This is an opportunity for you to see whether or not you are compulsively stuck in doing the maximum, or if you have a choice in regulating yourself as you wish.

After a while, decrease the movements until there is actually no more movement in space, and only in your mind the idea of the pendulum continues to keep the beat.

Sit this way for a while without movement and listen to the way you are sitting now. What is the alignment? What is the sensation? Notice whether or not the feeling of comfort in your sitting has become more pronounced.

After resting as long as you wish, bring back the image of the cord of hair carrying you upward. Relinquish responsibility for your uprightness, and sit comfortably.

Imagine that the wind is blowing on you now from behind, and after a while see yourself being carried slightly forward. Each time you move forward, stay for a while bent like that, reminding yourself to breathe. When you are open to feeling how the weight of your shoulders tends to pull them differently in this reclined position, allow them to revise their hanging and come slightly forward. Wait until the righting forces, on their own, bring you back to wherever they see fit.

Continue swaying like this several times. Then rest for a while.

Imagine now that the breeze is coming from ahead of you, pushing your torso to withdraw backwards. Take all the time you need till the image comes alive in your mind and you can respond to it passively, ever so slightly, without assisting it. You are likely to discover that it is not easy to maintain your stability when leaning backward. Go gently and gradually, breathing easily.

Leaning backwards means exposing your most vulnerable parts. See if you are willing to enter this position in the state of mind of voluntarily exposing yourself to risk, as though you like the challenge, and invite your chest to expand to its full length and breadth, allowing your chin to lift slightly. Remind your weight, in this position too, to search for support from beneath you while the cord from the skull reassures you that you are being held up.

Continue this way, alternately bending forward and backward. Let the movement forward imitate the careful and slow movement backward, until there is no difference in feeling between them.

This is not a symmetrical movement. Your structure of course is different, front and back, but you have an innate wisdom to equalise the style, the quality and the willingness to create a movement which feels symmetrical, despite a structure that is asymmetrical. This uniformity in the quality of operation leads you to harmony.

Rest and listen to the results.

Now combine both movements into a full, flowing motion. Once again recall the image of being suspended by your hair tied high to the ceiling, so that your head and spine is being pulled up and your weight collapses down.

Imagine that you are prepared to remain that way at rest, but feel how the height of the cable allows the wind to play with you, blowing you around and around.

Begin to move your entire body so that your head traces a circle on the ceiling. Go very slowly, as if every place you come to you are prepared to stay there, to settle and feel comfortable, but the wind takes you to another place further on around the circle.

Every point on the circle is an opportunity for adaptation, for re-alignment, for a more faithful response of the weight to gravity downward, and for reinforcing the image of being carried upward. The benefit comes not from the movement but from your adjustability to the movement. When the movement becomes smooth, allow yourself to increase the size of the circles.

Gradually bring the movement to a stop, and rest.

Next, imagine the whole movement being done counter-clockwise. When you feel ready, slowly begin to explore a small circle in the opposite direction and develop it gradually. Allow yourself to surrender to the repetitive movement again and again as the tail bone and the crown of the head tend to extend away from each other.

If you like you may place one hand on the top of your head and with the other hand touch your tail bone, to have a better realisation of the connection between them.

After a few circles, when you reach a quality similar to the other direction, begin to reduce the circle until eventually it revolves just on its own axis, between your two hands, until no actual movement takes place in space and only the idea of the movement continues to whirl in your head and carry you upward in a spiral.

Sit with this sensation for as long as it lasts. Release your hands and listen to the way you breathe now.

Finally, scan once again the way of sitting which fills you now and tell yourself what you have learned about straight sitting.

People who search for tranquillity in meditation often find the aspect of sitting to be a constant hindrance. The intention of taking a break from the turmoil of the intellect and being in a void, which offers potential for renewed activity, becomes totally impaired by the physical preoccupation of having to sit, thus preventing the meditation from being a period of tranquillity.

The tradition of Zen Buddhism knew that a number of alternating motions from side to side before sitting could pave the way for you to accept the still sitting.

Another tradition knew how to elicit non-resistant sitting by use of a metaphor: visualise your spine as an unbendable bamboo shoot, and invite yourself to lean on it, comfortably.

Aligning while standing: an experience of trance

You can apply the same process in all its stages to the standing position, and enhance your posture on a more realistic plane. In standing, the relationship between the legs and the back also comes into play. There is more to risk and more to learn.

The imagery of being suspended from above reaches its full effect in standing. When your head is held by the imaginary cord at a fixed height, you have an opportunity to loosen your vertebrae one by one, allowing them to sink down, beginning with the tail bone and ending with the atlas at the base of the skull. In addition, your shoulders and pelvis are invited to rediscover the comfort of being suspended by their weight alone.

This suspension provides your most authentic and effortless vertical alignment. In this straightening you are free of the toil of pulling the weight of your body upward, as is conventionally perceived. The idea of straightening downward instead of upward can be useful for you in all daily situations when you feel that your back is collapsing under its own burden. While washing dishes or sitting on a chair, all you have to do is imagine that a cord is holding your head at exactly the level at which it is located, trusting the weight of your body to filter down in complete passivity to organise you in the least compressed and closest-to-desired vertical uprightness.

When you begin to sway in standing, as you did in the chair, you can sense clearly how the motions of the torso are congruently reflected in the shifting of pressure on the soles of the feet, between the inside of the sole and the outside, in the right to left movement; or between the heels and the balls of the feet, in the forward and backward movement. You can verify through your own sensation how every oscillation of the body in space is interdependent on the direction of pressure in the soles of the feet.

Your balance while swaying in the standing position is more precarious than in the sitting position. The motion cannot be as large in range, but it can relate far away to the edge of the horizon. You sway from side to side and think about the winds of the heavens towards which you move. Your trajectory in space when you transfer the weight from one foot to another is tiny and barely perceived by an outside observer. But the repeatedly pronounced thought — east-west — gives your movement a significance of the vastness of the universe. You sway forward and backward and contemplate in your mind — north-south — and make contact with an orientation sense which navigates migrating birds or guides butterflies to arrive at the same particular trees annually from across the planet, without anyone from the previous generation to guide them. Being mindful of the relationship of your movement to space, you restore within you an extinguished radar for global interaction.

The movements of the torso while standing are reminiscent of the movements of prayer, and the final motion of drawing a circle in search of its centre can indeed generate a remarkable experience of trance.

Neutral standing: the innocence of doing nothing

The most impressive thing about the new standing which emerges from the process is that you are not doing anything deliberate in order to stand that way. The arrangement of your posture comes about of its own accord. You are comfortable, not interfering, and taste a way of standing in which you have to do nothing in order to stand.

Only then do you understand, retrospectively, to what extent you always used to add and try, to compensate, hold and invest. The neutral experience of living at peace with your body brings you a spark of insight into your inner wisdom which knows well what is best for you, to a greater extent than you could ask for. You realise that something in your organism is wiser than your intellectual thinking, surprising you with its notion of what an ideal posture is.

You are tapping into that kind of intelligence that knew to send the cells to the appropriate places when you were being created in the womb, and knew to urge you to practice and refine yourself stage by stage after you were born. This is a moment of standing in awe of Creation.

Only then, when you are not doing anything, can you sense how your social strategies drop away. As long as you are engaged in doing, your activity is subjected to the patterns you set aside for doing. When you have nothing to do, your habitual strategies in life becomes unnecessary. You don't have the need to protect yourself; you don't have the need to outsmart; you don't have the need to flatter or attack, to be reserved or shy, or to adopt any other habit. This is a feeling as though you have been cleansed of all those qualities that perhaps accompany you unconsciously when you do your best to make your way through life. This is a moment in which something might seem to you to be missing, and perhaps you even feel embarrassed. You stand at the end of the process comfortable and without the personality you are familiar with, learning the innocence which lies beneath your history.

To every person this new way of standing might be perceived as dramatically exaggerated to the opposite extreme of how one is used to trusting him or herself in daily life.

A woman who was accustomed to impressing others, and relied upon her talents to elicit appreciation, which she always expected, said after the process: 'I feel like a clumsy girl who doesn't care at all how she looks, doesn't care what others say ... what a liberation!'.

A businessman with a rigid, over-emphasised way of holding his chest was standing, at the end of the process, with his ribs hanging loose, breathing softly, and he said: 'I feel as though I am helpless and at peace at one and the same time'.

With permission to be yourself — as you are — there is an echo of a primal sound from a time when you were small, helpless, not yet brilliant, and still knew you were loved unconditionally. A measure of humility is required to allow yourself so vulnerable a state of being, and to learn from it.

It is useful to take the new posture into movement and to pay attention to the kind of walking which emerges from it. And it is even more instructive to begin to run with it — not in the way you know, but in the way it comes to you on its own. For many people this is an experience which brings up the association of the running of an animal, a running in which there is a willingness to keep running without getting tired, a running which has something authentic about it, does not try to be better than it is, and knows where the earth is.

A posture which sits in the middle of the six directions

To east, west, north and south you can also add the third dimension of up and down, arriving thereby at a posture which stems out of all the cardinal directions of movement in space.

You already know that your most balanced posture, in terms of having equal and easy access to both stability and mobility, can be found in the middle of your movement range. You already know that the quality of your posture depends on the quality of moving in your functional domain.

To the extent that you train yourself to reach efficient movement in each of the fundamental directions, you will increase the reliability of your posture make-up, and the empowering of your interaction with each direction can be achieved by performing, out of this direction, an actual task of daily life.

Like many of his other stratagems, Feldenkrais' process of the six cardinals has the genius of profound simplicity.

Walk around in your usual stride. Then choose a moment to descend as if about to kneel, lowering one knee slightly towards the ground without breaking the pace of your walk or altering it in preparation for the descent, without holding the breath, without making a big deal out of the gesture.

With the same ease, rise from the beginning of this semi-kneeling and continue to walk. At your own intervals, repeat this a few times until the cardinals

of down and up are clear and available to you as a simple part of life. Then take a rest.

In a similar manner, while walking in pleasantly fluid strides, assume that you are interested in seeing something over one of your shoulders. Without stopping your walk, direct your eyes and invite the rest of yourself to assist them by rotating the neck, spine and pelvis, adjusting the direction of the knees, while the ankles continue to make sure that your stride continues its progress forward. Contrive to do all this several times without changing the pace of your walk, without needing to stop any of the other things you are doing, thinking, feeling, seeing, hearing or talking.

While taking a few steps of simple, daily walking, in your own style and your own time, you can remind yourself of accepting equally easily the cardinals of forward and backward. Without any preliminary planning, you change direction. Instead of continuing forward you put yourself in reverse without needing to pause for any length of time to reorganise. You retreat more smoothly and fluidly than any motor car you know. Your body is able to set itself up for change with the speed of your thought.

You can alternate between backwards and forwards, unpredictable in pace, and train the adaptability of your entire being, until it makes no difference to you whether you are walking forward or backward.

When you stop everything and stand still you will sense the posture which has crystallised within you. Sense how the memory of the multi-directional readiness puts you at your optimal body tone, the optimal alignment for your unique body, giving you the feeling of your vitality readily available to respond to and participate in life with a flexible mind. It may be one of those moments when you can once again believe that life is indeed easy and that you are perfectly built to live it.

The more you go beyond the six fundamental directions and enrich your movement competency in general, refining your response to varying situations, not only will the functions that you perform improve, but you will also be continuing to cultivate and enhance your uprightness.

This holds true provided that your style of movement is acceptable to your organism, that you feel carefree in your moving, that you present movement to yourself in a way that will give you pleasure in performing it and curiosity to explore and discover more and more of its components and coordinations until you feel at home with it.

Movement is the context in which it is wise to invest. Movement is your element.

If you want good posture, go to movement and you will gain them both.

Bring out your best through a spark of imagination

To cultivate multi-directional openness in your functional programming, you don't need gross movements. You can recall each direction by minor turning of the head. While walking, see if you can forego your usual watch ahead, as though it were your eyes that were directing your progress, and instead look sometimes up at the sky, sometimes at the ground, sensing how you adjust yourself for frontal walking even though the eyes do not accompany it.

What is important is not your success in diverting your eyes to the side, but the maintenance of the uninterrupted flow of your stride as you do it. It may be advisable in the beginning to do this slowly. It is up to you to determine your learning pace.

You can also apply this while sitting. Instead of correcting the way you are sitting and trying to find at once the desired straight and appropriate alignment as you sometimes feel the need to do, you may take a journey through all the deviations, or just visualise such a journey.

The mere thought of movement already organises you into more efficient body carriage. You can reach the same accomplishments in posture if you do all the preliminary movements only in your imagination. Visualising an image, using the brain language of dreams, gives you a reminder of expanded possibilities and grants you a level of vitality that has in it more power, more colour, depth and presence. Taking a minute each day to reconstruct in your imagination the image of yourself moving in each direction, with the same ease, could be your hidden process for rehabilitating the optimal posture of your starting stance.

If you imagine that you are jumping, the thought alone takes your body to its best. In a jump there is no escape; there you have a bio-mechanic need to align on the vertical — otherwise you will fall. This urge to organise yourself straight up in a jump is a superb teacher for upright posture. It is sufficient for you to intend to jump and you will realise that your body is already beginning to re-organise. If you want to know what is the best possible posture for you today, give yourself the motivation to jump, without actually jumping, and look at the alignment which your torso takes upon itself.

The image of yourself functioning diverts your attention from the trouble or defect (the crooked back or any other complaint you might have about yourself) and transfers you to a constructive domain where the correction takes place spontaneously.

To deal with the hunched up or the crooked back in terms of hunching up and crookedness gives the negative the power to become dominant. To shift the confrontation to a perspective of service to life, to see yourself doing what you would like to do, paves the way to a healing atmosphere and invokes in your organism the knowledge of how to align yourself congruently with your aspirations. Skip over the hunched back and the dropped shoulders, the immobile chest or the stomach which may protrude arrogantly even though you are ashamed of it, and see yourself in your mind's eye one step ahead, as though you had already accomplished what you wanted. In your imagination be there at your best, in leisure, generously succeeding in performing your tasks and operating as you know you are capable of doing. You will be amazed what such a moment of 'as if' simulation can do. The instant you succeed throughout your entire self in becoming the image, you will feel that something within you begins to migrate, to shift and to move towards a different self-carriage.

You realise once again that there is something intelligent within, that you do not have to tell it what to do — just give it the picture of the destination and it already knows how to take you there. The road leading there is a multi-lane highway. You can choose at any time the lane which is more suitable for you — the mental lane or the movement one — provided that you let the posture emerge for you on its own as a response to the prospective journey.

An entanglement of compensations

At this stage you may ask with concern: 'But what can be done if the crookedness has already become fixated in the bones?'.

For example, if the area of your shoulder-blades is rigid in a hunchback hump, how indeed can the delicate motions from side to side, to say nothing of the imagination, unravel the massive rings around the ribs and shoulder-blades and loosen the vertebrae there so they can straighten?

What you perhaps do not know is that even were you to succeed in convincing the bones there to alter their deployment, you would still have a problem. All the other parts of your body have become accustomed to adjusting the balance between them according to your individual structure as it is. Until you train them one by one to alter their way of functioning and re-organise according to the local correction, there is little chance of the change catching hold.

Suppose that you 'clean out the rust' from the ribs-spine-shoulder-blades intersection and this area is open to manoeuvring and can now be arranged straight and vertical. This correction might perhaps give you the feeling that you are going to fall backwards and you begin to tighten your stomach in defence. The back of your neck then would immediately be called upon to adjust accordingly the angle between the chin and the neck. You are likely then to feel a loss of orientation. Your legs, long accustomed to under-utilising their springiness as they relied on the work which the back took upon itself, would be likely to rebel against the new burden which has been placed upon them with the relief of the back. You would barely be able to appreciate the delicate relief sprouting in the back because the protest of your legs would be much more vocal and you would probably reject the corrected posture altogether.

An ideal body organises itself so that it does not have to invest energy in standing upright. The ideal body has the skill to align itself with the economy of a pillar which supports itself, layer upon layer. Each vertebra is free to come and go, adjusting itself to the only alignment in which there is no effort, to the medial line which is oriented vertically. When each segment is supported in uniform overlap on the surface beneath it, without emphasised focal points of sheering stress, the force of gravity acts to reinforce stability and the counter-pressure from the ground enhances it even more, on the same marked trajectory, from its opposite end.

Energy is invested by the ideal body only for the purpose of mobilising itself when it needs to deviate from the vertical. When people lose their adjustability to break through to a variety of positions as well as to find the way back to the neutral one, they adopt set deviations and deformations, parts which stick out and others which cave in, which they cling to as expressions of their identity. Only then is there a problem in holding everything together without falling, or in simply standing motionless.

Trying to deal with a distorted habit of posture, you cannot avoid taking into consideration your entire musculo-skeletal network that is involved in its entirety in any working plan. Every distortion came initially as a biological necessity to compensate for a deviation from the vertical alignment somewhere else in the body.

It was the sense of family responsibility of each member in the organism for the whole body which balanced every deviation with a counter-deviation, in order to enable the body to maintain its equilibrium. Standing thus became an exhausting project of complicated, and constant investment of energy.

Local correction in the context of the whole

Any attempt to correct one part is an intervention in this complex fabric of deviations and counter-deviations, these traditional interactions reinforced by the habits of years. You intervene at one end and there is not a part in the whole body which does not react to it — some more, some less — with relief or resistance.

Even if the rest of the parts in the background have the physical capacity to stand differently in order to adjust themselves to that same intentional improvement, the program of their co-behaviour in the brain might not accept this change, like any compulsive habit. Cultivating the willingness of your nervous system's headquarters to agree to local correction, and make all the required adjustments for it in the periphery, is your educational assignment.

It is like reaching understanding between all the members of the family and receiving their permission to alter the conventional rules of behaviour, so that the individual will be allowed to do something which he did not do before, knowing that he will have the full support of all the others.

How do you obtain this permission?

How do you intervene in the complex balance without undermining it?

Where do you begin?

Feldenkrais guides this family therapy within the body's community by working with the relationships between parts, relating each part to the whole. In these processes your attention wanders back and forth between the foreground and the background, the detail and the whole, initiating local action and listening to the feedback from the rest, making careful progress which allows each of the participants to update its response. Sometimes you approach directly and deal with a certain part; sometimes you go indirectly to its reflection on the fringes of the periphery. It means, for example, that sometimes you elicit change in the neck through cultivating freedom in the hip joints.

In exploration from as many different starting points as possible, and in your ability to assimilate the lessons which the various relationships bring up for you, lies your answer to a realistic and lasting change.

Squatting: healing the conditioning between the shoulder-blades and the pelvis

As a medium for loosening up the upper back area within the context of coordinating activities in the rest of the joints, explore the following process: the development of sinking into a squat. Squatting in a frog's crouch is perhaps the extreme polarity of upright posture. By now you are certainly not surprised that the Feldenkrais Method sometimes uses what seems to be a paradoxical approach.

The squat — or as it is sometimes called, the laundry squat — is a position in daily use in cultures which are not dependent upon chairs. If you know how to descend into a laundry squat and can stay there and actually do the laundry in that position, as well as ascend from it easily, then the communication between all your joints flows with fluency and sensitivity. The folding knees, the bent ankles, the rounded pelvis, each one of the vertebrae extending to bend to its maximum possible angle, and the neck which does different things in different stages — all cooperate in a coordinated distribution of labour and in smooth synchronisation. Many disciplines of body development have emphasised the performance of the squat as an objective of fitness.

Begin, as always, by observing your initial movement. Try once or twice to descend to a squat and ascend from it. Sense what this function means for you. Probably you are aware of the demand it places on the obvious joints of the knees, ankles and waist. You are perhaps less aware of how a differentiated mobility between the vertebrae in the upper back is also essential for descending to a squat in a quality of a flowing wave, folding the whole body down as well as pulling it smoothly up again under the pressure of its weight.

The Function of Squatting
To descend and ascend from a squat is an assignment of harmonious communication among all your joints. It is possible to facilitate the function by slight deviations from the frontal performance and twist the shoulders and hips alternately. Is the barrier in the knees, ankles, thighs? Have you ever thought that the responsibility of smooth squatting falls also on the rib cage?

A Straight Back or a Wise Back?

Assume a stepping position with your left foot forward and stand comfortably with your ankles springy and your knees generously bent.

Extend your right hand upward so that your arm is attached to the side of your head or face. With the left hand grab the right elbow from behind, so that the left wrist is also touching the head at the crown. The head is held steady in the frame of the straight right arm and the bent left forearm.

Keeping this entire set-up as it is, begin with your right hand to outline circles on the ceiling. Your knees remain softly bent at the same level. Your entire trunk moves as one unit without the head moving relative to the arms. Listen and discover at what level of the spine — between which vertebrae — there occurs an articulation reminiscent of coffee grinding.

In the same manner lead the circle with the same hand in the opposite direction. Then take your hands away and stand and discern the difference between the sides.

After you go through the same stages on the other side, stand with the feet apart, letting your weight be dragged along the vertical line downward; loosen the knees to a bend which will absorb the sinking of the body; extend both your arms upward; cross the forearms and turn the palms to face each other so that you will be able to interlace your fingers. Bring the arms to full contact with the head on either side so that you fixate it between them.

This is a device to neutralise the neck. Usually, when you lead your head in circles, it will be the neck that will bear the primary responsibility in carrying out the circle. Here on the other hand, you place your arms like wooden splints in a cast treatment, and the neck is obliged to rest between them. This is an invitation to another part of your body to enter into action.

With your intertwined hands, begin to trace a circle on the ceiling, as the knees and pelvis maintain more or less the same position in space. Remember that what is important is not that the circle be fast or large, but that what happens inside your body is within the boundaries of comfort and pleasure.

Circle slowly in each direction several times. Perhaps now you can identify more clearly where the 'grinding of the coffee' is taking place. The neck is in splints, the pelvis and knees are kept in place by your conscious intent, and thus it remains for a specific area of the spine — between the in-curve of the lower back and the in-curve of the neck — to begin to contribute its share. This

Mindful Spontaneity

is the only area that can do the work of the circle now, for lack of any other choice. This confinement does not allow that section of the spine between the shoulder-blades to evade activity, as happens in ordinary standing, and something now begins to change there. You may even hear sounds of friction there, which teach you that it is better to go more slowly and trace smaller circles.

Let the arms down slowly and rest.

Re-organisation of Distribution of Labour
The arms block the flexibility of the neck, the bent knees stabilise the pelvis and limit the lumbar in-curve. The rib cage is left with no alternative but to directly respond to the circle outlined by the arms, starting to articulate its own joints and relinquish its rigidity.

Stand and observe the quality of the new uprightness which sprouts forth in your chest, in the spine. Do you feel that it has become somewhat easier to be straight?

Now return to the frog's squat and notice how you accomplish it this time. Isn't the flow less interrupted than in the beginning? Does your pelvis tend to sink lower than before? Aren't your legs ready to fold more easily, to stay this way for a slightly longer time, as they bear your weight?

Take a moment to contemplate how uprightness improves together with the squatting. Make a note of the reciprocal connection between the ankles and the upper back region. In order for your heels to agree to descend more deeply and reach more secure contact with the ground in squatting, you had to open more freedom of movement not only in the knees, waist and neck, but more particularly in the vertebrae of the middle back.

This straightening in the upper spine region which gives the posture its uprightness remains in your body of its own accord, because you achieved it through negotiation with all your parts while performing the circle. All the joints which learned to move differently or to inhibit movement, as was required in order to perform the sensitive and varying task of the flowing circles, now know all the more how to regulate anew their involvement in a standing in which there is no movement. This is an authentic uprightness.

The back of the chair: touching the root of the uprightness issue

If the squat is still not in your range of safe movement, you can enjoy the benefits of the process from a position of sitting on a chair. In the Feldenkrais Method there are countless procedures which can be done while sitting.

The back of the chair, which usually bears the weakness of your back and reinforces your dependency, can be in this process a superb tool for promoting uprightness. If the edge of the chair's back reaches the area of your upper back you have an ideal setting for creating an influence right there.

As you sit and lean on the back of the chair, extend one arm upward. As you did when you stood, hold the arm attached to the side of the head. You can bend the elbow and bring the forearm into contact with the top of the head, so that the head is set in the angle of the elbow. Place the other hand on the seat of the chair for support.

Without allowing any motion between the head and the arm holding it, begin to draw circles with the elbow on the ceiling or on the opposite wall. Of course your whole torso is called upon to mobilise the elbow. All the while the edge of the back of the chair determines which level of your spine will articulate in the circle when you reach backward.

You can choose to attach any vertebrae onto the edge of the chair's back so that the 'coffee grinding' will happen in that particular segment.

Using the Back of a Chair to Open Freedom in Your Back
It is important that the arm is attached to the face in order to make sure that the neck will not absorb the circular movement of the elbow so that the movement will activate the higher resistance sections of the spine. Shifting your sitting forwards or backwards on the seat of the chair allows you to direct the articulation to intended different levels of the spine.

After you make circles clockwise and counter-clockwise with each of your arms, you can embrace the head with the two arms crossed together, so that your neck is completely neutralised from both sides — as though the head and the back were one unit — and in this way continue with the circles.

Every once in a while shift your position on the seat of the chair a little forward, and allow a higher vertebra in the spine to receive the experience of 'cleaning away the rust'.

In this way you get a result that you cannot obtain in free standing. If you have in mind, while standing, the intention of doing something to correct your posture, and you try to straighten yourself up, you are probably inclined to move in places where it is easier for you to move; and you do not move in places where you are not accustomed to moving. Possibly you are overdoing it in the vertebrae of the waist and the neck, but nothing happens between the vertebrae held together in the outward curve of the upper back.

All of the processes here are designed to inhibit the movement of the neck and waist and to direct the activity to the area which truly needs it.

The edge of the bed: systematic re-education for reluctant vertebrae

In the same manner, the edge of the bed can also serve as an educator for straightness.

Lie on your back so that your head and part of your shoulders extend beyond the bed. Support your head with your right hand, making sure to support the back of the head and not the hollow of the neck.

Extend your left arm in line with the continuation of your body, so that it faces the wall behind you. Draw circles with the straight arm, and allow it to pull with it the entire upper part of the body, with the head carried by the bent arm.

Move with care and sensitivity. Do not make an effort to lift the head forward toward the ceiling. Your benefit from this position comes when your head is drawn backwards, toward the floor, where your spine is being arched in a backward bow which occurs not in the waist nor in the neck, but, for a change, at the level of the shoulder-blades, where your vertebrae meet the edge of the bed. Each time you reach back with the head, slow down, breathe, and invite the rest of yourself to accept the new arrangement.

Crawl back onto the bed and rest, between changing hands and reversing directions of the circle. You can return to the bed in a gradual process of dragging yourself in a crawl-like motion, alternating one side after the other. When you begin to be sensitive to the quality of your movement not only in activity but also in the transitions from activity to rest, finding graceful and pleasant solutions for these transitions, you are truly no longer dealing with exercises, but beginning to develop a lifestyle.

When you go back to drawing circles, each time you can lean a different vertebra on the edge of the bed. This is an opportunity to give systematic treatment to your most neglected places. The treatment is so intense that you will have to use your consciousness so as to not give in to the temptation to try and straighten your back completely in one day. As always, remember that you progress only to the extent that you will still feel good the day after.

When during day-to-day living you are tired and have the chance to lie down for a few minutes in bed, you can utilise even this rest as an opportunity for improving your posture. With time, when you are already experienced with the circles, you will be able to find rest in this extended position, with the head and arms hanging beyond the bed without any movement. When your neck is securely supported by the edge of the bed and your head is slightly lower than it, the circulation in the face and scalp is gradually refreshed as well. You train your brain tissue, in small portions, to tolerate greater pressures than is usual and the blood vessels in your head become more immune to higher pressure.

Rest in this way for a while on your back — or also on your stomach, with your face hanging outside of the bed, turned to one side.

Lying motionless in this way with only the breath gently guiding the subtle adjustments in the body, invite yourself to reduce the resistance and to allow the new openness between the vertebrae to be fully accepted.

Do not be concerned that lying on your stomach on the edge of the bed will aggravate the rounding of the upper back. Any loosening between the vertebrae, wherever it can be achieved, whether in the direction of rounding or straightening, will work to free the spine and make it easier for you to assume any new desired position.

Return to lying fully on the bed and remain there at least until you feel that your equilibrium is restored. Then get up gently through the side and see what kind of posture awaits you. Pay attention to the positive; detect it. If there is a word or an expression that comes to mind in this state, make a note of it to yourself.

Some words that people have brought up to express their feelings concerning this state have been: light, floating, taking off, straight.

The ankle sets the tone for the posture: rehabilitating the springiness

You have surely noticed that one of the difficulties in descending into the squat position focuses on the area of the ankles, which refuse to make the acute angle which this position requires. Is there a relationship between the willingness of the ankles to bend and an upright standing position? What is the role of the ankles in posture?

The distribution of weight at the base of the foot dictates the pattern of organisation of the entire structure above it. For example, leaning with slightly more emphasis on the outer edges of the feet will shape the legs into a bow, while weight sliding onto the inner edges leads the knees to knock into one another, and will probably form a greater hollow in the lower back. A foot with toes which are twisted and folded beneath themselves, as though holding onto the earth, will dictate a parallel rigidity in the pelvis. Concentrated stepping on the heels will require the chain of vertebrae to withdraw into a rounded curve and will project the chin forward, straining the neck in attempts to avoid falling backwards.

How then should the pressure on the bottom of the feet be distributed in order to design the ideal posture? Obviously when the pressure of the body weight is distributed evenly and uniformly, without preference or foci, it is not held in the foot but continues to be transmitted through it into the solid ground. The body remains neutral, free of the need to react in a certain way, and the feeling is one of lightness. But in order that the body be able to make the complex changes required for movement in space, the distribution of pressure in the sole must be capable of migrating quickly and sensitively in accordance with the action required.

The foot meets this requirement of being a variant surface by giving the ankle control over the adjustments. Ideally the pressure of the body does not bear directly on any particular part of the foot, but is primarily channelled to the arch of the foot. From the elevated position of this bridge-like top, it is easy for the ankle to distribute the pressure to wherever it is needed, as well as to withhold it or change its direction.

In order that the knees do not project beyond the toes or the heels, or on the inside or outside of the foot, but rather on the top of the arch of the foot, the ankle must be bent at an angle sharper than 90 degrees. This means that one of the clues to ideal standing is a flexible ankle which is capable of bending generously, an ankle which knows that it is a spring and not a bracket.

When the ankle is lazy in performing its sophisticated task of regulating the pressure on the foot, and is paralysed in reluctant rigidity, the knees have to take upon themselves this concern for distributing the weight on the foot, and sure enough they will become tired and worn out. The pelvis will be affected by the difficulty in the knees and will not be able to rely upon them sufficiently to suspend freely. It will need to distort somewhat its way of standing and for this purpose will draft the lower back, which with every movement will have to take into account the limitations of the legs beneath it. This is the well-known domino effect of compensations, which involve every part from the foot to the head.

Sometimes the ankle itself is quite able to bend to the desired angle, but people choose not to utilise it in this way. This is one of those habits formed by monotonous walking on flat floors. In order to refresh the attitude in the brain it is enough to imagine, from time to time, the springiness of the ankle — this permits openness to suffuse the whole body. For some people the mere thought of the springiness of the ankle will induce in the back a response of letting go; for others, the shoulders, jaw or eyes will loosen up. A significant change occurs in the knees. They, too, find their forgotten springiness.

Below is a mini-process which reminds the ankle how to enhance its participation in walking.

> Go down on your hands and knees. Lift your right knee and heel, and step on the toes of your right foot. Begin to move the knee forward and backward, parallel to the floor. Then draw complete horizontal circles, keeping the distance between the knee and the floor constant. Invite your pelvis to assist the movement. Listen to the bending possibilities of the ankle.

> This is a training in the interaction between the ankle, knee and pelvis, done in a context which is different from the usual, in which the ankle is free of the body weight which usually bears down upon it, and is also free of being the initiator of the movement. Unlike their role during the act of walking, the toes are now anchored in the ground and it is the pelvis which moves towards the ankle.

> Change the direction of the circles for a few moments. Then stand up and listen to the difference between the sides. You may be surprised at the conspicuous change brought about in the ankle by just these few movements.

> It could be that the leg which did not work seems to you now like a stiff pillar for which any change is inconceivable. Meanwhile the side which worked has been altered throughout its full length. You feel that it is softer, willing to sink down to the depths of the earth, and at the same time is open to straightening up as well. The foot perhaps finds itself pointing more straight ahead than is its habitual pattern. You are witness to a new quality of elasticity in the knee, ankle, hip joint, lower back and even in the ribs.

> And above all else, it is as though all the parts on this side have a deeper knowledge of belonging to each other, and they maintain a sensitive communication among themselves.

> Go down to the floor now, and give the other side the opportunity to be refreshed in the same way.

> Eventually, stand on your legs, which now perhaps remember a sensation you had when you were a child. Walk slowly and see how you perform simple daily tasks with this openness in the joints.

It might take a while before you can feel safe with this open springiness in preference to legs stuck like rigid scaffolding supports.

Walking while sitting: a glimpse into an ideal posture

Stand behind a chair with your back to the back of the chair. Sit on the back of the chair in a way that is halfway between sitting and standing. You will have to find a chair whose height will enable you to place your sitting bones on its back, fully supporting the weight of your torso, while your feet can rest comfortably on the floor.

Begin to lift one heel from the ground, let the pelvis bear down and sink its full weight on the back of the chair. Put the heel down and repeat it several times.

Put the back of your hand on the lower back. With each lifting of the heel, protrude backward the lower back vertebrae that you are touching. Mobilise this vulnerable part of your back in utter gentleness. Your hand can feel and verify the motion of cancelling the depression there. Each time the heel returns to the ground arch your lower back in, ever so slightly.

After repeating that for a little while, put your other hand on the top of your head to stabilise it, avoiding its tendency to make all the adjustments in the neck only. Then reverse the pattern and hollow your lower back when the heel is in the air, and round your back out when the heel steps down. Go through the same with your other leg.

Move to the right edge of the chair, so that the right buttock will be in the air, totally unsupported. Each time the left heel lifts from the ground, the right side of the pelvis has a unique opportunity to sink even more deeply down. Let your head balance the pelvis by bending to the left. Then put your hand on top of your head and stabilise it in the middle.

Now add the cancellation of the lower back curve, directing the vertebrae against the contact of your hand as the heel leaves the ground. After a while shift to the other mode of interaction and arch your lower back in when the heel leaves the ground, stepping slowly from one foot to the other.

After you do this on the left side too, and again some more in the middle, with both sides supported move away from the chair and stand for a moment in order to feel and assess the change.

Mindful Spontaneity

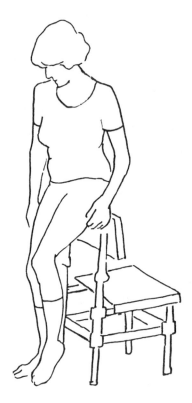

Walking While Sitting
You may need to tilt the chair so that it meets precisely the level of your sitting bones. While the weight of your torso is fully supported standing in the vertical plane, the nervous system learns to relinquish those parasitic efforts it is used to investing in during standing. When you apply to this context the function of walking in place, the new organisation is reinforced and integrated throughout your total self. Standing later gives you a taste of an ideal posture where the muscles are less involved and the skeleton carries you on its own.

You may find that your entire alignment has softened and rounded both in the lower back and in the knees, in such a pronounced way that it is nearly impossible for you now to return to your rigid stance with straight knees and an arched lower back. Once this rounding tendency is initiated it may not be difficult for you to continue to round yourself further to a squatting position.

Even if you do not squat but merely walk around you may discover a profound change in your walking style. All kinds of disturbances and tensions might have been erased. Your steps are quieter and follow one another more smoothly. You may feel how the springiness in the ankles is identical to the springiness in the knees, in the groin, in the lower back and neck. Your entire self is joined together with the same quality. Your eyes have also softened and you may be quite amazed at your new self.

The advantage of the change is that now the pelvis has learned the way to hang down with all its weight, sparing the spine the effort of holding it up. In a few minutes you have acquired a taste of a more functional posture, a feeling reminiscent of an animal trotting with an undulating, streaming gait.

Gap Between the Hands: awareness through touch

If you know what you do, you can do what you want. (Moshe Feldenkrais)

In the procedure known as Gap Between the Hands you know what you are doing due to the feedback which your hands give you when they touch your back. You learn to attach the palms of your hands to the hollow of your lower back, in certain ways and places, as will be explained in the following pages. You learn to conclude from the sensations of their touching and not touching each other how your back works, when you stand or move, sit or walk, bend or jump. Your hands reflect faithfully and in detail your individual way of organising your vertebrae while in action. They reveal to you the angle at which you hold your pelvis relative to the spine; they clarify for you where you summon up tension, and how all this changes during movement.

The sensation of the hands also guides you to activate specific parts of your back more precisely, and thereby bring your spine to an alignment which is free of vulnerability.

To Awareness Through Movement, you add awareness through self-touching. You lend to your blind back the rich experience of your hands, that are skilled in deciphering through palpating, and enable the brain to reach a fuller image of the way you organise yourself in space. Awareness through this direct sensation gives you an additional clue to generating a change for well-being in your way of standing. The same sensing mechanism which feels and examines also controls the correction.

This is a treatment you give yourself in the distressed zone of your back, the lumbar area, the narrow and vulnerable strait between the two solid parts of the body which become the victim of stress, tiredness and monotonous functioning.

With the help of your hands you can train each vertebra separately, at different levels of the slope of the lower back, reminding each one of them of the option, which is perhaps not sufficiently familiar, of how to move outwards, backwards. The ability to break through the immobility and protrude out of the in-curve, and to align on a more vertical line, within a more consistent continuation between the spine and the pelvis, is a contribution to the recovery of the back.

While walking with every step anew, you consciously give your lower back a brief moment of escape from the hollow, a short release from tension. When the pelvis suspends from the back by virtue of its own weight, it drags the lumbar vertebrae with it and pulls them towards the ground, along the vertical alignment, which is their safe place.

Instead of a frozen spine with an exaggerated and rigid in-curve, which is liable to be compressed in that same irritated spot, you educate a spine which recognises the freedom to manoeuvre and to create spaces of relief between the vertebrae. Throughout a trajectory of the full walking cycle you learn to take advantage of a special moment and eradicate the tension, a moment which is sufficient to grant the vertebrae recovery and refreshment before they return to the in-curve on the same wave of undulation in walking, which will continue to wind them alternately again and again between the hollow and its annulment, as an organic wave of motion is meant to be.

The use of the gap between the hands can accompany any function, and can be like a compass which directs you to the safe path. You can check with it not only your standing and walking, but also the dynamics of going up and down stairs, bending down to lift an object from the floor, the trajectory to and from a chair, as well as the sitting itself. This is a built-in guide, a friend for life.

The learning process may not be simple, and perhaps will not immediately become clear. Like a musician who requires countless rehearsals in order to train each finger to do as he wishes and coordinate them all, you patiently build the relationship between every vertebra and your consciousness. Through awareness, through listening to the movement and its reflection in the sensation of the touch of your hand, you acquire a new key to your well-being.

The adaptation of the release and the reaching of a stage where it becomes second nature may take a long time. The more you provide your organism with the information, in its own language of sensitive touch, the more you will tend to organise yourself in the way which guarantees safety. The more you use your hands in order to enhance mastery over the movement of the back, the better you will know how to do this later without them. You will arrive at a stage where your brain no longer needs the feedback from the hands.

The intentional mobilisation of the lower back, in addition to the trail of adjustments which follow it throughout every part of the body, will become clear to you. The manoeuvring of the lower back curve will take on the status of a voluntary movement in the functional map of your self-image. You will know how to shift a particular vertebra as simply as you open a fist.

The difference measured in centimetres is perhaps so minute that it can barely be detected by outside observation. But the difference in feeling and in the stamina of your stance in life is remarkable. Your walking becomes transformed; the lower back stops being a blind area charged with a frustrating problem and it begins to be alive in your self-image with a feeling of pleasure and liberation.

Here are some comments people have made about the Gap Between the Hands experience:

'I was standing and talking on the telephone, and suddenly I felt that I didn't mind standing. It's been years since I remember such freedom.'

'Yesterday I felt that my back was beginning to develop pains. I remembered the process and I walked for a few moments with the hands in a gap on the back. The pain went away and did not come back.'

'You taught me something for my whole life. I always looked for a way to stand that would be comfortable. Since then I have a clue which guides me. I walk differently, clothes look different on me.'

'I went up the stairs and felt as though my back was oiled.'

How to lend your blind back the orientation intelligence of your hands

Lie on your back and rest for a while. Begin to sense how the spinal cord makes contact with the floor. Observe where it is particularly remote from it.

Bend your knees and put your feet flat on the floor, comfortably apart. Place the right hand in the hollow of the lower back from the right side, so that the palm faces the floor and the thumb touches the waistline. The back of your hand supports the rear of the pelvis.

Leisurely and gently, begin to press the pelvis onto the hand, in the direction of the floor. Learn by the touch of the hand how to direct the pelvis to flatten itself more fully against the floor.

Repeat this a few times, cancelling the hollow of the lower back, without particularly lifting the tail in the air, without exerting the muscles of the buttocks or the stomach, without stopping the breath.

Take away your hand and ever so gently repeat the same movement without the assistance of your hand.

Take a rest, extend your legs, and pay attention to the changes in your way of lying.

Once again bend your knees as before. Place the right hand on the right side of the back below the waistline as before, and place the left hand on the left side of the lower back curve above the waist, so that the left little finger is located on the waistline and the rest of the hand supports the lower part of the ribs.

Push the feet gently to the ground and flatten the pelvis to the floor, slowly, softly, while breathing. Identify the protrusion of the waistline backwards in its contact with the hand. Remain this way and without changing the position of the pelvis, continue also to flatten to the floor the part of the curve above the waistline. Identify the cancelling of the hollow by the feeling of the pressure of the ribs on the left hand. Continue to breathe and allow the hollow of the lower back to return slowly to its usual shape.

Continue in this way, time after time, to cancel the hollow of the lower back in two stages — first from the belt and below, and afterwards pressing the area from the belt and above. The two stages enable the organism to accept the proposal more simply.

Switch hands and continue to practice cancelling the hollow of the back in two stages. Find a way to remain at ease in the shoulders, stomach and face, and in breathing.

Remove your hands and see if it is possible to continue to attach the lower back to the ground, in two stages, without the help of feedback from the hands. Take the time you need to locate the movement. When you act without suddenness, without coercion, there is a chance for greater precision. Take note of the clarity you have acquired in organising your back.

Let go of the movement, extend your legs, rest, and notice the way your back makes contact with the floor.

Now get up and stand on your feet. Pay attention to the difference in the way you stand. The rest of the process will be done in the realistic plane of standing.

In standing, place the back of the right hand behind the pelvis. The thumb is along the waistline and all the other fingers, more or less held together, are below the waistline on the upper area of the pelvis.

Begin to push the pelvis backward ever so slightly in the direction of the hand, especially protruding the area of the waistline backward, with the tail remaining in its place. Breathe softly and allow the clarification process of this movement to occur. It is important that you do not bend your chest forward and lose your vertical stance when the area of the waistline is carried backward. Listen to the feeling of the continuity between the pelvis and the spine, and see how much it can be accepted naturally. Remember that the knees stay slightly bent in order to make it possible for the back to be comfortable.

Go on to place the left hand above the waistline, higher than the right hand so that the left little finger is parallel to and touching the entire length of the right thumb. Take a slow breath through that arrangement, let your belly expand softly, and make yourself comfortable. Only when you breathe can your system 'own' the new movement and use it in life.

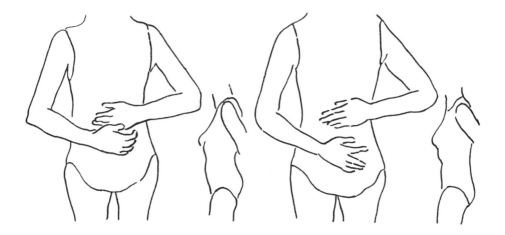

Gap Between the Hands
You lend your blind back the wisdom of orientation of your hands. According to the sensation of touching and detouching of one hand to the other you learn to feel how you compress your lumbar in a hollow and how you can create space between the vertebrae.

Continue to annul the hollow of the lower back in two stages, and be aware that each straightening of the vertebrae causes the hands to separate. Feeling the breaking of contact between the hands is your sign that your back has indeed moved from an exaggerated in-curve to a straighter continuity.

Each time you return the back to its place, the hands also go back to touching each other. The feeling of their renewed contact verifies for you that you are once again standing with your lower back shortened in a curve.

Continue in this way a number of times, annulling the hollow of the back and deciphering it by paying attention to the response of the hands as they detach from one another. Do it in minute, easy movements.

Stand this way for a moment with a gap between the hands and straight lower back, and slowly remove the hands without changing the back organisation. Assess the way of standing that your hands helped you to assume.

Notice, within this unconventional stance, the quality of comfort in the region of the vertebrae which connect the pelvis to the rib-cage. Feel how they can be suspended on a vertical line without stress and pressure. Pay attention to how the other parts of your body resist or accept the new situation.

Leave everything and stand as you normally would without interference. Feel whether or not something of the process has already been applied to your way of standing.

Once again place your hands in the hollow of your back, one beneath the waistline and the other above it, with the thumb of the lower hand touching the length of the little finger of the upper hand. Gently and without interrupting your full breathing in the stomach, invite your back to withdraw backward so that it separates the hands from one another. At the same time raise the heel of your right foot slightly in the air, with the knee bent, as you do when you begin to take a step forward. Return the foot to its place and let your back return to its normal alignment. Notice that your hands also returned to touching one another.

Continue in this way, taking the beginning of a step a number of times. Each time the right foot leaves the floor, round the lower back and protrude it outward.

Switch the arrangement of the hands. Lift the left leg a number of times. Pay attention to the way each side receives the movement.

Rest a little. Then combine the lifting of the foot with the rounding of the back while you actually walk. With each step, when one foot is in the air, lead the back to separate the hands. When both feet are on the ground, allow the back to return to its normal arrangement with the gap between the hands closed.

Pay attention to how it is possible to reshape the line of the back into greater continuity without giving up the vertical alignment of the entire posture.

Acknowledge the parts of the body which are called upon to do something different from their usual action so that the more ideal position of the lower back will be accepted with less resistance and without any loss of continuity in walking. Feel how a soft bending of the knees is renessary for the back to be able to re-shape. When you are able to fashion your back at will, with complete support from all the other parts of your body, you will have recovered your back's function.

One requires a lot of patience and a consistent supporting attitude in order to avoid the frustration of learning something new which may seem obscure and complicated. This is an opportunity to recover not only your back but your ability to learn. Give yourself permission not to succeed immediately; slow down to a rhythm in which clarity can grow, slow as it may be. Repeat a specific detail as many times as it is necessary for it to become clear, and especially give yourself appreciation for coping with something new.

The more the walking pattern in the process meets with a strange feeling, the more your organism has an important lesson to learn from it.

Go back to standing with your hands in the mould of your lower back, one from the waistline and below, and the other from the waistline and above. Leave the hands attached and the back fashioned in its usual curve, and in this way lift the right foot from the floor. Lower the right foot to its place on the ground and then, calmly and slowly, thrust your lower back towards the hands, cancelling its curve and letting the hands detach to form a gap between them. Continue in this same way, with the right foot in the air, the curve of the back in its usual place, and the hands touching one another. When the right foot comes back and steps on the ground, protrude the curve and form a gap between the hands. Sense how the step of the foot on the ground helps to push the waistline backward, aligning your spine without a curve.

Continue in the same way, lifting the left foot.

Bring this pattern to the action of walking, leaving the hands touching one another each time one foot is in the air. Be aware that you are still standing with a deep curve in the back. Each time you land the foot and take a step forward, push the waistline backward ever so gently to form a gap between the hands.

Continue in this way to walk slowly, taking step after step as though you were performing a magnified walking wave in slow motion.

Leave everything and rest a while.

Stand and place your hands joined together in the hollow of the lower back and cancel its curve. Slowly, without holding your breath, first push the upper edge of the pelvis backwards and then the hollow above the waistline. Identify the sensation of the breaking of contact between the hands. Leave the gap between the hands as it is and begin to walk around in your own way. Enable the lower back to undulate in a soft wave, as is required in ordinary walking, but do not allow the curve to deepen to the degree of closing the gap between the hands completely.

In this way, by maintaining the gap between the hands intact, you ensure that your back remains within the boundaries of more direct alignment with the pelvis. Feel how the motions of walking work this way to cancel the curve, while usually the emphasis in habitual walking is on its deepening.

Allow your walking to determine which phase will coincide with the cancelling of the lower back curve. You may discover that you complete each step with an in-curve, and then transform it into an out-curve towards the beginning of the next step. You have a full cycle of moving back and forth with each step. You begin to restore the organic wave-like quality of walking.

Occasionally you may shift the location of your hands a little higher up along the spine and give other vertebrae and ribs a chance to practice their voluntary articulation.

It is important that the protrusion of the lower back is not done with a sharp and sudden movement. Reduce it to a comfortable measure where it can be accepted as part of a natural walk.

Gradually release the pressure of your hands on your back. Reach a state where the hands barely touch the back and you still know how to organise the lower back wave motion independently of the hands' feedback. When you master the movement according to your internal kinaesthetic sensation, take your hands away. Continue to walk as if the hands were still there, allowing your back to behave as it would if the hands were touching it with a gap in between them.

A Straight Back or a Wise Back?

At this moment you may feel very clearly how different and strange is the involvement of all your other parts in this new walking. You begin to comprehend the kind of transformation that is required of your other parts, in addition to the lumbar region, in order to bring it relief.

You may sense what kind of knees go together with a comfortable back. You may find that your knees are less straight than is usual, and even wonder if it is possible to rely upon them in this condition.

You begin to sense what kind of ankles are related to a spacious back. You perhaps feel the difference in the way the feet step on the ground; the distribution of pressure on the sole of the foot is altered. It is as though you are stamping the feet on the floor from the heels to the toes, with the flow of rolling wheels, and you glide on them like a bicycle rider. You may comprehend then that for your back to maintain the comfort found for it by your hands, your feet need to step on the earth more gently.

You discover perhaps that your shoulders behave in a way that is almost impossible for you to recognise as your own. Through every tissue and fibre in your body you fully grasp the idea that what most prevents your back from being comfortable is not the damaged lumbar section, but rather the unwillingness of the other members of your body to give up their habitual patterns and learn how to accommodate the back.

Acknowledge any doubts you may have as to adapting this kind of walking to your life. The intention of the process is not to coerce you into following any righteous advice, but rather to make available to you an efficient tool for eliciting another option. You may use it when you feel a need to remind yourself of the clues for a more gratifying organisation. The application to life will take place on its own, at the pace of the nervous system and according to its subconscious logic.

Approval for achievement or for process

How is it that people who are close to Nature grow up straight on their own, without having to deal with correcting their posture? How does Nature do this? Where does the spoilage begin?

One of the famous Feldenkrais stories tells of a man who came to Moshe with his tortured back. Feldenkrais glanced at the X-rays and said:

'You are the first born in the family.'

'That is correct; how did you know?'

'It's obvious — look at this back.'

There is something about happy parents who are so admiring of their child's development, especially with the first-born, that they can cause distortion in posture for the child's entire life. When the parents, loving as they are, have a goal-oriented mentality, they tend to interpret the child's natural impulse to learn and move on to the next stage of progress as a matter of their offspring's personal success in a competition to achieve the norms. When they approach the child from a hurried and hasty world in which ideas are grasped with the blink of an eye over the headlines, they perhaps do not remember how much patience is needed for the repetitive practice of natural learning. Parents derive so much pride from their child's progress that with his first groping experiment to stand on his feet they give him compliments, approval and expressions of satisfaction, encouraging him to try hard to stand.

It is difficult to imagine how compliments can be so misplaced. When it is seen as important to succeed in not falling, instead of developing an agreeable way of standing, it is the child who sacrifices the chance of arriving at the ideal stance.

Perhaps you can remember how you learned to ride a bicycle. Do you recall your feeling when you made sharp and exaggerated corrections, which you most probably did in the beginning? In the same manner the infant distorts his spine in order to remain somehow standing. The curve in his waist is perhaps suddenly deepened, he waves his arms and strains his stomach, or any other thing that helps him not to fall at that moment. If he immediately receives admiration for this, then everything associated with this kind of standing will be registered within as something worth doing. Not only faulty alignment, but even the accompanying feelings of apprehension, discomfort, impatience to succeed, and aggressive response as if in emergency, will all be imprinted as necessity.

Every time life presents that child with a problem of stability while standing, the brain will call on the early emergency program, and will try to retrieve the atmosphere of struggle, with all of its accompanying attitudes. The recurring distortion in the spine will be identifiable in X-rays even fifty years later.

The natural learning process in early life is designed to take place within the presence of a witness, who observes and confirms the progress of the child in his or her experimentations. The growing child's nourishment is the feedback of attention from that witness. The child's little ears hear well which of all the things that are done bring approval and reinforcement. The child quickly learns to earn its social existence, learns the effectiveness of a smile, of a cry, of success in standing up on two feet and walking.

The social reward is much more important than body comfort. For whom is it not so? With inexhaustible energy a child will direct all effort to satisfying benefactors and parents, and to gaining more of their love and vocal praise, desiring to be the centre of attention.

Performances may change, but what remains is the accompanying feeling, the implied message that one needs to strain the body before the eyes of the people who are important, so that they should see, react and give high marks. Instead of the inner process of inquiry remaining open to advancement and refinement, it becomes important for the child to present an achievement and thus join the show-off racing club of Western culture.

The primal learning of the infant: its asset in organising its standing

In the first year, even before the acquisition of language, an incredible amount of learning takes place, which is more revolutionary and varied than all that a person can learn in all the rest of the years put together. From a passive state of helplessness, from dependence on a few reflexes which act to preserve basic existence, the child becomes a person with social status who negotiates with those around for the fulfilment of his or her desires. From a limited repertoire of movements over which the baby has no control, it arrives at the end of the first year at the systematic differentiation and directing of muscles and patterns of action which are effective in performing many intentional functions.

The quality of this extensive and complex learning process determines not only the operational style of the child, and the attitude to learning in general, but also the body posture. For example, the way in which the infant, lying on his stomach, begins to lift his head as he tries to stabilise the head above the shoulders, time after time, is part of the preliminary training for stability in standing. The way in which the baby acquires skill in each of the stages of development, as in turning from the back to the stomach, in rising to a sitting position, in repetitive undulations in a kneeling position, in crawling, develop in that baby a personal style of coordination, a resourcefulness in finding solutions which will serve his ability to cope with gravity and balance. All these traits will comprise his assets when, at the end of the first year, the child comes to organise himself for an upright posture.

Of utmost importance in the organisation of the posture is the level of cooperation between all parts of the body which the baby brings with it to the standing position, the extent to which all the parts of the body know how to assist one another to perform a task. For example, the quality of crawling is determined by the ability of each part to transmit the power from foot to head.

But if the baby did not have opportunities to develop this coordination between all the parts through an assortment of varied tasks in different positions, if the baby grew up on a soft, flat bed with poor stimulation, or remained for hours in a semiseated position, in monotony, strapped into a pram, instead of manoeuvring in space or being carried in a tilting bag on its mother's back, that child is likely to stand on its feet before all of the lessons needed in order to interact with the environment effectively have ripened within. The child will be compelled to cope with the force of gravity in the vertical and less secure position of standing before it has developed sensitivity to economy and precision in the more comfortable positions of the preparatory horizontal stage. Such a child will be tempted to resolve this difficulty by investing more strength, and thus, standing on its feet, enters the cultural habit of over-using clumsy aggression, the habit of losing grace, fostering the belief that standing on one's feet is a struggle. Joseph Chilton Pearce devotes an entire chapter of his wonderful book *Magical Child* to describing this shortcoming.

Uprightness which ripens in its own time — unconditional love

If the parents interfere and help in order to shorten the struggle, for example if they grab the hands of a baby who is lying on her back and pull her straight forward to sit up, there is a danger that they will limit the infant through the limited habitual pattern of their own functioning. They deny her the motivation to search for herself the ways which perhaps might have led her to better solutions, such as arriving at the sitting position by rolling over on the side.

Of course the support of parents, their concern, the devotion with which they cushion the child's way, are essential for its growth. This love of parents for the new-born child, when they are still its entire world, is an unconditional love, that even the ecology of the technological age has not succeeded in dimming — and it is the hope of the human race.

Without the encouragement of parents, children might perhaps never stand on their feet. It is possible that the very idea of standing on the feet and straightening into the upright position is a human invention which is passed on from generation to generation by imitation and personal tutoring.

There is evidence that in a number of cases in which children grew up among wolves, they were found in their teens to be crawling on their hands and knees, even though they had the physical potential to stand upright.

It might be that upright standing and walking is the fruit of human learning par excellence, for which there is no code in the prenatal program. Like every acquired attribute, it is more exposed to mistakes, mishaps and variety.

It could be that the standing position has less evolutionary experience than the other functions which preceded it. Actions such as rolling sideways, turning over and crawling, Nature ripens with a strong independent impulse; and they occur in the same order everywhere in the world. The closer the stage of standing on the feet gets, the greater the differences in the formation of function by different children. In crawling there are already different and strange styles, including total avoidance of this stage. In the absence of appropriate conditions, many babies are ready to skip this exhausting stage, especially if they are granted an elevated observation post from which they can participate in the life surrounding them.

It would be impossible to exaggerate the importance of crawling, of the indispensable lessons which the organism acquires through it for coordinating all of its parts in efficient cooperation. All the later stages of development — standing, talking, and even reading — are beset with difficulties when they are not founded on mastering the skill of crawling.

Appropriate conditions for crawling are not only a ground which is sufficiently solid that it can be trusted to return counter-pressure, and space which gives the imagination more scope than a one-square-metre playpen, but also parents who are not impatient to see their child successfully standing on her feet.

Nature imbued parents with the need to teach their children how to avoid hurting themselves, and upon children it bestowed the curious joy of testing these hurts for themselves. As in the imparting of other educational values, the parents face a task of delicate sensitivity, in which they try to know when to help and when not to help, when to allow and when to prevent. The sense of measure that is required of them can only be found through their unconditional love.

With greater respect for the learning process of the young human being, for whom everything is strange and new, with fewer expressions of love at the first signs of success — especially with regard to standing and walking, accomplishments so vulnerable to distortion — the child can ripen in her own time and arrive at the ability to stand when she is better prepared and trained, and capable of continuing to refine the process as well. The child can receive a firm foundation for her entire life, not only in the alignment of the spine, not only in the ease and comfort with which she relates to standing, as well as to physical activity in general, but also in the sense that she stands a better chance of growing and going through the obstacles of life with a feeling that she is forever free of having to earn love through actions which she does or does not perform. Such a lucky child could believe that being born is sufficient reason for being loved.

Primal Moving: reconstruction of the process by which Nature prepared you for mature functioning

One of the outstanding paths of learning in the Feldenkrais Method is the reconstruction of the baby's model of development. The process of Primal Moving is a source for precise information on the dynamics which evolution utilised in order to develop the newborn's system of judgement and to prepare him for mature independent functioning.

Each lesson of Primal Moving is devoted to a different basic function, and can actually include any movement which a baby performs, such as sucking, lifting the head while lying on the stomach, raising the pelvis while lying on the back, turning over from stomach to back, holding the ankles in the hands to pull the legs, rolling over from side to side as well as forwards and backwards, bringing the big toe to the mouth, butting the head against the bed, rhythmical rocking, shifting from kneeling to sitting, and a variety of locomotion patterns from the twisting of fish and the pecking of chickens to crawling in the style of reptiles, monkeys, bears and panthers, all of which have an echo in human walking.

Mindful Spontaneity

Arching the Spine
Raising the pelvis in the air, vertebra after vertebra, and moving it in circles in three dimensions, is to do systematically and with awareness what every baby had to do spontaneously, endlessly, in order to acquire mastery over its body. When you experience those same preliminary stages through which Nature prepared you for standing on your two feet, you get up from the process with a body that is more prepared for life.

In these processes you are instructed to undergo once again those stages which preceded upright standing. You systematically return to the movements which you once knew how to do and have long since forgotten. This time you discover in them possibilities which you might have skipped when you were a baby. You cope with each of the challenges as in the original process, searching for equilibrium in various positions, navigating the effective outline for the task and for your structure, adjusting the rhythm to suit yourself, integrating breathing, coordinating the eyes. When you take into account all of these sensitivities, you are likely to arrive at sophisti-

A Straight Back or a Wise Back?

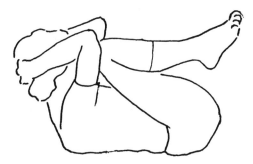

Relief Through Moving the Spine in One Block
Simulating your spine like a wooden wheel, printing it uniformly onto the solid ground, ever so slightly from right to left, is an advanced assignment of coordination. The weight of your body works to realign each vertebra to its proper place. You may wrap a long cloth around your knees and head to secure constant distance between them, to substitute reaching the elbows to the knees.

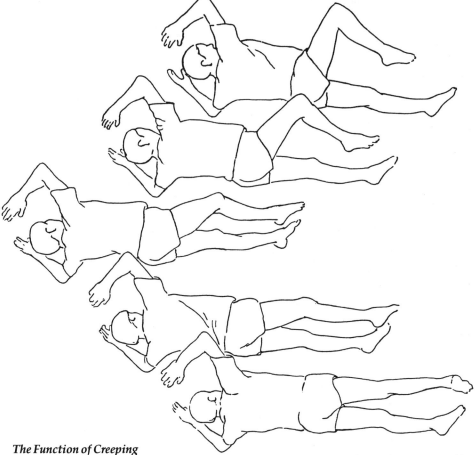

The Function of Creeping
In terms of surviving in Nature, you are fit for life to the degree that your pelvis and spine are capable of serpenting in a way that will transmit without a loss, the propelling force generated by your foot interacting with the ground all the way up to the head.

cated solutions in performing these early tasks. Unlike during infancy, you are now passing through this process with your awareness present, observing and taking note of your perceptions.

You emerge from the process with new conclusions, new insights, and with a new way of standing as well. Your updated posture is more authentic because it rests on a fuller functional exploration, within the perspective of Creation's intent.

The processes for reconstructing Primal Moving are an extensive and fascinating theme which requires an entire book of its own. The examples included here are not full instructions for experiencing, but only a taste to give you an idea of the possibilities hidden in this trend of work.

Recovering the link between the knees and the back through primal swimming

In this process you are guided to gradually experience the dynamics of primal swimming, and to mobilise your knees in the way that they were designed to move in the original function. While lying comfortably on your back, you reconstruct the pattern of movement which was at the time performed while lying on the stomach, 'way back when' in the ocean. You move your knees to the sides, bent, in a frog-like shape. You return to using them as you used them when you were a baby, before you walked upright and began to bend them only forward.

The difference is that in the horizontal position, the knee being bent to the side is not at the same time also required to lift the weight of the thigh, as happens when standing. This can be a meaningful relief, as anyone who has an injured knee would most certainly testify.

In the process you first draw only one leg to the side, a number of times, and you reveal how the knee which moves to the side elicits a certain rotation of your pelvis and spine. You encourage this interaction and repeat it until it becomes easily and pleasantly coordinated.

You find within yourself the softness which allows you to create an atmosphere as though this movement were done in water, as though you were smoothly paddling through it, without getting tired, in a motion which refines itself through its repeated cycles.

When you continue and move the knees to the side, one after the other, you sense how your pelvis swings softly from side to side, in coordination with the knee and the head. All the parts of your body are integrated in participation in the rhythmic flow.

When you move the two knees simultaneously, on both sides, your back has a cradle in a different dimension, from front to back, and you feel how your pelvis becomes more and more skilled in discovering its options, more intelligent.

When you restore to your knees their functioning in the context of the whole

A Straight Back or a Wise Back?

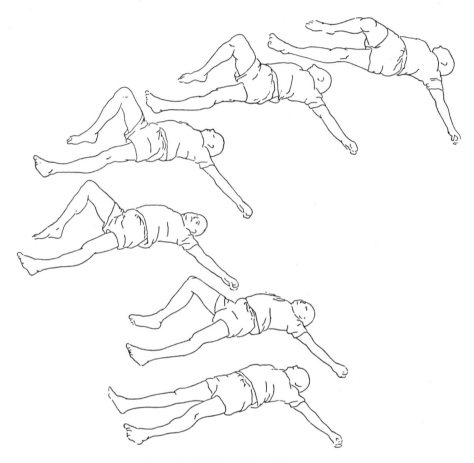

The Knee as a Handle to Activate the Pelvis and the Spine
The rotational motion of the pelvis leads to the elongation of the spine in each and every one of its articulations, while being done moderately and safely.

body, in accordance with the original intention of Nature, you bring them relief from the tensions produced by rigid frontal walking on concrete floors. You realise how your back also benefits from this original relationship served by your knees.

By descending to the ancient hierarchies of development you always find comfort and correction. What sifts the superfluous from the fundamental activities of existence and makes them into efficient activities, in evolution as in the reconstructed process, is the orientation to seek out that which is comfortable, the talent for coordinating the participation of each part in the appropriate measure and in the right time, without waste — a kind of functional gravitation.

This is the same willingness to mobilise yourself through sensitive teamwork which later vertically aligns your body in an upright stance, making each of your parts responsible for and connected to that thriving posture.

The effective trajectory for extending an arm: sensitivity instead of a map

Even a simple movement like extending an arm can be the theme of an entire research study in the awareness laboratory seeking efficiency.

How to Raise an Arm in the Least Resistant Pathway
You facilitate the beginning by first bringing the hand to the mouth, which is basic to the function of eating and therefore simple, and then you allow the rotation of the arm to facilitate its extending.

When lying down, or later in standing, you raise your arm like a baby who extends his hand to grab an object. The process guides you to experiment with a number of possibilities. You are attentive to subtle details and discover the path of least resistance.

You realise that the trajectory which brings you a continuous uniform movement with a low level of tension forms for you shapes which flow through space in curving lines winding around themselves. No-one can give you in advance the map of this pathway; you can only discover it yourself by your sensitivity to varying shades of ease.

You may discover that the most comfortable way to coordinate your scapula, shoulder, arm, wrist and hand into an integrated function is to first direct the hand toward the mouth. This primal existential motivation sets you into a moving pathway which your body readily accepts.

From the mouth you continue to lift your arm with a certain rotation and reach a full extension of the arm above the head. The whole time the sensation of your own weight guides your elbow to hang loosely and to seek the lowest point below. If you allow yourself to touch your body you can pass through part of the way with your hand restfully brushing your chest, neck and head. Even a painful shoulder which made it impossible for you to comb your hair is liable to consent to move more than before.

This is the orientation to navigate to the practical and the easy which later stands you up on your feet with greater efficiency and simplicity.

Transition from prone to supine: integrating all dimensions

When parents leave their baby lying on his stomach and later find him lying on his back, it is not only cause for a celebration but also a confirmation that the motor development is on the right course. The function of turning from prone to supine and its reverse integrates the use of all three dimensions with precise balance between weight, intention, direction and the inter-relationship between all parts of the body, with a special challenge to the rib-cage.

If you are not suffering from a serious problem you are surely capable of turning from back to stomach. But are you capable of doing it in a continuously smooth, flowing motion so that no vertebrae or rib fails to articulate at the right time, in accordance with your eyes, your breathing and your interaction with gravity?

After you explore the transition from supine to prone in many different fashions, you feel you have touched a potent clue for moving that can improve any of your functions and postures.

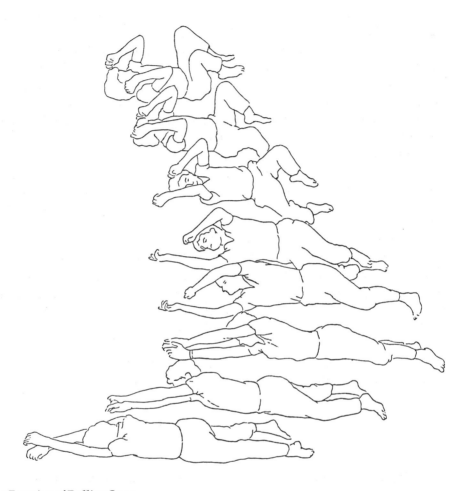

The Function of Rolling Over
Rolling from the back to the stomach is a complex skill that requires the sensitive cooperation of each and every part of the body within, precision of investing power, and configuration in space and timing while coping with gravity. Learning to roll over in harmony, you enhance your movement intelligence for every other function in life.

Cyclic motions: sifting of investment and precision of timing

There are movements in infancy which repeat themselves again and again in cyclic rhythm. Such are the swinging from side to side, and oscillating back and forth which babies do countless times. The repetitive rhythmic cycle refines the coordination of the movement.

In the reconstructed process in Awareness Through Movement, you decipher the details of this cycle one by one. For example, you lie on your back rolled up like a

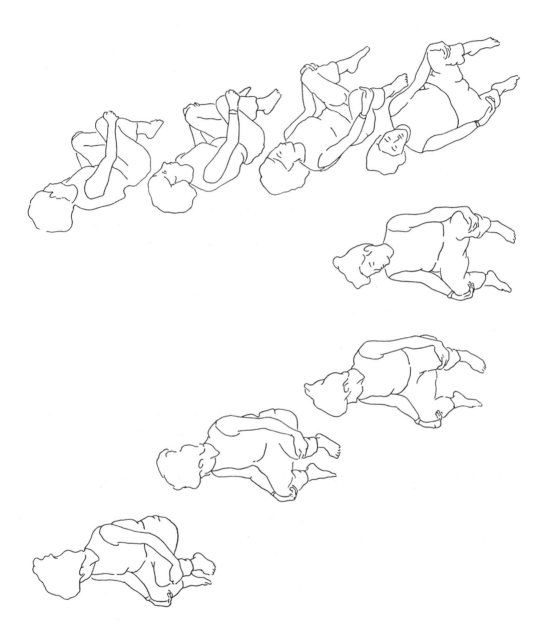

Rolling from Side to Side

Listening to the dialogue between your back and the floor in the symmetrical rolling gives an opportunity to each section of the back, even though for an instant, to reach the reconciliating experience of making contact with the ground. You can gently lead a slow roll, steering it by the eyes or the periphery of fingers and toes. Or you can whip a quick and dynamic roll, generating it from the axis of your spine and pelvis. The more you enrich your movement vocabulary with alternatives the more stable and free your standing will be.

ball, with your knees folded up to the chest, and begin to roll to the side. You discern in which member you should invest intention to activate the movement, and in which member to allow the response to happen passively, so that your back will stamp itself fully onto the floor without deletions or pitfalls. From the rolling you learn to sift parasitic tension from your body.

Or you explore the rolling backward and forward when it is magnified through slow motion. You learn to prepare your back so that it simulates itself into a wheel which can allow the movement to flow in a smooth stream. You observe how to use your legs, when is the right moment to detach them from the ground, when to take the momentum. You try different ways of correlating your head and feel how each of these ways influences the continuity of movement.

Finally, to enter into the rocking motion, first holding only one knee and only later, both, you increase the range of the swinging motions until the rolling forward brings you to a sitting position and the rolling backward returns you to lying with your legs over the head.

The actual momentum, which does not allow you slowness or reversibility, teaches you the resourcefulness of agility. You guide the flow of the function from one part of the body to the next without the pace of the rolling being disturbed. You learn to feel when it is the right moment to invest strength, in the right place, and when it is the time to let go of it.

All these are lessons in economical organisation in the dynamic context of a given frequency. When you develop the sophistication and sensitivity of appropriate timing in a course of rapid movements, then how much more easily can your nervous system find the appropriate tuning for standing, when it has all the time it needs.

Anchoring the head: how turning upside down contributes to posture

There is a special stage in the development of a baby in which one finds him or her rolling on the head from a kneeling position, time after time, in different ways and for long periods of time. When you reconstruct this in the lesson your head is fixed on the ground and you feel how your neck needs to readjust itself in a totally new orientation. After such an adjustment the neck will align itself by standing in a freer way than the usual.

In the course of the process you may take a rest in this position of kneeling with your head supported on the ground. After rolling you may find the softness to accept this gathered-in position. Babies indeed love to sleep like that. The folded kneeling induces a feeling of intimacy with yourself. You are protected from the world and remote from it. You are in a state of non-verbal serenity, neutralised from your thoughts and excitements. It is inconceivable to get angry in this state. When you are ready to get up again and stand on your feet after this meditation, you

A Straight Back or a Wise Back?

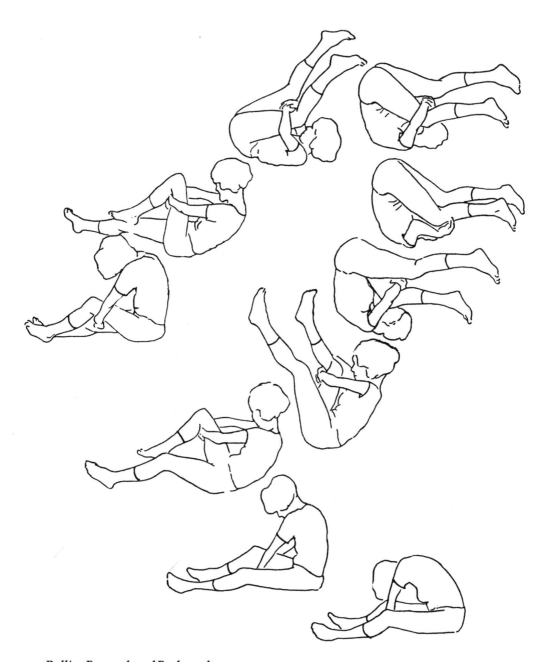

Rolling Forwards and Backwards
There is a distinction between the reversible preparatory stage of bending the knees to shape the back as a ball and the non-reversible stage of swinging the legs over the head. To monitor each vertebra with uniform quality within a given frequency is a high functional resourcefulness of organising fluency.

indeed feel that you are turning over a new leaf.

The sensation of anchoring the head in the ground is a rare experience for an adult. Years can go by without giving the head the opportunity to encounter pressure against a solid ground and to recall the joy of primal butting. A neck which has become tired of always having to find for the head a place in space relative to the body is refreshed by reversing the relationship, and can participate in standing in a different way afterwards.

Reconstruction of crawling: a renewed choice in the fundamental traditions of the organism

Perhaps the most extensive lesson for stable standing is the reconstruction of the crawling stage. Successful and coordinated locomotion by crawling challenges all of your movement properties. In the process of exploring different types of crawling you focus each time on a different aspect. This could be an exploration of how to anchor the foot in the ground in a way which enables you to spring forward effectively. You use the foot as a lever to mobilise the body. This places a special demand on the hip joint. The angle which is formed between the thigh and the pelvis is one that does not occur in ordinary walking.

All the other parts of the body also have to organise themselves in a certain way so that the thrust of the foot can be transmitted through each one of them up to the head. You discover in which area the flow is blocked, and you become aware of your less functional joints, which you can then give more opportunities for exploring their possibilities.

You discover how different your sides are from each other. When you focus your attention on the performance of each side separately and track it for a while, you may discern that generating the motion from one leg comes easily and smoothly, while from the other leg it seems strange, as though the link between the leg and the head is blurred and lost along the way.

There are differences which are difficult to distinguish in the rhythmical alternating crawling; its dynamic works to compensate for what is lacking on the retarded side by over-involvement of the competent side. The systematic process clarifies these fine distinctions for you in extreme magnification. The mere awareness diminishes the gap between the sides and prevents you from accumulating distortions which are full of tension and liable to become problematic.

You learn to activate within you an innate biological wisdom — the ability to create the required changes from within in order to produce a symmetrical movement in space, despite a non-symmetrical structure. You learn to create a rhythm of symmetry.

This work directly affects the correction of deviations in the posture. For example, if one foot is accustomed to bearing down on its entire sole, then in the process of crawling, which directs it again and again to produce the primal spring forward, you realise that it can be utilised differently and it later carries you in a different way when you stand. The chain of compensations in all the parts of your body, which in the past had been required for the previous way of using the foot, now loses its basis. The reconditioning is so total that you might even feel it as a confusion.

You have an additional experience of reconditioning in the shoulder girdle, which in crawling on all fours serves as a kind of upper pelvis. In crawling, your shoulders and shoulder-blades are enlivened to take on the original role of front legs. You listen to the dialogue between the stepping hand and the ground. You learn to distinguish the difference made by landing with a bent or rigid elbow. You listen to the dialogue between each of your shoulder-blades and your spine, as it creates a compression which does not take place in the upright position when the arms hang freely.

Sometimes, the most complicated thing in reconstructing patterns of crawling is the ability to concentrate when planning the movement. Every activation which is organised in a non-habitual way, or which tries to reconstruct the habitual pattern but more slowly and with awareness, is a significant intervention in the fundamental traditions of the organism. Extending the right hand and the left foot when the head turns left or right are simple and easy movements when you do them absent-mindedly. But when you try to produce them under conscious command you are liable to feel perplexed and confused.

This is an opportunity for you to check your attitude to learning. Instead of being like a pupil who hurries to correct himself in a panic even before he clearly understands what is expected of him, you can take permission to proceed at your own pace and to repeat each coordination as many times as you need in order to reach clarity and mastery. You find then not only the pattern, but also the climate in which the process of self-perfecting can take place .

Patience brings you to the clarity and simplicity of a well-coordinated, flowing performance — until you no longer need the conscious performance itself. When you feel as though the movement flows on its own you once again entrust it, enriched and improved, into the realm of absentmindedness.

You receive approval from Nature itself. With the transition from conscious movement to spontaneous movement, your whole state of mind alters. Without exception in a session of crawling, at a certain moment in the process, people begin to laugh a healthy and contagious laugh — an echo of the joy of the child within — which liberates a carefree mischievousness. This is such a rare revelation for adults.

Standing on the feet after crawling brings an experience of relief. Every part of you is joyous from the permission not to do anything. Your standing is clean — it is your ideal standing for today. You sense readily that all the crawling manoeuvres that you struggled with on the ground were exactly what you needed, so that afterwards you could feel so good in standing.

Mindful Spontaneity

In essence, it may be that life did not at the time give you enough supportive conditions to explore, to experiment and practice in order to reach the best choices for your posture. It is never too late to improve, to a smaller or greater extent. You can always go down to the floor and give yourself the systematic opportunity to cope, to reach new conclusions, to refresh the mechanism which knows how to invent solutions and to fill in that which is missing. You have a mechanism which is always capable of learning, unlearning and learning anew. This engagement with learning is the most fascinating entertainment there is for the human soul.

6

Resourcefulness in Times of Trouble

In this chapter you will find an abundance of useful processes through which you will learn how to help Nature help you. As with your collection of music records, you can feel what is desirable for you today and repeat what is meaningful to you as long as you are learning from it. Gradually, in your own pace, you may progress to experience the full repertoire.

The lumbar vertebrae — between the hammer and the anvil

Bending the knees plays a key role in the safety of the back. Straight knees are the product of the flat surfaces of the civilised world. Imagine that you had to walk along a path full of pitfalls, or cross a stretch of land that is rocky and uneven. During which portion of your walk in these conditions would your knees be able to remain straight?

Springiness in the knees induces springiness in all the other joints. When the knees vary their level of height, each vertebra along the spine has the chance of a game of expansion and compression. When the knees are constantly fixed at the same level, it's much more difficult for the back to continue the animated game of springiness. In other words: your back is agile and alive to the degree that your knees are agile and alive.

When your knees straighten into a fully locked position, the pelvis is being pushed upward and it tightens itself to the spine. In this way, pressure is created on the lumbar vertebrae from the bottom upwards. This is in addition to the pressure applied by the upper torso's weight, which also accumulates in the lumbar area of the back, and compresses it constantly, from the top to the bottom. Thus, your lower back is caught in a trap of pressures between the hammer and the anvil, and has no outlet for the redeeming expansion.

You have no ability to change the body weight that compresses the waistline from above. You have more options in modifying the angle at which the pelvis joins the back, by decreasing the curve between them, so that it makes a more fluid alignment, flowing with a continuity that allows the weight of the upper torso to be transmitted unhindered from the spine to the pelvis, and from there to the legs, and thence to the ground. The critical angle at the conjunction of the lower back and the pelvis, which may become like a dam blocking the flow, can be successfully changed when you stop holding the pelvis in an elevated position by the force of your straightened knees.

Mindful Spontaneity

Only when you bend your knees and lower them is an outlet cleared for the pelvis to sink into the depth, in a more fluid continuity with the back, with less protrusion to the rear. The pelvis is then released from the back's hold and behaves like a pendulum, suspended passively by its own weight.

The pelvis gliding downwards releases the lumbar vertebrae from their pressure and frees the painful blockage. The weight of the body can then transmit easily through the lower back and be supported by the ground, as should happen in a healthy body.

Feel with your hand the dependency of your back on your knees

You can find out for yourself, through a direct experience of the touch of your hand, to what extent the bending of the knees determines the fate of the lower back.

Hand Resting on Lower Back
By means of the hand resting on your lower back, you detect the response of your back to the behaviour of your knees. You learn from the sensation in the hand how your chance to be comfortable in your back is conditioned on your willingness to release the rigidity in the knees and bending them like springs. You train to initiate the ever so slight protruding of the lower back out, at the same lightness and clarity of deepening its curve in, reviving the primal wave of movement that propels your walking step by step.

Take a moment to first scan the contour of your torso. A mirror will help. See to what extent this outline is drawn in a continuous flow. Pay special attention to those curves that break the continuity. Observe and sense the nature of the juncture between the skull and the neck, between the neck and the back, and between the back and pelvis.

Stand the way you're always used to standing, and place the back of your hand against your back along the beltline. Use the hand to learn about the make-up of your posture. With the back of your hand, sense the area of your lower back, and get an impression of the angle that the pelvis forms in relation to the spine. Feel the texture of the tissues in the waistline, in the sacrum, in the lower back, and on either side of the spine.

Begin loosening the knees and let them bend ever so slightly. Feel what's happening in the lower back. See if you can learn, through your own touch, how your back responds to the change in the knees.

Repeat this process several times. See if you are prepared, each time the knees are bent, to interpret the experience as an opportunity for the pelvis to suspend itself and sink down.

Now straighten your knees fully, and lock them in a backward sway. Notice what this does to the back, to the pelvis. Let the touch of your hand tell you how each straightening of the knees calls on your back to stiffen, and causes the lumbar to curve in and the tail to stick out.

Continue straightening and bending the knees back and forth, and clarify for yourself the interdependence between your knees and your back. Feel how the tension in the lower back unwinds each time the knees bend down, and the back becomes strained once more, each time the knees straighten out and become locked.

If you're in the habit of standing with absolutely straight knees, you are placing an exhausting assignment on your back which may expose it to vulnerability. This is perhaps the most important piece of information for you when your purpose is to heal your back. If you forget all the rest and just remember that straight and locked knees are your back's worst enemy, then you will gain remarkable relief for both your back and your energy.

At the beginning, standing with knees that are slightly bent may feel strange to you and not at all steady. You may imagine that your knees are failing and that you're about to collapse. Perhaps you aren't ready to accept the relief for your back at the price of renouncing your self-image.

Nevertheless, allow yourself to observe that even like this the ground faithfully supports you, and sense the advantages which this way of standing provides for you. Take a moment to reconsider whether the habitual effort in locking the knees is actually necessary.

Let your ankles reconcile your back

This way of standing that is comfortable for the back, with the knees neither straight nor bent, can also be attained with ease and acceptance, when you entrust to your ankles the initiative of manoeuvring of the knees.

To understand this, stand up on your feet. Imagine that you're standing on a varying surface, like the deck of a ship on the ocean, ready for every shock and shift, and sense how your ankles accommodate the image.

Feel the change of tone in the joints of the foot; notice not only the change in the effort involved, but also the change of attitude. It is not so much an actual bending movement of the ankle folding in, as it is a readiness there to respond with agility to unexpected changes, which the environment may provide, and to flex accordingly.

Then remind yourself that you're standing on solid ground, and notice how your ankles respond to the quality of the floor and organise themselves accordingly, becoming more stiff.

Alternate between one state and the other several times, and remain in each arrangement for a while in order to absorb its meaning.

Notice that each time the ankles respond to the varying surface and utilise their talent to open up in readiness to maintain equilibrium, the knees are also loosened up and become slightly bent. With the flexing of the ankles, the knees find the desired position by themselves, where there is no exaggeration either to straighten or to bend. In addition, this way of unlocking the knees does not feel artificially imposed.

When you don't think in terms of exercises, but rather in terms of coming to serve the function of adjusting to the pitfalls of reality, your organism is ready to accept the bending of the knees.

Place the back of your hand on the small of your back and let your hand tell you to what extent your back is conditioned by your ankles. Feel how, as soon

as the ankles soften, the pelvis stops working at carrying its own weight and instead, becomes a passive mass which is fully suspended. Observe how the sinking pelvis releases the lower back from its trap of compression. Sense the delicate and subtle flow that is streaming along the lumbar region, spacing out its vertebrae, as the pelvis drags them after itself into the depth, by the force of gravity alone.

Take note that each time your ankles stiffen to the point of inflexibility the knees can't bend either, and everything that is dependent on them becomes stuck too; the pelvis can't sink, the lumbar area has no outlet for its compression, and you feel your back tensing up. If your ankles remain obstinately stiff, your back has very little chance of being comfortable.

Repeat the movement of flexing and fixing the ankles gently, time after time. Find out how much bending in the ankles is truly needed in order to unravel the pelvis from the back. Search for the minimal movement that makes the big difference. Continue until you can see clearly that your back actually begins in your ankles.

Remove your hand from your back, and have a look at your way of standing. Identify the sensation you have in your leg muscles, which perhaps are now working more than usual. And don't ignore the sensation in the lower back as well, which by now has perhaps succeeded in relinquishing its chronic over-involvement.

Begin walking about and check the possibility of stepping on the soles of your feet without stiffly fixating the ankles or knees. Land on the sole of your foot with your ankle continuing its spring-like surrender, and your knees ready to accept the idea of bending. Imagine that you're walking across a bridge made of ropes that is unstable and unpredictable, and see if you are capable of developing a live dialogue between yourself and the ever-varying earth.

While in this mode of walking, strange as it may feel, direct your attention to the way your back is responding. Can you feel that its response to the springy walk has been enriched with more dimensions, more vitality, more health?

Imagine how, with your knees in this unlocked state, your legs are capable of ascending, climbing and groping, lingering over, or gliding unimpeded between obstacles. In conditions inherent in a natural environment, the knees

are, most of the time, in transition between varying degrees of flexion. The straightening of the knees to the extreme of locking is reserved only for brief and specific instances.

To gain further clarification, you may explore the reverse — walking so that with each step the knee at the rear is thrust backward into a full lock, and the heel is rigidly pressed against the floor. Can you imagine, then, how you could carry out the previous tasks with legs that function like wooden crutches? Acknowledge the penalty your back is obliged to pay, when flat cement floors discourage your legs from functioning like springs.

Altering a deeply rooted habit, such as your characteristic manner of standing or walking, is an undertaking that requires awareness and repeated practice. You may need a prolonged period of time to become familiar with the non-habitual mode of organisation, until you come to prefer the arrangement of unlocked knees and ankles as a more efficient stance for daily use in life.

When you have mastered a soft, gliding walk, with your legs springy and your back relaxed, you'll discover the intrinsic power of the bamboo that repeatedly straightens out after each bending, without ever submitting to it.

It probably won't be as simple to also convince your personality to foster the message inherent in this way of walking, and to imagine yourself passing smoothly through life's challenges, with higher adjustability and less conflict.

In essence, if your back hurts, the easier way to approach it is through your ankles. Leave the irritated area alone and first check out its carefree, remote partner. When the ankles assume their full flexibility, the intense rigidity of the back will also be more ready to melt. It is the ankles that can reconcile the back, simply by remembering their talent for springiness, and their willingness to surrender and bend.

How the legs fail the back

The way in which you straighten up from a bending position has special significance for the safety of your back. To straighten up from a bending position without your knees doing their share of the work may be critical to your back, especially if you bend down to pick up something from the floor and increase the burden on your back with the weight of the object you are trying to pick up.

How do the legs fail the back?

If you stand with your knees straight, they lose their manoeuvrability and their ability to exert a sensitive pressure towards the earth, and they cannot in turn transmit the upward counter-thrust, so that it will pass, unreduced, through the rest of the body.

If the functional memory has lost the option of bending the knees to different degrees while in a standing position, then the elastic forces from the ground that raise one upward cannot be utilised, and the back is obliged to raise itself by the bounce of its own muscles. The effort of the body's muscles plus the weight of the object that is being picked up, from a position that is originally stretched by the forward bending, is liable to activate such an extensive stretch, that the entire organism becomes defensive. With the same force that causes the back muscles to stretch, they will react with the need to contract and shut off. For a long period of time, they will recoil from stretching again, even to the slightest degree, and will remain contracted.

You can spare yourself all this when you remember to keep in mind that your ankles and knees can function as submissive springs.

Knee-back interaction

There are cultures in which enormous numbers of people walk through their daily life without ever completely straightening their knees. If you recall the traditional walk of the Japanese woman who flows forward with tiny steps, you'll acknowledge that this, too, is a human option. The sole of her foot resembles a wheel that prints its lower half a short distance till the second foot steps forward, continuing the same function. In this form of walking there is a consistency of rhythm and a consistency of outline. The head remains, nearly all the time, at the same level in relation to the ground, the differences in height that are inherent in the swinging motions of walking being absorbed by the pliant joints of the spine, the knees, the hip-joints and the ankles.

After a session in Awareness Through Movement, people spontaneously organise their walk with slightly bent knees. The single objective of this mode of walking is to bring the trunk slightly forward, which in turn triggers the sole of the foot to step forward, like a supporting peg that restrains the fall. You can glide more smoothly and quickly with this mode of walking than with a common walk that is hindered by each transfer from foot to foot. As a walking style it may perhaps look sloppy, with the feet seeming to come forward at the last minute, treading with loose knees and springy ankles. However, the advantage of this form of walking is that the back can completely relax in it. The pelvis is suspended by its own weight in a continuation of the spine, with no demands put on the junction between them.

People who suffer from back pains have an advantage in testing the various methods. With their very low threshold of sensitivity, they can receive faithful and accurate feedback on the efficacy of every method or part of it. The feedback given by people in pain who tried walking with loose knees was that in this manner the back indeed ceased to be a focus of trouble. It is interesting that when they returned to their habitual manner of walking, the benefit previously gained continued for a while. The message is deep and encouraging. Finding a way of moving which bypasses the damage works as a corrective within other contexts too. This is because human beings are learners. We just need the chance to experience another manner of organisation, which makes sense to us, and our brain will stop being compelled by the detrimental manner of operation. The slight change which we have learned to apply to our knees and ankles puts us into the category of having a choice, and this is readily reflected in all our activities.

A simple way to remind your knees of their springiness

Stand in a step position, right foot forward, left foot backwards. Put your left hand on a table or the back of a chair for support.

Draw your legs close to each other so that the left knee digs into the pit behind the right knee.

Invite your left knee to bend so that it will also gently push the right knee to bend. The rear knee is the active one, and the one in front is totally passive.

After a few times change the roles.

Eventually stand and feel the readiness in your knees to float now in the intermediate state of springiness.

For further learning, place one hand behind your lower back. While one knee bends the other, gradually and gently deepen the hollow of your lower back.

Later on do the reverse as well, so that with each bending of the knees you round out your waist and protrude it ever so slightly backwards. It is important to leave the stomach soft and continue to breathe lightly so that the new integration will have a chance to register as natural.

Roller under the foot: a lesson in springiness

A simple way to remind your ankle of its full spectrum of mobility is to place the sole of your foot on top of a cardboard or wooden roller about 8–10 cm in diameter, and roll it back and forth along the length of the sole, and then across its width. You can practice this any time you are sitting, reading or watching television.

At first, put one foot on top of the roller and roll it forward and backward for a while. You do not need to roll all the way from the heel to the toe each time. You may stay at any specific area of the sole, and cultivate its surrender to the shape of the roller in small motions.

Then stand up, and assess the effect. Sense whether one foot spreads out differently from the other.

Now roll the other foot, and observe to what degree this foot tends to deviate from the front, in what way it is different from the other.

You may place both feet parallel on the roller and activate both ankles simultaneously. You may find it easier to place one foot slight forward and the other slightly backward.

Stand up and walk around. See if you notice any difference in your walk; feel whether or not your step has become a little more springy, more refreshed and airy.

Selective inhibition by a touch of the hand

Selective inhibition by a touch of the hand, or as it can be simply called, 'pinching a muscle', is the most immediate and effective strategem you can do by yourself, for yourself, when you are standing in the garden and your back is killing you, or when you are walking around the museum and your back won't let you enjoy it, or when you are sitting at work and can't find your place on the chair, or when you are in bed and you know there are certain movements you have to be careful about, and so on.

Through selective inhibition by the touch of the hand you achieve a reduction of pain through a manoeuvre of neutralising the problematic muscle, by pinching it while the rest of the body goes on with its functioning. This intentional pinching enables you to carry out, without pain, the very activity that usually causes you pain when done without the intervention of pinching.

Isolating a single factor and preventing it from taking an active part in the production of the general movement is one of the principles of the Feldenkrais Method for Functional Integration. This is applied throughout individual lessons by touch as well as in guided processes for groups. I have attempted, in the following instructions, to merge touch with self-mobilisation, so that you can give the lesson-treatment to yourself.

A change of proportions in the division of labour

It isn't easy, simply by a conscious effort, to alter the proportions of the division of labour among the various muscles that are involved in an activity. For example, when a muscle in the neck has become chronically over-tense, and every attempt to turn the head to the side triggers pain, it will be very difficult for you to discover another way of carrying out the turning movement of your head on your own, without making use of the same tensed muscle, and without using it in the same way that repeatedly elicits the injury.

Many times, when people feel a need to loosen up the neck and relieve it of its burden, they tend to move their head in a circular motion, round and around, and they probably also do it with impulsive haste and force, in spite of the grinding sounds of outcry. The same painful muscle is then taking full part in the activity while it is subjected to even more demanding requirements than is usual. Indeed, very rarely does the imposed circular motion of the neck bring the desired relief. People repeat this movement time and again, out of habit, without considering its poor results.

It is a tenable idea that shaking the body through a movement can bring relief. However, the approach that demands the neck to complete the circle while struggling against resistance does not explore any significant change in the mode of operation, nor does it bring about any proportional change between one part and the other. The mechanical circling of the head around itself does not invite the thoracic upper vertebrae into awakening and participating in the activity. The back remains stiff, just as it always is, and the entire effort of articulating falls again upon that same sore area at the curve of the neck. When force is used to perform a painful movement, it only intensifies the pattern of organisation which first caused the pain.

In the Feldenkrais Method, the pain-free path becomes clear through a conscious tracking that explores the non-habitual zone of moving. When a person himself, or with the help of his instructor, pinches the injured muscle and prevents it from participating in the movement that continues to take place throughout the rest of the organism, a chain reaction of role transfer is set off, and the organism, of its own accord, finds new ways of re-organising and bypassing the pain. The direction of this learning process goes from patterning the movement in space on to the brain.

Swimming and walking: changing the pattern or establishing it

Just swaying the whole organism around does not necessarily produce a specific change which brings about relief. As long as there is no intentional selective isolation of the painful muscle, it is free to participate in the movement, while being subjected to the program as dictated by the brain, which in this case sentences this muscle to difficulty.

Even swimming, a whole and natural function which brings humankind closer to its roots, gives little possibility of changing asymmetry in form, or differences of functional discrimination in which one side is accustomed to do most of the work while the other side is like a parasite. Even if the swimmer is very supple, and is capable of changing and shaping the body with a choice of options through conscious intention, still the nervous system will tend to return consistently to the same individual channels of functioning that are characteristic of the person swimming. Diligent and mechanical swimming, in which the number of lengths and the time taken are the objectives, will even reinforce the establishment of the same biased pattern of the division of labour, and will continually recreate the same individual asymmetrical structure.

Walking does not guarantee improvement either. Throughout life a person walks absentmindedly, and even though the mobilisation of all the limbs presents new opportunities to change and utilise oneself differently, a person remains attached to the characteristic form, faithful to the selectivity in which certain parts are activated and others avoided, even though this arrangement may not be best. Repeatedly leaning the weight on the same focal points in the foot — and this may differ from one foot to the other — one continues to turn each knee at its set angle and reaches with each knee its same degree of bending and straightening.

While breathing, the same region in the chest is mostly used. The head may be slightly tilted in a certain direction, and this preference is repeated with each step taken. Faithful to the same rhythm, the same emphases, the same frictions, the same synchronisation of the various parts, the spinal cord will repeatedly align the back in the same manner, preserving the same deviations, curves and levels of compression between vertebrae in various sections. The pelvis will outline each time the same configuration in space, with the same relationship to the legs and back. Even from a distance, friends can identify a person by the characteristic, individual style of walking.

The invisible partners of habit

It is the nature of habits that you consistently act according to a dominant inner agreement that engulfs you. It's as if the brain is attached to that multi-claused agreement that has been acquired through its own experience. How, then, is it possible to reach a more beneficial agreement that can serve life more successfully — one that can become a substitute for habit, and be continually endorsed as a method of operation?

This is the very entrapment of habit. Although habit spares the energy required to make decisions, and saves time, when life-threatening emergencies arise, that is precisely when the organism needs to be rescued, needs a resourcefulness that may be different from its habitual pattern. But the defensive system itself, needing immediate security, holds on in panic to the familiar and available, which has indeed appeared to save it before, and does not allow itself the risk of seeking out new ideas that come from another direction.

The support which the masterful instructor can give the student is to escort him or her through the threatening situation, and help create a more secure atmosphere in which openness to new discoveries may be feasible. Without this support, a suffering, stricken person confronting distress will only increase his or her defensiveness through familiar forms of reaction, and thus aggravate the trouble.

In order to uproot a habit that adversely affects a specific area, one must take into consideration that the roots of this habit are intertwined and interwoven through-out all the other parts of the body. For instance, if a person suffers at a specific verte-bra in the lower back, the entire organism must organise itself to protect against activation of the injured part. If the injury were to occupy a less central location, then it is most likely that the person would achieve the reduction of pain at the cost of relinquishing the function, whether for a short or long period of time. However, the lower back junction is involved in every action. Even during situations of rest, the lower back area maintains its tension. It will be considered an advanced achieve-ment in organic honesty when in the supine position the lower back is able to cease working and spreads out fully flat on the ground.

When walking with a painful back, besides the muscles that are contracted in an attempt to prevent any movement in the distressed area, the foot will also step on the ground with a certain self-consciousness and the ankle will block its own elas-ticity. The time span of leaning on one side will change, and shifting from one side to the other will become emphasised with additional effort. The knee will accumulate stiffness in trying to stop the exaggerated movement from reaching the back. The pelvis will cut off its movement in space and the chest will become immobilised as it holds the breath at the critical moment of anticipated pain. One shoulder or both will be tensely held on guard. The look in the eyes will become hardened. The head won't dare to move freely to the side which is bearing the weight for fear of aggra-vating the distressed area. There are endless adjustments through which the organ-ism will try to avoid pain. This is such an all-pervasive and complex weave that no single part of the body is untouched by the effect. Its message is that the fear of pain sets the tone for all other manifestations of life.

This all-encompassing distortion, that emerges from deep existential need, is reinforced with every step and becomes a mandatory pattern for dealing with the pain. This pattern may remain intact long after the original injury has passed. The problem for many people is how to get rid of these by-product effects which serve an injury that no longer exists.

Dealing with injury: dealing with the interaction between injury and peripheral functioning

Pinching the muscle directly addresses this interaction between the localised injury and the response of the rest of the organism. The pinch meets the need of the organ-ism to protect the injured spot, and its advantage is that it accomplishes this without the rest of the body undergoing any distortion. Pinching tissues so that they are brought close together presses the muscle to recoil inward upon itself. Actually, the hand is carrying out the act of contraction which the muscle itself tends to perform as the defence against pain demands.

When the nervous system gets the message that its task is already being done, it is ready to cease investing further effort in it. The muscle which previously anticipated the pain, and was ready to contract, need not and indeed cannot now respond as it used to. It finds itself neutralised, in a certain repose. The rest of the system experiences a forgotten taste: how it might function had there not been trouble at that specific point.

Since the movement of the rest of the body continues, other muscles are awakened to participate in the performance of the function. They probably don't retain the prejudices of unavoidable pain and the fear of frustrations. In this way the organism can arrange its movement from a more innocent state. It can realise how an action that usually causes pain is now able to occur safely. The neutralising pinch introduces the organism to an experience of altered differentiation, with precision and simplicity. Instead of having the irritated and over-stimulated muscle move relative to the static body and pull it to distortion, the vector is reversed. The muscle rests, and the entire body revolves freely around it. Instead of the threatened muscle needing to elongate in spite of resistance, the hand protects it and takes it out of the game.

The elongation, as needed for the movement, will be provided by the other muscles surrounding the focus of injury. All those members of the body that weren't injured but did limit their movement as local pain dictated, begin to shake out the rigid scaffolding of defensiveness, to give up the distortions, to function more fully and freely. As more and more parts function in a way that is relevant to reality, and are less subjected to localised trauma, a real transformation — which gives a chance for healing — begins to take place.

This is the moment in which people begin using a choice of alternatives that they didn't dare make use of before. The fact that Selective Inhibition takes place within the context of ongoing functioning creates the inner conviction that things can indeed be different. Thus, the pinch acts like a mentor who instils confidence in times of distress. Quietly, it directs the organism to navigate new paths which may lead not only to release from pain, but also to the rejuvenation of functioning in general.

Parable of the anxious boss

The stratagem of the pinch can be explained as a system for teaching the tired boss to let go of his anxiety, which undermines his abilities and the productivity of his employees.

If the boss is someone who believes he is irreplaceable and is always worried, always making an effort to do everything by himself, convinced that the task before him is very difficult and that he must sacrifice the pleasures of life for its sake, he becomes chronically pressured until he can no longer relax even when he isn't working. He ceases to initiate successful ideas, and all his workers feel pressured too, and can no longer work at top productivity as they did when they weren't pressured. Sending him on vacation will ease the pressure on him to a certain extent, but there is no guarantee that when he returns from vacation he will change his attitude towards work, and that he won't once again be swamped by the gathering tide of fruitless tension. Relaxation alone is not yet a transformation in the pattern of work organisation. How, then, can he be helped?

Imagine for a moment that this executive could be seated in the centre of his plant, after agreeing that he will not interfere. He can see for himself how the work is being carried out without him, how all the workers manage to deal with the tasks at hand and present ideas of their own. Perhaps, then, there is a chance that he will begin to see his destructive tension in its true light. Perhaps he will now be convinced to reduce his anxiety, his over-involvement, and curb the non-relevant neurotic part of him that doesn't know when to stop, that undermines the efficiency of the plant.

To pinch in your hand the muscle which causes the trouble, while the rest of the body remains in motion, is like seating the executive director, rendering him inactive, forbidden to interfere, and letting him see that the activity can be carried out without him, and in a smoother and more pleasant manner than before. The nervous system can discern that which brings it success and can absorb the advantageous suggestion. The proof: when you release the pinch in the back or in the neck, you may be surprised to feel how the pinched spot seems to have become relieved. The entire side of the body feels elongated, more vibrant and airy. The shoulder descends comfortably; the foot bears the weight differently. After a process of 15 minutes, people arrive at sensations in which one side is so profoundly different from the other that their self-perception seems schizophrenic. The side that didn't receive the touch reflects how they are holding themselves in life — with chronic defensiveness, an attitude of being on guard. The side that did receive the inhibiting pinch offers them a glimpse of the freedom and innocence they can attain.

Local neutralisation within functioning

You can pinch a muscle wherever your hand can reach. You can neutralise the tissues in the vulnerable area of the lower back, the pelvis, on either side of the coccyx, behind the neck and on its sides, between the shoulders, on the knees and at the jawjoint. Daily activities such as walking, climbing steps and sitting on a chair can be used as a context for renewed differentiation, in this way enhancing the organism's discovery of new ways of coordination that are more beneficial to living.

The combination of inhibiting-while-activating reaches extraordinary effectiveness when applied to the face. Pinching the corners of the mouth, the roots of the eyebrows or the crests of the cheeks, and challenging these muscles through their daily functions such as talking, smiling, eating or sucking, is capable of blurring the wrinkles of personal facial expressions and reversing them to a more innocent aspect.

Localised protection in conjunction with overall movement is the main principle behind the various support belts and splints. In the old days, when people only had access to simple household items, backaches were conveniently treated using a similar method. Long strips of wool were wrapped around the hips in several layers. With the back thus strapped, a person in pain would be put on a horse which trotted at a rhythmic pace that fell between a step and a gallop. Combining the immobilisation of specific vertebrae with the passive swaying motion of the rest of the body succeeded in releasing the back from its affliction.

Pinching a muscle: self-treatment of the lower back

Pinching a muscle in the back can be easily done in positions of standing and walking. Please stand up. Close your eyes and sense the manner in which you are standing.

Listen to your back and hear its complaints. What is the critical point at which it repeatedly fails; at which level does its strength give way?

Stand at ease with your knees softly bent and place the back of your hand on the more sensitive area of the lower back.

Offer your hand to your back as if it were a wall, and invite your back to lean towards it.

After a while, let your back return to its original position, and even exaggerate its arch.

Repeat this procedure several more times and then direct this sensitive part of your back to extend itself backwards in a movement that cancels its curve. Each time, stay with the lower back protruding like this towards the hand, with a sensation that it has a support there. Don't forget to breathe through the stomach, to flex the knees and to allow the shoulders to find their own comfortable level. Continue with these slow, fine and gentle movements — in a way that involves intention more than action. Visualise the vertebrae and see them striving to expand backwards.

This slight back-and-forth movement is the essence of correcting the back's function. During this process you will repeat this movement dozens of times. It is important that you find a way to do this moderately, without accumulating fatigue in your back, so that you will feel good the following day as well.

Remove your hand and take a moment to observe whether or not there is already a marked difference in your standing aptitude. Feel how this contact has affected the lower back. See if you are ready to promise yourself to grant your back this hand contact from time to time, despite society's veiled taboo against touching oneself.

Pinching while walking

With both your hands, begin feeling the tissues on the right side of your waistline behind you, or on the side that is hurting at the back, near the spine, between the ribs and the pelvis — some place that is meaningful to you. Gather the flesh there in a pinch between your fingers. It can be held between each thumb and index finger with the fingers of both hands facing each other. The thumbs can be above, on the rib side, and the fingers below, on the pelvis side. Keep the muscle pinched steadily.

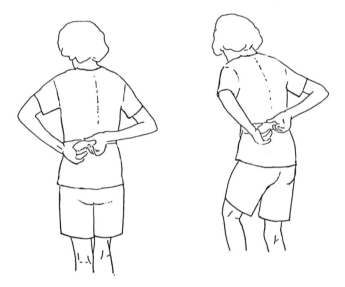

Selective Inhibition
You can pinch the hurting muscle to inhibit its operation while the rest of the body continues functioning in stepping from one foot to the other. This is a way to register in the brain a distribution of labour that does not challenge the pain.

Begin walking gently on the spot. Notice how the stepping interacts with the pinch, as if each step were trying to release the tissues from your fingers' hold. Continue this for a moment or two and then let go of everything.

Notice the sensation in your back. You may feel a sensation of airiness spreading out at the spot that has been released. See if you are willing to interpret this as the beginning of a thaw.

Again, pinch the flesh on the right side of the lower back, with both your hands coming from behind you to take hold. In this procedure you sacrifice the comfort of your arms for better mastery of the back.

If you find it difficult to reach the spot to pinch with your hands, you can clench your hands into fists, and place their snail-like facets next to the back wall of the pelvis. Either with your thumbs or with the knuckles of your index fingers, pull along the tissues from below, going upwards, and hold them slightly raised. Support them in an area just a bit lower than the focus of sensitivity.

By gathering and moving them closer to the sensitive area, you neutralise the tension and give it a sense of relief. This support provides the sensitive area with increased muscle length and thus allows it to manoeuvre its movements through tissues that are not as tense or as limited as they used to be.

Encourage your Tendency of Shortening the Back
A slight dragging of the tissues from down to upwards makes a difference in the tone of the lower back from defensive tension to trustful letting go.

A pinch while cancelling the curvature of the lower back

Stand with your hands pinching your lower back or supporting it with your fists. Allow your ankles to flex and your knees to slide forward. Remind your pelvis that it has permission to suspend by its own weight. Explore to what extent your shoulders can relinquish their tension.

Once again, invite the area that you are pinching or supporting to thrust itself backward, into your hands. Concentrate on protruding and rounding outward the area being held, as if it were trying to push the hands away from it. Do this slowly and gently, not all at once, and remembering to breathe. The movements can be so slight as to be barely perceptible. Sense their significance from within rather than making them observable on the outside. In your mind's eye, follow the movements and see how the vertebrae slowly shift towards cancellation of the lower back's concavity, and align themselves in a more directly continuous line between the back and the pelvis. Feel how instead of two separate parts colliding at a tension-ridden angle, a quiet unified continuation has been created.

Try the opposite option as well. Each time your back returns to its original position, continue increasing the concavity, as if the spine were trying to escape the touch of the hands and migrate inward towards the front of the body. Listen to that sensation while breathing.

Continue guiding the back gently from a slightly greater in-curve to a slightly greater out-curve. Each time you thrust the right side of the lower back backwards, rounding it out, lift one foot off the floor, alternating. Raise one heel and allow the knee to bend slightly, and in this position, round out the pinched back as if you intend to begin sitting down on a chair.

After a while do it with the other foot.

Eventually alternate, as if walking. Continue walking on the spot in this manner and softly sink into the beginning of the sitting-down movement each time one foot comes up. There is no need to exaggerate the mobilisation of the spine. Make the smallest movement that creates a change in the sensation of the tissues pinched between your fingers.

Very slowly, lighten the hold of your hands until you totally remove them; continue pushing the same area of your back backwards, even though it receives no directing touch from your hands. Feel whether or not some budding of a new orientation begins to emerge and the movement now knows its direction by itself. Ask yourself if it has become clearer to you how to activate certain vertebrae that previously were out of your control.

Use your hands to seduce your back into releasing its length

If the task of cancelling the concavity of the back through voluntary choice is still unclear in your consciousness, once again use your hands and pinch the tissues in that area. Allow yourself to use your hands for as long as you need their help. Make them a hothouse for the growth of your independent competence. The day will come when you will no longer need them for this task. After you provide your nervous system with the conditions in which it can learn this idea, you will know how to mobilise a specific vertebra into a more sensible alignment just by the hint of a thought. You will be capable of bringing relief to your tired back while walking, standing or sitting on a chair, through movements so intimately fine that they don't look like exercise at all.

Let everything go and take a full rest. You can determine your own rest rates. You don't have to perform all stages of the process at once.

It might be a good idea, every once in a while, to lie on your back and bring your knees up to your chest, placing your hands on your knees and sensing how the lower vertebrae can enhance their relaxation as they rest on the floor.

You can also draw your knees closer to your chest in gentle and rhythmic movements, and through these vibrations reach a clearer sense of how your lower back makes contact with the floor.

Stand up once more. Notice whether standing up means for you locking the knees automatically. See if you can stand up and leave the knees free of stiffness. Let your stance soften around the ankles, knees, hips, shoulders, eyes and jaws.

Once again, pinch that area on the right side, where the back joins the pelvis. Notice if the tissues respond more easily now to the touch of your fingers gathering them up.

Gently push out the pinched or supported area and protrude it backward in back-and-forth motions. While doing so, begin walking on the spot.

With each step, as one heel is raised in the air, round the lower back backward toward your hands. As before, with each such convexity, allow your pelvis to sink downward as if you are about to begin sitting down. Visualise your coccyx being pulled to the ground as if a weight were suspended from it.

Now apply this pattern while walking around the room. Very slowly, with each step forward, round out your back and sink towards the start of a sitting position. Feel how the walking movements challenge the pinch and refresh the entire inner formation of the lower back.

Let go of everything, and remain standing where you are. It may be that this time you have less need to lock your knees when standing. Be aware of how the area of your lower back has come alive in your consciousness. Does a sense of relief begin to emerge?

Walk around for a while, and notice if you witness greater freedom of movement in the area that was held. Give yourself credit for having learned to differentiate a single meaningful element, and to improve the behaviour of your back.

You can apply this lesson in full to the other side of the lower back, or to grabbing both sides of the spine at whatever level you feel a need to bring relief. It can be at the skirt of the ribs, behind the pelvic wall, near the coccyx edge, or at the very depth of the lower back concavity.

Releasing the lower back from its constant compression trains the organism to manoeuvre its structure towards well-being. It is a significant change in fostering your personal ecology, especially since it is done within the full context of a basic function, such as walking. It may take one or two hours at first to achieve this, and perhaps quite a number of patient repetitions. Later, you will be able to simulate this within a few minutes, during your daily activities, and add the pinch to any function you may want to improve.

Circles with a leg: movement within sustained weight

Another variation to achieve freedom in your lower back can be through circular movements of the leg. In a standing position, pinch the sore area, perhaps on the right side, with both your hands.

Shift your weight to the other foot, to the strong left side, allowing the left knee to be slightly bent.

Free the right foot and begin to outline with it circles on the floor's surface, without quite losing contact. Do some counter-clockwise circles as well.

Take a moment to rest, to stand upright and be with the sensations in your back.

Now again pinch the area on the painful side and shift your weight to the same side, onto the right foot. Bend your knee slightly and invite yourself to lean on it till you are ready to clear the left foot off the floor. When you can, begin to slowly move your left foot in circles, parallel to the floor, barely touching the floor, to the extent that your painful side is capable of independently bearing your body's weight.

Feel the changes taking place in the tissues that are pinched between your fingers, as a result of the circular motion of your leg. This is a training for your back in fulfilling the task of stabilising your posture in the context of varying motions of the pelvis and maintaining a springy stance.

Let go of everything and be attentive to your manner of walking after the process.

Pinching a muscle while lying in bed

When you are lying in bed and see no possible way of moving comfortably, you can still grant yourself relief through the pinching process.

Lie on your side, with the painful side — let's say the right one — leaning upon the bed.

Be certain which movement causes you pain. Search gently, and try to either round your back or increase its in-curve, moving your knee closer to yourself or pushing it further away, so that you can locate the point in which the pain is focused.

Extend your upper hand, the left hand, behind your back, and gather with your fingers the tissues around the painful area on the right side.

Slowly, repeat the same movement which previously induced pain. If it still awakens the pain, shift the pinching location about, until you find a spot at which the pinch neutralises the pain, while you continue the same movement. Find the patience to seek out this key point whether it is at the waist, the buttocks, the swell of the sacrum, or at the side of the coccyx. While holding the pinch, slowly and gently search out possible movements.

If pinching is hard on your fingers, you can use your fists to fasten the tissues of the pelvis towards the waistline, from below upwards. Pinch like this from only one direction, as you curve the back inward and outward alternately.

After several repetitions, remove your hand and try again to begin moving without the pinch and observe if any improvement is being made.

If you like, rest on your back for a moment or two before turning to lie on the other side.

Now lie on the side that is not bothering you, let's say the left side. In this position, the sensitive area has far more manoeuvrability, but is also more vulnerable. It helps to lean your upper knee, the right one, on a pillow to reduce the painful pull.

Again, pinch one area after another, while at the same time curving your back inward and outward with very fine movements, moving your upper knee forwards and backwards. In this way you can now systematically locate the focus of disturbance and neutralise it.

Each time you curve your back, allow your mouth to drop open. When the mouth is slightly open, it not only clears more space for movement of the back of the neck, but also helps you break your pattern of recoil from possible pain. Check that you haven't tightened your stomach, your buttocks or rectum.

Remain like this in comfort until you can breathe in this position, and feel your body's response to the cancellation of the hollow of your back.

When you feel you've had enough, let go of everything and rest. Remove your hand and notice the sensation as you once again begin the original movement, this time without the pinch. If indeed something has changed, and the movement becomes free, don't exaggerate it while doing this test.

Also when you return to your daily activities, do only the minimum that is required of you. The change is still a young and fragile suggestion. Any threat will bring a return of the previous pattern in its stead. Your goal is to find for yourself a balanced progress towards what is possible, without dramatic exaggerations, or setbacks.

Pinching a muscle while lying down became for many people the breakthrough from a frightened and helpless back to one with the self-confidence to return to activity.

Self-treatment of the neck

There is no-one who wouldn't be willing to receive a little more softness and comfort in the neck. The neck is the bottleneck of your functional honesty. Relatively gentle and fragile, at the junction between the two massive bodies of the torso and the skull, it has to compensate for the many movement omissions and drawbacks of all the other components which make up the body's alignment. The neck is conditioned by the functional behaviour of the rest of your body.

You can utilise this conditioning from the opposite direction and manoeuvre the torso through the neck. Although it may be difficult to alter the movements of the major mass of the body by mobilising the most delicate section of the spinal chain, still unless the neck changes it will be difficult for the other vertebrae, pelvis and limbs to convert their harmful habits into more useful ones.

What can be done is to remind the neck of how carefree it can be locally, and thus create space for the other parts of the body to re-arrange themselves in a more sensible way.

You can administer self-treatment to the neck in a sitting position. Sit on a chair; lean back in full comfort, and more or less straight. Devote some time to arranging cushions and supports so that you will be able to sit for quite a long time without getting tired.

If you prefer, you may sit on the floor. You can make it easier on your back by sitting on a pillow, which raises your seat while letting the knees slide diagonally down to the floor. Elevating the pelvis spares your lower back some of the elongation required in order that the pelvis reach the floor.

Take a moment to become fully acquainted with how your neck feels when it is not moving. Then begin turning your head to one side and then to the other, observing how it goes on each side. Refrain from trespassing into the domain of difficulty, and repeat time and again only that portion of movement which comes with total ease and without any threat. Take note of the boundaries of the comfort zone available to you on each side.

If you perceive a stop signal earlier on the right side, place your left palm on the right shoulder, at the juncture between the shoulder and the neck, with your left elbow bent in front of the chest.

Let your fingers gently palpate and explore the tension-loaded area for sev-

eral minutes. Softly, without any pressure, stay at each spot long enough to discover how you are built. Go over the shoulder crest, explore the shoulder-blade protrusion and feel the texture of the tissues between the shoulder-blade and the spine. Touch the spine, monitor the vertebrae of the neck, look for the edge of the skull, identifying all those strips that hold the head onto the shoulders.

Your fingers will tell you where the centres of tension are located. Take the patience to touch them softly, without confronting their rigidity, without trying to break them apart by force. If you come across a hard knot, give it a touch that does not come to criticise or rectify, but to feel — being ready to wait for a while until this feeling becomes clear.

Let go of all that. Allow your hand to slide along your chest so that it finally drops to rest in your lap. Allow a breath of relief, a time to reorganise yourself.

Listen inside and notice the sensation in your neck, on the side which has just received the exploring touch. Compare it to the sensation on the left side. Possibly you feel as if the right side is more aired, more full of life. Contemplate the chance to alter your self-perception by a few minutes of touch alone.

Once again hook your left hand beyond the right shoulder. Very gently, begin gathering the tissues and gradually grasp them between your fingers and the heel of your hand. Prolong your grip for a while. Hold the muscles with gentleness and determination, but without causing them any pain.

Check whether it is possible to give up unnecessary tension in one shoulder, then in the other, and allow them to sink downward into comfort.

Let the right arm suspend freely downwards, extended towards the floor with its elbow straight.

While you are steadily pinching the muscles, begin raising your right shoulder ever so slightly, and bring it closer towards the ear. Gradually, release it and let it sink down to its place. Repeat this movement of the shoulder time after time. The pinch hold is steady, and the shoulder moves within it, in minor movements.

Be attentive not to drop the shoulder suddenly. Escort the movement of the shoulder as it sinks downward. Follow it and see where it chooses to reach each time, through its own weight.

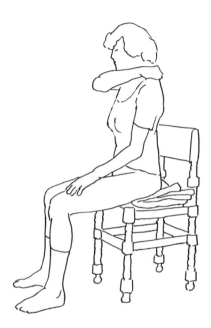

Neck Relief
Pinching the tension-loaded muscle excludes the possibility of activating it. When, in addition to the pinch, you execute a function like raising the shoulder to the head slightly and slowly, time after time, the nervous system becomes convinced that the specific muscle is not essential for the movement and it releases it of the tension. The contrast between the shoulders shows you on one side, how you could have been and on the other side how actually you are carrying yourself in life.

As you raise the shoulder, rotate the whole arm around its axis so that you turn the back of your hand towards your body. As the shoulder descends, allow it to unwind.

After repeating this for a while, gently try the opposite rotation: each time the right shoulder rises into the pinch, turn the palm out, and as the shoulder sinks down turn the palm in. Each time do a little less than before. You can arrive at a token movement, using only a small part of your capacity, within a slow motion that does not seem like an exercise.

Let the movement come to a stop. Gradually release the pinch of the muscle. Spread your fingers and let your hand glide into your lap, all along keeping contact with your body. In this way you use the brushing motion of your hand upon your body to compensate the fingers for their cramped condition.

As you rest, allow your breath to pass through the entire chest. With your eyes closed, be attuned to your right shoulder. Feel whether or not it has learned to respond more sensibly to the force of gravity, and is more ready now to remain on a lower level than the left. It is not a minor thing if, in a few minutes, one succeeds in convincing the shoulder to relinquish its habit of wasting unneeded power in holding itself against gravity.

Once again come back to pinch with your left hand the tissues on the right side where the neck and the shoulder interact with each other, where you feel the seat of the tension between them.

Each time you raise your shoulder in a certain rotation, bring your head slightly closer to the shoulder. The head and the shoulder need not touch each other, but merely salute one another. Let them alternate between meeting and separating in many different ways and directions.

Each time, turn another part of your face toward the shoulder — sometimes your nose, another time the ear — always in minor subtle movements absolutely free of tension. Invite the head and the shoulder to dance towards each other, around the pinching hand, in a slow, unpredictable, seaweed-like flow.

Eventually leave the shoulder raised and attach the rear of your ear to the hand holding the shoulder muscle. Hold the head and the shoulder in this position, joined together.

Begin moving your full torso through space, without disrupting the relationship between your head and shoulder, as if they were one solid unit. Gently swing the body in circular, pendulum-like motions, bending forward as well as arching backward, without any force and without letting the head move away from the shoulder.

Let everything go, and take a full rest. Close your eyes and wait until the image of your shoulders becomes clear in your mind's eye.

Observe the balance between the shoulders now. What is the direction of the right shoulder; what is its length? If you were to draw the outline of your shoulders, what sort of picture would you make? What is the sensation of this imbalance? Possibly you hear the pleas of the left shoulder, asking to be led to freedom too.

The transformation in the shoulder's alignment is not only the change of releasing the length of the neck on that side, but also a change in one's attitude towards life. Can you discern the difference in state of mind between one side and another?

Be attuned to the mood of the right side; what is its message? How does it differ from that of the left side? You may feel how your right side now knows that life is meant for enjoyment, for permission to be carefree and comfortable, while the left side seems to believe that life is hard, that one must always be on guard, and that there is no escape from tension.

This is a rare moment, in which you can view yourself split between two choices: one side reflects the way in which you carry yourself through the day-to-day coping with life, while simultaneously, the other side gives you a glimpse of what you could be.

Before you go on to apply the process to the other side, take a moment to check how your neck moves now.

Begin to gently move your head to the right and to the left. Has the range of mobility expanded since the beginning of the process? Does the warning signal appear after a more extensive run than before? Has the quality of the movement changed too; does it flow more smoothly now, more simply, in a way which is less imposed? Does the neck live in greater harmony with the shoulders, the spine, the eyes? Has it ceased being a separate problem-ridden section and become more integrated with the rest of yourself?

If you acknowledge that you have enhanced yourself in a desired direction, take a moment to program the ways in which you can apply what you have learned for future use. If you leave it up to chance, your logic may interpret the accomplishment of the neck's comfort as if there is no more need to take any further action in this matter. Remember that your neck found relief as a result of a process, and especially due to the awareness that you invested in it. You can rely on both the process and the awareness to lead you to new achievements each time.

Create your own model for carefree movement

You can derive your own model for recovery from any one of your many movements, and not only from the specific suggestions recommended here. In order to set a model atmosphere that your nervous system will be able to imitate, choose a movement that hurts you, that from experience you know is difficult. It can be drawing the knee to the stomach or twisting the back towards the pelvis, turning from your back to your side when lying down, or any other function.

Repeat that movement gently, several times, so that you can closely follow its route, its components. You may be surprised at times that it isn't so easy for you to spark the pain by wilful intention. That's good news for you, though.

When you have found such a movement that elicits pain, let go of it. Recall all those times you tried to overcome the pain, to pass through it forcefully, to suppress it by using more power. Make contact with the feeling you had when you were pretending to keep it under control, while inside you were crying out.

Tell yourself the truth: did using force ever help you heal the movement? See if you are willing to try something different, if you are willing to invest your good intentions in quality instead of force. The fact that there is a certain movement which gives you a feedback of pain provides you with an accurate landmark for orientation. The pain can be your guide out of the maze.

Take a moment to review the procedure of the motion in your imagination, and then gently begin to actually do in space that part which does not trigger pain. Do less and less, even if you have to reduce the movement to 20 per cent or do only its mere beginning. Just as in sensitive cooking you adjust the rate of heat with care for the success of the dish, so in this movement, seek that level of involvement which maintains your well-being.

Move very slowly — not with a forced, impatient slowness, but with a slowness characterised by intervals filled with listening, a slowness that gives your organism time to recognise where it can ease up and respond with reconciliation. Your organism will let you know when you reach a place of consolation, by a deep breath of relief that emerges of its own accord. Repeat the movement at that level several times, pausing once in a while for a breath of integration, and tell yourself that it wasn't actually this specific function which caused you the pain, but its full volume. Are you willing to check once again the relevance of your need to always perform at the maximum?

The movements that bring healing are delicate and fine, and they are sometimes not even perceived from the outside. They need many repetitions to regulate the nervous system according to their message, just as loading a magnet demands repetitive feeding.

After repeating ten or twenty times a comfortable miniature version of your specific movement, return to the initial movement in its entirety, and notice how it is carried out now. Be careful not to overdo your inspection and don't forego your gentleness when you leave the safety of the comfort zone.

If you are sensitive to subtleties you may observe a change. Perhaps you can now carry the movement somewhat further before it signals you to stop. Perhaps the pain itself appears less intense. You can say to yourself that you went down from a pain rated 7 to a pain rated 4, perhaps.

People who are not yet sensitive to subtleties may be disappointed the moment they find that traces of the pain are still there. Training to heal the communication between you and your organism teaches you not only to understand how to move without harming yourself, but also how to respect the rate of learning this organism can integrate, and allow the change to be a gradual process which lasts as long as it needs to.

Take a free ride on the momentum of primal patterns

Movements that imply walking, crawling, swimming — even if they are minimal and slow-paced — can serve as a superb context for creating a climate for recovery. For instance, if you are lying on your side in bed and have difficulty in moving your back, remind yourself that you don't have any problem in moving your ankle. Start flexing one ankle, without force, back and forth. This is already a hint of walking. You can continue, signalling with each flexion of the ankle a fine, responsive movement of the shoulder, raising it ever so slightly towards the head and then lowering it down away from the head. After a while, you can develop the movement of the shoulder into a slight rotation that pulsates together with the motion of the foot and the jaw.

When the synchronised movement develops a comfortable rhythm, it will signal in your brain the familiar program of full walking, which elicits springiness in all your vertebrae, from the pelvis to the skull. Bit by bit, your back will find itself participating in the alternate wave of rounded, subsiding movement, in protruding the lower back backwards and then drawing it upright into height. Of course, if you think the objective is to reach a large rotation with a strong movement of your shoulder, or to twist your foot with exaggerated effort, you will only place yourself in a stressful situation. The pattern of walking, being associated with softness and struggle-free flow, won't be able to identify with the aggressive action that you create. Instead of forcing yourself on your ankle, shoulder, back, or any other part, trust them to know how to participate in walking, by themselves.

In the organic body, the orchestral score for harmonic functioning is written in every one of your cells. Your assignment is to tune your motions to the authentic frequency in which vitality flows, and which is thus capable of reaching the problematic area where it had been blocked. This doesn't happen all at once. It doesn't occur just because of the right formula of the movement. It takes place through your sensitivity to seek that which is easy and feels appropriate; through your ability to discern the artificial from the natural.

Meet your need — make the struggle unnecessary

If you're standing, and something within you is reluctant to straighten up and is holding you bent in a strange way, see if you can stop fighting this tendency, and instead begin obeying it. A good way to stop the struggle is to find support that will release your body from the effort of holding itself upright. A reliable support you can find in kneeling on all fours beside a bed, with your knees on the floor and your torso fully resting on the bed.

Come down on all fours very slowly at the beginning; you may support your hands on a chair.

Bend more in your knees and less in your back. Go first on one knee and then on the other, so that in going down you turn yourself somewhat sideways.

This is not a kind of descent that comes out of determination, coercing you in a jerky and painful way, but rather a descent that comes from surrendering your weight, sinking into what is more comfortable, where and when it is possible. While improvising motions of minute turns to the right and the left, with your knees bouncing like springs, you may feel where the path is open for further bending. Every exhalation is an opportunity to sense where else you may let go of holding and allow yourself to become drawn downwards into the depth.

This kind of sinking down doesn't have to occur symmetrically or directly. It's as if you aren't interfering with it; you allow yourself to stay in whatever position that's meaningful to you, as long as you're comfortable in it. You are waiting for a signal from your body, to inform you when it's ready to go on. Be tuned inside yourself, kind and tolerant, free of criticism, accepting for a few minutes this collapse. For a while suspend any considerations and pretensions. Let each moment be a discovery without trying to control it. Make this descent a project for a few long moments.

Eventually, you will find yourself with your knees on the ground, kneeling beside the stool or the bed on which you can rest the upper part of your body.

In this arrangement, the relationship between your back and your legs assumes the fundamental pattern of crawling, while your chest and belly are

safely supported from beneath, enabling the back to stop working and begin resting. Give yourself permission to receive comfort and support from simulating this early stage of development, a stage with which you might not have had enough practice.

Listen to the way in which your body accepts this kind of support. You may be surprised to discover a position that you have forgotten about, a position in which you feel relatively comfortable and free of threat. You even allow yourself to take in a full breath — perhaps the first in a long time.

Your breathing is a faithful feedback concerning the response of your organism to the way you use it. Possibly the breath of relief is telling you that your organism is now ready to accept its present state, a position it had long craved for, entering a path towards improved balance and healing. If this breath has emerged spontaneously, it is a confirmation that you are on the right path.

On all fours — comfort at home base

Put your hands on the tender area of your lower back and give it a touch that induces soothing. You can, with your hands, move the pelvis ever so gently towards your head and in this way further reduce the tension in your lower back. Use the back of your hands or the thumbs and knuckles of the index fingers. Continue to drag the tissues of the pelvis, and each time remain in that position for a while, to adjust to it. In this way you spare your back the need to contract, through its own effort, to protect its injury.

Kneeling might be a good position for simply resting. Stay in it for as long as you find it comfortable. At a certain point, you may feel a need to begin to shift and move. Remember that movements done while in a vulnerable condition are beneficial when carried out in a passive state of mind. If you move in your accustomed manner, you take the risk of activating all the habitual prejudices that perpetuate the pain. To move without activating the harmful programming requires finesse and sensitivity. You have a better chance of attaining it when you move slowly and gently, with a minimum of investment, in a passive way.

Possibly, one of your knees will tend to rise from the floor. You may increase the pressure of that foot into the floor and feel how your whole back is softly being mobilised toward the head. In this way you give your lower back an opportunity to be less tense. The thrusting foot does the work instead of the back, thus eliciting the relief. If this movement is done gently and harmoniously, it will be confirmed by the 'amen' of the deep breath.

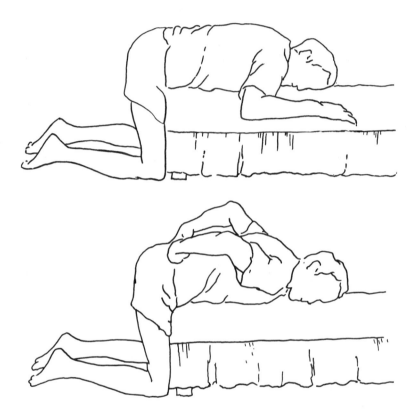

Comfort on All Fours
Kneeling near a bed, with the angle between the body and the thighs, allows the pelvis to find a comfortable state. While the full weight of the torso is securely supported on the bed, the lower back begins to let go of its strenuous holding. You may gently drag the tissues behind your pelvis, gliding them towards the belt line, thus bringing the muscles of the lower back to a less tense condition. The more gently you do the movements, the greater chance you have to convince your system to relinquish its defensiveness.

You may find that the movement in one knee brings you that sense of relief, while in the other knee it evokes a threat. Certainly, stay and repeat the movement only on the side that feels comfortable to you. The purpose of your exploration is to encourage that which is possible and not to force that which is impossible. Probe various directions with the knee. Moving a few degrees to the right or to the left will have a different effect on the back. Find out for yourself what suits you best.

You can also raise the foot in the air, keeping the knee anchored to the floor. When you move your lower leg about, in soft, rounded movements, you can feel how a corresponding movement is taking place in the vertebrae. Perhaps in this position of being supported, in between the bed and the hand, your back will be willing to enter into mobility without arousing pain, and this mobility marks the beginning of its recovery.

At a certain stage, your head may begin searching for another arrangement for the neck. Slowly turn it at your own pace to the other side. You may arrive at this in tiny repetitive movements. Perhaps you will find that you can turn your head at the same time that you lift the knee, and your foot thrusts the thigh, which thrusts the pelvis, which in turn thrusts the spine that thrusts the head forward, in a flowing motion that re-connects you all over.

It's not important to perform many movements. Do the little that elicits in you a sensation of acceptance. It's not important to aim at any specific configuration. You move in order to follow something inside of you that remembers how to find comfort. Let yourself be led by the movement, as if you're being carried by hidden currents, smoothly and slowly — as smoothly and slowly as can be. Without planning, wait until some movement from within emerges to guide you on.

In this way you communicate with a deep inner wisdom that steered your life before you knew how to talk or understand. You are inviting it to express what it knows, after years of having its subtle message drowned out by the loud voice of habits. When you respect the pause needed for listening, inside you begin to feel what it is that you need. To give up intellectual initiative and become passive for a few moments seems to be one of the most difficult things to do in a culture of hyperactivity and manipulation. However, it is through this quality of passive listening that you can pass through the movements in safety.

When you are ready, come to the standing position very slowly, stage by stage; open to turn yourself to one side or another, so that at any point you can stop and readjust yourself, go back or move on. Eventually, stand up and feel whether or not your back has indeed learned something about how to be a little more comfortable.

Upside down on all fours

The same 'on all fours' position can be assumed upside down. You lie down on your back and rest your lower legs from heel to knee, on the seat of a chair or on a bed. In this way, you form the same right angle between your trunk and your thighs as in the crawling position. Long-term sufferers who for a long time have been unable to find for themselves a single position of safe remission, are pleasantly surprised to see how leaning their legs on the chair can unravel their backs from the tangle of defensive fear and enable them to become ready to rest and flatten themselves out.

Indeed in this arrangement, the entire weight of the body is distributed between the legs and the back, and the over-sensitised area reflects right away the decreased pressure and responds by relaxation. The elevation of the lower legs also hints at an upside down suspension of the lumbar area, so that gravity alone works to reduce the compression between the vertebrae, while they find support on the solid ground. It's even possible to sleep in this position, if this is the only way to find relief.

Lying on the side: your safe refuge

Lying on your side with your body softly curled is your certain refuge. A pillow placed between your bent knees will further reduce the pull on the back, induced by the weight of the leg.

You can also find comfort by crossing the knees. For instance, if you are curled up on your right side, move your right knee backward, and bring your left knee, which is on top, in front of you. If you feel the need to, support the left knee on a pillow.

When lying on your side, you can also place a pillow or a rolled blanket behind your back. The supportive touch of the blanket, even if your weight doesn't lean upon it, gives your back permission to relinquish inner tension that is usually present when the back lies exposed and isolated in space.

Reclining thus on your side, you can perform several useful movements, even if your back is sore. Place a cardboard roller, about the size of a bottle, between your knees, so that it leans on the thigh and calf of the bottom knee, bent as it is.

Slowly begin rolling the upper knee, which is leaning across the roller, back and forth.

Sense how this soft movement of the knee gently swings your pelvis and your back. In this way, you allow the upper hip to experience its freedom of movement relative to the rest of the body, in a comfortable and supportive way. The roller supports the weight of the hip and traces for it a smooth, consistent

**route which perhaps the hip could not have undertaken on its own in daily
life, especially with a back that hurts.**

**To further enhance the comfortable atmosphere, you can use your upper
hand to help roll the roller back and forth, so that your back remains totally
passive while experiencing the movement.**

Changing positions

Sometimes the problem is how to manage turning to the side with an injured back,
without getting the warning signal of sharp pain. It is often the case that a person
can walk, stand, lie down, lie on the back or on the side without causing any pain.
The difficulties begin with shifting from one position to another.

Just as you should consider every unsuitable food you may have eaten when
your stomach protests in pain, so should you consider the warning signals of certain
movements liable to cause pain, and look for ways to bypass them. Every pain is a
regression, and you have the right to aim at consistent advancement without setbacks. Passing from lying down to sitting, or from sitting to standing, or turning
over on your side, are all functions that should be given full attention with sensitivity and patience.

Even such a simple task as bringing the straight legs, while lying on your back, to
a bent-knee position, can be carried out either comfortably or harmfully. The knees
need to be bent before you can raise them or lean them on a chair, or before rolling
over to the side in order to get up. If your back is caught in a spasm, how can you
safely go through the bending of the legs when the slightest movement of the knee
causes pain at the other end of the thigh bone, in the problematic area of the hip
joint-pelvis-spine? How can you move your legs and at the same time leave your
back safe?

Knee-bending as primal swimming

Imagine that you are lying on your back with your legs stretched out, and you want
to change positions and bend your knees so that the soles of your feet will stand on
the bed. Are you aware of how you usually do this? For instance: do you bend both
knees and pull them upward simultaneously? Do the soles of your feet pass from
the stretched position to the bent position by relinquishing the support of the bed
and moving through the air, detached from the surface on which you are lying?
Surely if this is your trajectory, then a sharp pain in your back will notify you that
this is a forbidden movement. Before coming to the conclusion that bending your
knees and raising them has to hurt, see if you are willing to explore another way of
moving that may bring you to the same place but will bypass the pain.

People who have sensitive backs, who know how to be attuned inwardly, doing only what is comfortable and safe, may find this path by themselves.

At first, they turn to one side, to the right for instance, so that both feet are pointing towards the right. The right knee becomes more and more bent, still facing the right; the sole of the foot is drawn along its outer edge, all the while touching the bed, so that the back is not called upon to carry its weight.

Before Getting Out of Bed
The transition from extended legs to bent knees can be done with no threat to the lower back. You find the safe trajectory by your own sensory appreciation as you drag each foot along the bed surface, tilted on its outside edge. First on one side and then the other, while your full torso assists the rotation from side to side. Repeat the alternating undulation a few times for an easy start of your day.

When the angle of bending in the knee is sufficient and the sole of the foot upon the bed has come close to the level of the left knee, it is easier to raise the knee from the side and then bring it toward the ceiling. At this stage, the entire surface of the right sole comes to a standing position upon the bed.

Then, veering the torso and both legs to the left, the right bent knee is inclined above the body, assisting the turning movement towards the left.

The left leg, still extended out, points leftward with both the foot and the knee. When it is thus rotated on its side, this is the time to draw it along the left side and deepen the bend of the knee, keeping it still close to the bed, at a comfortable level.

Using pillows to support the extended knees will facilitate the pulling motion along the sides.

When both knees are sufficiently bent and the back responds and becomes round, you can raise both knees one after the other to the upright position, the back returning to a balanced middle position.

To summarise:

Draw the right knee from the right side and afterwards stand it perpendicularly.

Turn it, bent over, to the left.

Draw the left knee from the left side.

Raise both bent knees to the middle. The feet are at all times in some contact with the bed.

In this way, the knees are brought up one after the other, each from its own side, in a kind of alternation in the pattern of breast-stroke swimming. The back is being cradled gently from side to side without a single threatening moment. The weight of the legs is sustained by the bed throughout the entire movement, and the back is free of that responsibility.

During the learning process, when people do the motion of drawing up the knees repeatedly from side to side, the motion swings the entire torso as if it were a silk scarf, simulating an amphibian dance of fins in water. The generous harmony of this wave-like movement appeals to people on a very deep level, beyond any explanations, and they enjoy doing it again and again.

Just for a moment you can compare it to the conventional arrangement where people detach both their feet from the bed, bending both knees at once directly toward the ceiling, and feel how your back is summoned sharply to hold up the weight of your legs in the air. Many people simply forget that there is another option. They do it the hard way, absentmindedly, without ever putting it to the test of efficiency. This is a mechanical habit; its statement is that movement is a project in overcoming and one must learn to accept its penalty just as all of life is a struggle.

This approach leaves no room for searching out comfort and a reduction of tension. Even with an injured back some people won't consider the idea of moving their legs up through the sides, and allowing the planet to carry their weight rather than inflicting it on their aching back.

Paradoxically, those few people who have relinquished the habit and found the compromise that allows them to move safely from straight legs to a bent position, don't give themselves credit for having found the easy way. They tend to see themselves as spoiled, because of helplessness and a lack of choice to do otherwise. The movement that bypasses the difficulty just works to reinforce their sense of injury. They don't realise that the easier way is also the right way, and that everyone else should learn from them a lesson in grace and efficiency.

Creative caution: between obsession and abstention

When something begins to hurt, Nature is calling out in the language of pain, giving warnings to stay away from self-injury. The same readiness to be attuned to the finest discriminations of pain is also the compass that points the way to healing. This creative attentiveness should be fostered. Such cautious sensitivity may seem to be a withdrawal from life, because everything is done slowly, listening more than doing, having as much patience as is required and for as long as required, until one feels more secure and can be less cautious and more active.

The trap is, though, that suffering people may turn their sensitivity into a habit of fear, and establish caution as a lifestyle, and so become stuck in wariness as with any other habit. Attentiveness has then ceased to be a creative searching, and has become merely a means of surrounding all action with an attitude that screams out one big, undiscriminating 'NO'. Instead of a sensitive dialogue with movement, movement has become an enemy to avoid. Such avoidance is degenerative and does not produce a climate for recovery; the damage may even increase. Other parts of the organism, which have no reason to hold back, begin restricting their movements as well in order to protect the injured area. Knowing how far a gratifying movement can go, and where to stop, is a wisdom that comes only from self-exploration, through movement that is oriented as far from compulsion as it is from avoidance.

This constructive equilibrium is one of the values acquired through prolonged work with Awareness Through Movement processes. Through every such process, you train your resourcefulness in discovering more and more of what is feasible for you for at present.

Turning over in bed without setting off the emergency alarm

At times the most blundering self-injury occurs while you are in bed. You rested all night, you feel relaxed, and you want to get up. Entering mobility costs you a sharp pain that cancels all your hopes for progressing with your recovery today. This also happens to people who don't intend to get out of bed, but only want to move and shift position. Let's have a look at the very beginning of the movement. There is one typical movement that people do easily thousands of times when they are healthy, and which they aren't willing to give up even when their backs suffer. This is a twisting movement of the spine which starts the transition from lying on the back to lying on the side, or from lying on the side to lying on the back, or any other rotational movement that a person does around the axis of his or her own length.

For example, you are lying on your back and intend to turn over to the side. Instead of removing the blanket and allowing yourself to roll over, invading the adjacent area of the bed, you are captive to the idea that you must remain in the same warmed-up spot in which you have been lying, so that you raise up your pelvis and twist your body around itself; your shoulders remain flat on the bed, and only from your pelvis and your sensitive lower back do you demand the sudden twisting motion, while raising your weight in the air. You are doing the most difficult thing for your system, and demanding it of that part of you which has the greatest difficulty in carrying it through — your lower back. What's more, this is done without cooperation from the rest of your body.

When you are ready to explore the efficiency of your rising habit, first of all make a point of removing the blanket from you, so that it won't hinder you from rolling further along in bed. This is not so much because it is a physical hindrance as that the very idea of the blanket over you blocks your imagination from considering the possibility of rolling over.

You can help your pelvis to drag the back after it safely if the back remains passive, while your entire self remains in contact with the bed. Let your hands and legs do the job. Bend your knees one after the other, pulling them along the outer edge of the foot.

Turn both knees to one side, and place your hands on your groins or on the sides of the pelvis. Let your hands direct the pelvis and assist it to roll.

Turn your head to the side before the pelvis does, thus involving your eyes in steering the entire spine.

The process of finding the safe trajectory

The best path for you may emerge not by receiving advice about one or another outline, but through a process of self-initiated minor movements that are repeated over and over again, in varying conditions, within the same segment of the function, until it becomes clear. To be able to move yourself from one static position to another and to succeed in doing so on the first try, without wasting aggression and without provoking the injured area, takes sophisticated skill.

How, then, can you perform the turning motion as a gradual process? If you tried to turn over all at once, and if, as you feared, a sharp pain flashed, try again; but this time do only a very tiny bit of the beginning of the movement.

Begin moving only one knee slowly, and find out how far you can turn it before receiving signals from your back. Be aware of the angle of turning, the distance the knee traverses. Locate the precise boundaries of the safety zone.

Again, move the same knee to the side and bring it back to the middle, back and forth, several times, without being tempted to go beyond the safe zone. You are moving your knee to gain your organism's trust, to make the fear unnecessary, to give the rest of your body time to participate in the twisting movement with the best possible coordination.

If your movement virtually creates an atmosphere of support and security, you will receive confirmation from your breathing. After several movements, your breathing will become open in fullness and relief. If you don't receive confirmation of the relieving breath, it means that you have to further reduce the range of the movement and slow down the pace.

At times you will have to continue reducing the initial movement until it is barely hinted at, almost imaginary. As you decrease the intensity and the ambition to achieve the end result, so you increase your chances of keeping the emergency program of your functional memory turned off.

Graded involvement: first grade of learning

You may be concerned that the above implies that this is how you are supposed to act all your life; but, in fact, the instructions for this style of careful activity only apply for the first stage of dissolving the trauma. After you have established a quality of comfortable movement, accompanied by a breath of relief, you can test your movement to find out if you are ready to widen its scope. You will be surprised to discover how much further you can reach, and this time, without frustration. In the same manner proceed with the next segment of the function.

It is important for you to remember that during the first stage you deal only with what is possible. Your objective is to reach there a level of ease and freedom from worry. After you have made the possible easy, you can address yourself to the problem zone and search within it carefully, feeling whether the impossible begins to yield and become more possible. The more credit you build up in movements that bring you satisfaction and pleasure, the more you are liable to succeed in transforming the impossible into the feasible.

You create ease through ease, and safety through safety. Your movement is rewarded when you give your commitment to quality, to a sense of comfort, to what demands the least effort, to a pace that doesn't push you to ignore yourself.

Perhaps these aren't your rules for the game of life. Perhaps you are anxious to give your all without reserve. This self-examination that doesn't allow you to exaggerate may seem to you a stingy approach. Perhaps you would prefer anything to this contained involvement. Are you willing to ask yourself honestly what is the price you are paying for this?

When you are tempted to give yourself a hard pull by a sudden force of your muscles, which your body is not prepared for, you threaten your system and intimidate it. It must then defend itself and become further entrenched in the traumatic pattern, with greater suspicion of any change. So what did you gain?

To drive your body with lack of consideration is like a short cut, in the children's game of slides and ladders, to the top of the ladder — only to find that you are compelled to return immediately to the starting point. There you have to sit and wait until the right conditions occur that will allow you to once again be in the game.

Your true problem is perhaps to what extent you are ready to mobilise yourself without pressures and without coercion. To what extent do you trust the innate wisdom of your organism to let go of its critical hold when it is convinced that there is no longer any need for it? In essence, this is a matter of self-tolerance.

Foreplay that ripens the movement

You will find instructions as to how to continue your roll to the side and proceed to a sitting position in *Chapter I: Functional Honesty*. Rising into a sitting position is more gratifying when it is done as a process of repetitions, as a preliminary game of to and fro which enables the movement to take place of its own accord.

When lying on your back, all rolled up with knees bent, and intent upon rising, you will do well to begin by moving only your head. Roll your head from side to side, and repeat this several times.

Gradually invite the rest of your body to become familiar with the idea of rolling. It needs time to organise itself.

If you respect its need, your torso will begin to respond, slowly, until it too begins to move from side to side, in small motions, almost imperceptibly, more in the imagination than in reality.

Choose one side that comes easier to you and continue to roll there.

Be with the state of mind of alternating, rolling to the side and coming back to centre, without any pressure to reach end results. Think rotation and the idea of moving your nose to face the ground. After ten or twenty motions you will be ready, by yourself, to go much further, on either side.

At a certain moment, you will feel that you are able to rely on the rolling momentum to lift you into a sitting position; but don't be determined to make this happen.

Let the rising happen of itself; let it take a ride from the inertia of the rolling. The less there is of your intentional involvement, the less will be the defensive restraints in your back.

Roll until you face the ground with your head continuing its rounded trajectory, brushing its motion on through space.

Keep rolling, without holding your breath, trusting the bed to continue supporting your weight along each segment of the movements' route.

Use your hands for support and you will be likely to find yourself sitting without your back having summoned any pain.

From sitting to standing: a free ride on the spiral

If you intend to move into a standing position from sitting on the bed, or on a chair, and are concerned as to how your back will react and how it will sustain the compression of your body weight, give yourself permission for gradual beginnings. Devote some time to practising the very beginning of the process of getting up, again and again. To get up immediately, safely and harmoniously, especially when rising straight up frontally, demands any person to have superb skill at a level of perfection. At this stage, it might be easier for you if you place one foot in front of the other and hint to your organism that you are operating according to a walking pro-

gram. The stepping position immediately places the process of rising into the familiar context of walking, in which your organism is highly experienced.

**When you sit at the front edge of a chair with one foot forward and rock your
upper body forward, you may notice that your upper body has a tendency to
rotate to one side. One shoulder, on the same side as the forward-stepping foot,
gains on the line of the opposite shoulder and your entire body actually tends
to rotate to one side.**

**This organic diagonal contains the initiation of a spiral, and that is its
advantage. Any diagonal in the pelvis will elicit a spacing-out on one side of
the vertebrae, and will draw them near to each other on the other side. The
expansion that is thus formed on one side of the spine is much greater than the
expansion that can take place when both sides work at one and the same time
during a frontal 'getting-up' trajectory.**

How do you Cope with Gravity in Getting in and out of a chair?
*Ascending, you allow your weight to rest fully on the planet, imagining its depth, evoking the
counter-pressure from the earth to assist the raising. Descending, you empty your feet of weight and
imagine the height of the sky surrendering to sinking down without interfering with it. Going up or
down through the spiral, one can do more easily, gradually and smoothly what is difficult to do in
frontal uni-dimensional movement.*

While walking, this alternating expansion takes place of its own accord, and thus enables each side in its turn to contract and expand as it moves fluidly from one function to another. To experience full expansion and full compression, through the entire springy spectrum between one and the other, means, in terms of the organism, to be more vital and effective.

After several repetitions, change the arrangement of the legs and continue with the rocking motion. Find out with which foot forward it is more comfortable for your entire organism to enter into the upward-spiralling twist. Pay attention to the differences and continue in the comfortable arrangement.

From every rotational motion return a little before you reach the barrier. Spare yourself any frustration.

When the movement acquires the trust of your organism, you will find yourself moving forward to the point where your weight will shift to your feet.

This is the moment for your feet to take over their task and to lean fully on the ground. This is a kind of thrust to the ground, solely by the weight heaped upon them, for which you don't have to do a thing to make it happen, except to be aware of it.

You can also lean your hands on your thighs, so that their weight is also finally transferred to the ground. It's as if you have enrolled, for your benefit, the use of four posts well anchored in the ground to handle the sudden uprooting of your weight against gravity. In this position you fixate the spine into the frame of the limbs, and in this way you spare your back any threatening articulation.

If you have any need to protect the knees as well you may, with your hands, get hold of your lower legs beneath the knees.

The more you engage your hands and feet to take part in this project, the more your head and your sight are adjusted to lead your entire skeleton into the configuration of the rising spiral, and the more your back can remain passive and not signal the pain, which is now the only thing it can do when called into action. If, in addition, you don't forget to breathe, you have a good chance of standing up on your two feet without your back being summoned into any effort.

You may be self-conscious about looking awkward, standing up in a manner that changes course by 90 degrees. You certainly have the choice: to consider what people around you will say, or what your own flesh and organs are saying.

The tendency towards the diagonal on stairs

The principle of the diagonal can be of help to you in many varied situations. While standing you can achieve the rotation of the pelvis to the spine by bending one knee. You can facilitate prolonged standing by placing one foot on a raised stool. You can ease your back when lying on your stomach by dragging one knee along the surface of the bed closer to the pelvis, in a creeping motion. Work in the garden can be less exhausting to the back if you carry it out kneeling on one knee. It is possible to do all kinds of jobs in the kneeling position — even vacuum cleaning.

The diagonal makes a significant difference when going up stairs. Try going up stairs by turning your front from the stair-line by 45 degrees. This angle, approximately, serves to bypass the difficulty inherent in frontal climbing. Your vertebrae, in the diagonal mode, can enjoy a gradual and varied twisting game, instead of a sharp emphasis always on the same spot.

A critical moment for the lumbar hip area, when going up stairs, occurs when you raise your foot to carry the weight of the leg in the air while lifting it to the next step.

Another critical moment for the lower back is when the foot behind needs to become a reliable axis for leverage. Each one of the joints on that side of the body is then required to sustain the sharp, increased pressure, and that immediately reveals any weak point.

When you are willing to relate to the four winds of heaven as open space for your movement, and do not perceive yourself locked into your old orbit, you know that your raised knee need not remain facing the front, but that you can also raise it facing slightly to the side, either in or out, an echo of the undulation of primal swimming.

You can feel how turning your knee to the inside, relative to yourself, allows your back to elongate in a spiral which is always easier than a frontal elongation that works upon both sides at the same time.

It is also easier for the leg serving as axis to sustain its task of lifting the body when the movement develops gradually, and the timing of pressure is more diffused.

Mindful Spontaneity

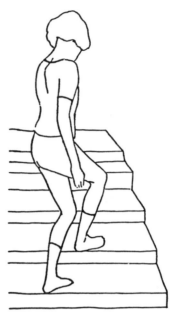

Going Up and Down Steps Within Rotation
When you respect every nuance of well being, you allow the comfort of your spine and not the structure of the surroundings to determine the design of your movement.

The other leg, which is turned outside, assumes the soft diagonal stance as well, and serves to assist the initial twist from the other side.

Turning the knees sideways and twisting the torso need not be over-exaggerated. Just the permission to visualise these possible directions already makes the difference. To go up steps like Charlie Chaplin or with both knees facing the same side, while the side of the body is parallel to the steps' slope, can be a refreshing and amusing change for sound, healthy people. For sensitive people, it can be a matter of survival.

Another suggestion that will make a huge difference in climbing steps is the reminder that you don't need to straighten the axis leg to its extremity even when you complete the raising to the next step. If you pay attention, you may realise that it is possible to cease straightening before locking, and leave the knee somewhat bent.

From this bend you receive the springy momentum to thrust and take off to the next step, until the other leg takes over the role of axis. When the knees give up that final locking, all you need to do is just lean your body forward, with the feeling of falling uphill.

It can be helpful, when walking up steps, to extend the 45-degree turn to a full 180 degrees. Did you ever try going up steps with your back facing upward? Or going down steps backward? Mountain climbers know that one of the ways to restore ease to exhaustive climbing is by reversing the front of their body for a few minutes, so that they climb with their backs facing the upward path.

During traumatic stages people with back spasms are amazed how, when climbing stairs, anticipated pain fails to occur in this way. This is the power of non-habitual options. When going up backwards, you are not activating the same set program and the same set of muscles that are usually responsible for the suffering in this function. You carry out the function with another group of muscles, which perhaps has no defensive history. The message that comes through again and again is: it isn't the back that hurts, but the manner in which you utilise it. It isn't the computer, but rather the software programming.

The healing diagonal when lying down

Cultivating the diagonal when lying down may be your way to find freedom from pain. If you are lying in bed and can't move your back without hurting, you cannot turn around and you certainly cannot raise your pelvis.

You can still lie in such a way that the knee on the side that hurts less is bent and perpendicular, for instance, the left knee. Then, the right leg, on the more sensitive side, is stretched down with a pillow supporting the knee.

Gradually and gently begin increasing the pressure of your left foot on the bed, and give your knee the intention to draw further away from your head, which is turned slightly to the right. Repeat this several times.

Then, bend your right foot at a right angle and draw your entire straight leg in, pulling it towards the pelvis, with a slight rotation of the heel outwards.

Take a moment to see in your mind's eye if you can move your left, bent knee further away from your head, at the same time that you are bringing your right, outstretched leg closer to you, in a kind of pincer movement. Slowly do the actual combined movement, but minimally, and each time stay in this position for a while, for a period of adjustment.

Listen to the posterior of the pelvis on the right side, the troubled area, and feel how it is re-establishing its contact with the bed.

You can add to this a diagonal formation in your upper body as well. To the above arrangement, add the extension of your left arm above your head on the bed, in a continuous line with your body. Let your right arm rest alongside your body.

Each time your right leg is pulled in towards the body, continue the process of shortening that side by reaching with your right hand towards your foot.

In counteraction, your left arm is being gently pushed further upwards, within a slight rotation, turning the palm towards the floor.

To the overall twisting you may add an ever-so-slight turning of your head to the right. In this way, your two pelvises, one at your hips and one at your shoulder-blades, are both carrying out the diagonal manoeuvre. The entire right side contracts as the left side expands in relation to the spine. Quite a number of vertebrae, as a result, gain more space between one another.

Rest, and feel the difference in your way of reclining. Feel the difference in the way you are functioning. Is it easier for you now to turn around? Or perhaps it is even possible to begin raising the pelvis with less pain?

It is important to remember that you are not applying the diagonal elongation in order to pull yourself as far and as strongly as possible. You are applying the diagonal elongation in order to achieve a specific effect on the injured, right side. In shortening the right side, you fulfil its need to protect and contract. You provide it with a sense of security as the movement attaches it to the bed's surface. After such reassurance, it is more readily inclined to move once more without defensiveness.

Cultivating the diagonal by means of the roller

In times of severe pain, you can make meaningful progress with the aid of a small roller: a rolled-up towel will do, about 10 cm in diameter and 30-40 cm in length. When you place the roller under the right half of the pelvis, it serves as an extension of the bed platform, effectively moulding itself to the unique shape of the right side of the lower back.

In order to place the roller, turn a little to the left until you have sufficient room to place the roller where the right buttock had been lying.

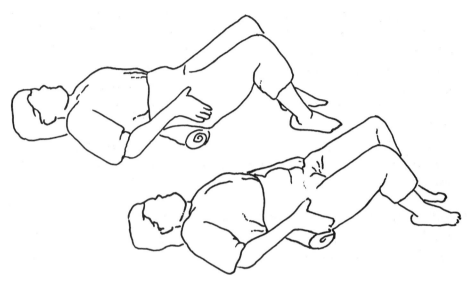

Support the Vulnerable Hip
A small rolled-up towel placed diagonally under the hurting hip provides it with restful support. The movement is being done by the free hip as you raise it from the floor ever so slowly and slightly, several times, breathing all along and sensitively moderating the effect of the movement. When you remove the towel, you may find a surprising relief.

Return to lie upon the roller so that the right half of the pelvis and lower back, all the way to the lower ribs, recline on it. Your knees are bent and perpendicular. Take a moment to adjust to the support of the roller in all those places that aren't used to receiving contact.

Place your left hand underneath your left buttock, and your right hand on the right groin. With the help of your hands, raise your left side slightly, and begin balancing your pelvis on the roller. Repeat this process gradually, each time ever so lightly, for a few times.

Each time you raise your left side, pause to breathe with a soft, expanding stomach. This breathing will ensure that lifting the pelvis is not done through the back's efforts, which you wish to neutralise. Each time you slightly raise the left edge, look for the height that allows you to soften yourself all over and accept the movement.

Sense the dialogue of pressure between the roller and the problematic zone of the right lower back. You may experiment with placing the roller in slightly different directions.

After repeating this process several times, remove the roller. First, drag the end of the roller from under the waist, then remove the rest of it from under the buttocks.

Remain lying for a while, and feel the difference between both sides. You may discover that the right side has learned to organise itself in comfort and is able to remain flat on the bed, with a sense of security that it did not have before.

Gently, check out your capacity to move now, perhaps by raising your pelvis into the air ever so slightly. See what it feels like to turn on your side after this process.

The diagonal in the complete context of walking

The most fundamental confirmation of the diagonal arrangement is achieved when you apply it while walking.

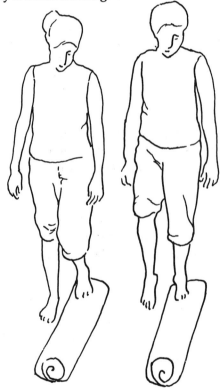

Communicating with the Back through the Feet
Stepping with one foot on the rug challenges your adjustability to reorganise your total self. The function of walking, with your preferable arrangement, works to reassure the security of your troubled side while in motion.

> Roll up a rug into a long roller, and walk along its length with one foot stepping on the raised rug and the other foot stepping on the floor, sort of limping on purpose.

> Try one side, then another, and you may well discover that one side is easier for you than the other.

> Continue walking like this on the more comfortable side only. Walk forward, then backward, with the same foot continuing to step on the rug the whole time.

> After repeating this a few times, take a moment to sense the way in which you are standing, with both feet flat on the floor.

> Then try walking with the other foot on the rug. If it now feels easier, then continue walking with that foot on the rug. If, however, it feels as difficult as before, then leave that side. You may have to practice on the comfortable side alone for several days, until the other side is ready to do likewise.

By now you are certainly not surprised at how, in Functional Integration, you avoid wrestling with difficulties — a concept which may initially have sounded paradoxical. You turn an easy movement into a pleasant, fluent one wherever possible, and eventually the difficult movement becomes easy as well. It's as if you are searching — where it's convenient for you, under the light of a lamp — for something you lost in the dense forest. Amazingly enough, for the organism, it works.

Initiated limping by walking along a raised step is an effective device that refreshes the total torso-leg-ground interaction. A Feldenkrais practitioner, Linda Tallington Jones, applies this idea to the healing of horses.

Symmetrical functioning

In times of severe pain, when your back becomes 'locked', you try to stand up and you feel as if some deformity has been moulded upon you. Something is out of line, and you are locked into it with great tension. You are specially concerned about being crooked. You believe that if only you could straighten up, the problem would be solved. You try walking and the broken rhythm of your walk reinforces your sense of how crooked you are.

An injured back indeed usually results in the loss of symmetry in the body's posture between the right and left sides, the loss of symmetry in the range of possible functions on each side, and the loss of symmetry in the time required to carry out functions on each side.

A body in a state of disturbed equilibrium does not only reflect the injury, but putting it to use in such a state works to reinforce the damage. Muscles, by their nature, are quickly enlisted to strain, while their release is slow and gradual. The more sudden and tense is their enlistment to strain, the slower will be their release. In cases of extreme contraction, they seem unable to find a way to release their hold at all. In a threatening situation, as in a sudden stretch — especially if the lifting of weight is also involved — the organism is immediately summoned to organise itself in emergency defence, and it contracts. This defence comes from a deep and vital urge for survival, beyond conscious consideration. The muscles involved in this defence remain contracted long after the original cause has ceased to exist.

This is characteristic of trauma: the organic complex is not easily convinced to let go of its state of emergency, even after the cause is no longer active. The trouble is that as long as the body's scaffolding is predominantly engaged in expressing defence, it feeds the same initial fear that created this defence. When you are afraid and your entire musculature is organised in a frozen state of fear, you are unable to consider other modes of organisation even though they might have brought you more benefit. This is a vicious circle.

Whether the body's distorted hold is relevant or anachronistic, the person's suffering is just as real. Such a person needs help to cease reacting to life out of fear, to cease using himself in a prejudiced and unbalanced way that has no longer any basis in reality.

How, then, do you dissolve fear and return to a symmetry that expresses this reconciliation?

Reconciling symmetry in the Feldenkrais approach

Feldenkrais' way of thought is characteristically original on this subject as well. The Feldenkrais approach is derived from a deep respect for the organism's inner needs, which are revealed through it's apparent external design in space. If a person is distinctly bent to one side, Feldenkrais won't attempt, as many other therapies do, to forcefully eliminate this bending, in order to straighten the person's structure. Feldenkrais will help this person to increase the bend and deepen the deviation on that side. Gently and gradually, this person will be guided to move in accordance with the body's deflection, and the guide's own hands will further organise the entire body, time and again, to help the person feel more comfortable with the crookedness.

What happens after a few moments is that this person takes a deep breath of relief and begins spontaneously to fall into a much straighter posture than he has had in a long time.

How does this paradox work?

Feldenkrais trusts the innate intelligence of the nervous system. This system has experience that has been sifted for thousands of generations and is equipped with everything it needs in order to cope successfully with the challenges of reality. If it appears that its need is to bend, to protect a certain part, the teacher won't pretend to know better than the system what its needs are. Rather, he will help it carry out that need.

When the system comprehends that someone else is working to do its job, then its effort becomes redundant. This is the moment when it ceases to invest in defence and deflection, when the person takes a deep breath and is able to straighten up by him or herself. If indeed the defensiveness is no longer relevant, the person will begin to adopt the new, more upright alignment and will no longer return to the pattern of trauma.

Instead of demanding correction, which is a direct confrontation that provokes the organism to entrench itself deeper in its strategy, Feldenkrais creates a situation in which the tendency to protect has already been manifested. The nervous system is ready to cease activating its strategy from the brain to the muscles, when it is being established from the muscles to the brain.

The message is that if you are willing to be attuned to your deflection, to follow it and fulfil its need, you will be able to find your way to freedom. Asymmetrical differences are a rich source for sharpening one's capacity to listen inward and decipher the organism's orientations. All processes of Awareness Through Movement pass the trial of symmetry. Each movement is carried out separately on each side, and you learn to discern how one side is different from the other. You become sensitive to the nuances of preference, avoidance, deviation, and the inner feeling that accompanies the doing. Through your examination of one side as compared to the other, you learn to read what your organism is broadcasting to you.

You can remedy that which is manifest on the exterior only by that which you sense inside.

Functional symmetry despite asymmetry of structure

Symmetry is the characteristic ideal state of the organism, but none of us is ideal. Aren't we entitled to full well-being in whatever structure we presently hold?

This right to fulfilment and pleasure in a body that is less than perfect is provided by the Feldenkrais Method in that it does not concern form as much as the process of creating functional quality. It does not deal with judging structure, but rather with the dynamics of activating each side with awareness of the sensations this activity elicits.

When you bring about a closer similarity between the sensations accompanying your movements on either side of your body, you will have a sense of harmony and your body structure will begin to approach symmetry, whereas if you are determined to produce movement on one side that is measured in range and appears outwardly identical to your movement on the other side, you may perhaps achieve symmetry but you won't feel in harmony; you will feel coerced. Objective symmetry is a frustrating goal.

You have the sensory tools to develop subjective symmetry — the symmetry of equalising the sensations. Humans are gifted with the ability to perform movement that is symmetrical in its perceptible quality despite a structure that is not symmetrical.

If you have one problematic side and one perfectly sound side, which of them would you want to equalise to the other? It would seem that your goal is to improve the problematic side, so that it will be able to perform like the sound side; however, this is exactly what the problematic side is incapable of doing — it is an impossible, wishful demand. If you persist in striving for it, you will intensify the limited side's defensiveness — on the level of its muscles as well as on the level of your self-image — and the gap between both sides will only increase.

You can achieve symmetry between your two sides when you equalise the configuration of your movement in space, the course of the movement's flow, the idea of the outline. However, you do not try to make their quantitative dimensions strictly equal. You can reveal a symmetry of sensation when you equalise the level of comfort for each side when involved in a movement, if you are willing to forego the attempt to produce an equal range for both sides. You can bring both sides to a level of equality with the common denominator of functional honesty. Each side does what it can, and the sides feel equal in their degree of ease while so doing. It is similar to equality in terms of social justice, in which, for example, each person pays taxes according to his income and not according to a pre-established quota.

Symmetry of rhythm

How in practice do you attain functional symmetry? For example, if you are standing and the right side of your back is tender and sore and highly vulnerable, you will probably also find it hard to lean fully on your right foot. It won't be as simple for you to disconnect your left foot from the floor and manoeuvre it in space, as needed when walking, climbing steps, dancing or kicking.

In walking any step on the right foot will probably bring in its wake some distortion throughout your body. Very quickly, you will shift your weight again to the more reliable left foot. On this safer side, you remain longer. If you pay attention, you will realise that the difference in the rhythm of remaining on each side while walking faithfully reflects the difference in the condition of those sides.

How do you create balance?

Obviously, you cannot demand of the injured side that it behave differently. On the other hand, your sound side does have the choice. You can stand on it in the way that you are used to, and you can also utilise it in other ways, including — if you wish — the request that it behave like the injured side.

Take a moment once again to lean on the foot of the injured side, and attentively follow the response this leaning elicits throughout the various parts of yourself. Gather information, with more and more details concerning the ways in which the difficulty is organised in each part, from the sole of the foot to the facial expressions.

Move to stand on your injury-free side, but this time simulate there an imitation of the injury pattern. Apply there, time after time, all the details you have been gathering from the other side.

Begin walking in place very slowly, and each time you lean on the free side, limp on that side the way you observed yourself doing on the limited side.

When you limp on both sides and twist in both of them equally, your brain registers the symmetric balance, which in organic language is reserved for a condition of well-being. In this manner, you upgrade yourself to a frequency of recovery, and healing progresses at an amazing rate. From one step to another, you find it easier to step on the previously reluctant side.

This process can be applied to any condition involving a one-sided injury, such as a sprained ankle, a confined arm, a backache, a sore hip joint, or imbalance of sight. The guiding principle is to establish uniformity, not where you wish to, but where you can.

Scoliosis: create it on your other side too

The well-known problem known as scoliosis is also tackled in the Feldenkrais Method by the same way of thinking.

In scoliosis, the spine undergoes a spiral deformation that develops the ribs on one side, projecting them outwardly, while the ribs on the parallel side are less developed and become sunken inward. Working with the asymmetrical back in the Feldenkrais Method begins with confirmation of the existing condition of the back, reinforcing it through all its manifestations that connect it with the pelvis, the arms, the legs and even the eyes.

During the next stage, students may learn to trace the configuration of their own movements in space and assess their inner sensations. In this way, they will acquire a more precise definition of the difference between the right and left sides. In the course of a long, educational process, they will gradually learn to train their movements so that the side that is freer will imitate the way the same movement is performed on the more limited side. Emphasis is always on the nature of the dynamic behaviour and not on the quantitative static design of the structure.

It is as if people learn, through awareness, to act and respond through a body in which they themselves have created an inverted scoliosis. Instead of a struggle to correct towards ideal alignments, the process creates functional symmetry, which works to trigger the organism's consent to change its entrenched course to one based on a better logic and balance.

As you've made your bed, so shall you sleep

What is the influence of your sleeping habits on your condition?

On what kind of bed should you sleep? On a hard mattress? A soft mattress? In a hammock? On a waterbed?

When you are healthy and capable, you can sleep well on any of these. Nonetheless, you are influenced by all the factors with which you interact. In ancient Sparta, youngsters were trained to be instantly ready for action; they were taught to sleep on hard floors, so that even during sleep they would not experience a state of complete indulgence. Soldiers must be on the alert, ever ready to defend.

A hard mattress can indeed become a constant struggle. If your body isn't prepared to soften and surrender its weight in each of its parts, then even the hardest of mattresses will not guarantee that your body will align itself to the flat surface of the mattress. It is more likely that your body will develop chronic resistance and centres of tension.

On the other hand, a mattress that is too soft will absorb you as you are, in any kind of deformation, and will deny you the chance of becoming acquainted with a more ideal method of organisation.

Perhaps the solution lies somewhere in between. Imagine being in a lap that holds you firmly and at the same time is sensitive to your personal topography, giving where necessary and supporting where necessary. Perhaps, then, your bed should be of a texture that lets your hills feel as plains and your valleys as crests.

When you use a wooden board as the base of your bed and place a soft mattress on top of it, you get the feeling of unified quality all over, as if you are equally levelled out, while being comfortable.

The art of pillow arrangement

The pillow under your head also dictates to your back its various options, and you would do well to give it some thought. The mutual relationship between the curves of the spine, at the neck and at the lower back, is such that a hollowed neck stimulates the lower back to flatten out, and a flat neck stimulates the lower back to hollow in. If your pillow raises the back of your head together with your neck, your lower back becomes tense in its need to deepen its in-curve. On the other hand, if you form a depression in your pillow into which you can recline the back of your head, with the curve of your neck equally supported, you will invite your lower back to flatten out in greater comfort.

A synthetic pillow that doesn't submit to your individual structure imposes upon you an arbitrary arrangement. If you get up each morning with discomfort in your neck, you had better check your pillows. A down pillow that moulds itself to your individual shape is the pillow for people who respect their well-being.

The principle of reserving straight knees for necessary transitional stages only, holds true for other positions besides standing. When you're lying down, too, your back will feel more comfortable with knees slightly bent. This isn't only because of the mechanical conditioning between the direction of the legs and the readiness of muscles to elongate, but also because of neurological conditioning, subjected to a specific program of operation.

Lying on your back with straight knees will be registered in your irritated back as a threat. However, if you support your knees with a pillow it will give your system the idea that you're no longer in the framework of straight knees and its ramifications, and you'll feel immediate relief.

You probably know from experience that lying on your stomach pulls your back in a manner which it can't always sustain. However, lying on your stomach can become more acceptable simply by cancelling the straightening of the knees by supporting your ankles with a pillow, so that your calves are slightly raised, and your toes are off the bed. Your back receives the message of the bent knees as a release from the demand to stretch and it loosens up with ease.

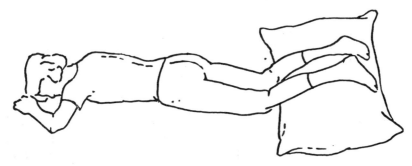

Bend Your Knees to Comfort Your Back
Elevating the feet on a pillow, while lying on the stomach, brings immediate relief to the lower back. The flexion of the knees spares you the necessity to elongate the back's muscles beyond their willingness. This is the same motor connection as in standing, which conditions the comfort of the back on unlocking the knees.

Sometimes, the solution is to bend just one knee. In that way, you tune into the pattern of crawling and raise your entire self to the level of organic efficiency.

Knowing how to place supports while lying in bed is an art. You can play with a variety of pillows of different sizes to support an aching shoulder, congruently filling the gap between it and the bed. You can accommodate in a similar way the back of your neck, your hips, your ankle, elbow, the curve of the lower back, or the sacral protrusion. As you make your bed, so you lie in it. You may sentence yourself to a procrustean bed, where the bed is fixed as it is and you have to adjust to it. Or, with clever supports, you can design your bed to meet your individual needs.

Lying on the back, knees to the chest, a pillow placed on the lower legs helps press the lower back to the floor. Your fists placed on your chest will remind your breathing to flow all the way to the top. Pillows beneath each shoulder and elbow help bring the fists to your chest without any tension and induce the feeling of lying in a nest.

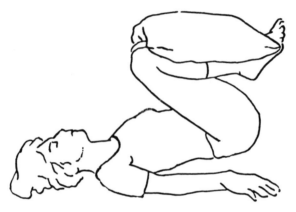

Another Practical Use of the Pillow
Allow the weight of the pillow, plus the weight of your legs, to flatten your back to the ground. In body language 'to flatten down' means to heal the response to gravity.

Lying face down, a pillow placed under the chest and stomach eliminates the curve of the waist and connects the spine to the pelvis in a more continuous alignment. This elevation of the torso allows the neck to suspend freely and be lengthened by the pull of gravity; while both knees can be bent simultaneously, in the way that a baby rests, you can allow yourself to curl up softly.

Satin sheets: smooth out the pain through pleasure

Have you ever considered the influence that the texture of your bedding has on your movements and your attitude towards your moving? The most delightful remedy that I ever heard of, which helped to relieve the backache of a long-suffering man, was the use of satin sheets. Can you imagine the atmosphere which satin sheets give to your sleep? Can you imagine how they smooth out and indulge your every movement and enhance your capacity to be pleased with yourself?

When your consciousness is drawn to the periphery, to the surface of your skin, the inter-muscular tension is reduced. The harshness of certain movements resonates with the tone of the peripheral fineness, and the discomfort begins to dissolve and disappear.

Every night, satin sheets can be a source of relaxation and pleasure for every part of your body. Every movement is enveloped in the flowing lightness. When you learn to savour the generous ongoing pleasure of this atmosphere, which resembles the sensation of swimming, you will reawaken the forgotten romance between you and your body. You achieve this reconciliation without any effort and without any exercises. All you need is to be in the presence of the right agent that sets the tone.

A waterbed: learning to be like water

A waterbed can give you a first-hand lesson on how to be receptive to changes in patterning your positions. Resonating to the water that supports you, you begin to reproduce its qualities. Like the element of water, you become more responsive to the changing moment and adjust your configurations congruently, without too much preparation.

This is possible only when you have reached the stage in which you know the way to surrender, and you can enjoy a game of variations. If you perceive your body image in terms of a set structure, and you are attempting to block the changes which take place in the variant surface, you may well wake up in the morning after a night in the waterbed feeling battered and broken.

Oscillations in travel: resist or surrender

The same holds true for the turbulent motion of car travel. You can attempt to hold your posture stiffly intact and try hard to block the tilting that threatens it, as if you are holding your body in a cast by the force of your muscles. You will most likely end your trip feeling stiff and exhausted, developing the opinion that in your condition, travel is harmful. On the other hand, you can welcome the unexpected vibrations and allow yourself to receive a free massage all over your body — both external and internal. When you surrender yourself to the rocking motions, letting go of the fears that tense you up, then you are like a baby — the softer the baby, the less he is injured.

A microcosm

In Nature, every springy step in an animal's walk sets off a response that echoes in a gesture of the head, in a wave that is generated from the feet, transmitted through the knees and the hip-joints to the pelvis, and passed throughout all the spinal joints. It isn't just a motory, mechanical relationship; it's a neurological relationship, a connection derived from a primordial program of teamwork.

The living body isn't like a machine made up of many different parts, but rather it resembles a constellation with members which are conditioned by one another and interbalanced, like the celestial bodies in the solar system. The organic complex conceals the miracle of each of its parts, reflecting its relation to the whole. Every cell embodies the structural and functional code of the rest of the system. Every group of cells that forms a defined organ or a functional system contains within itself the program, the perspective and the characteristics of all the other various organs of the body, and is interdependent with them all.

There is no part of the organism that doesn't represent a microcosm of the entire organism. Understanding this amazing trait — the organism's microcosmic reflection — opens up wide vistas for unique forms of therapy.

This principle lies behind medical diagnoses in which a person's whole condition is deduced from a small sample of one of the organism's systems, such as the blood. Similarly, a hair test can testify to the composition of the tissues and indicate a deficiency or excess of certain nutritional elements and the body's capacity to assimilate them.

In ancient times, as well, before the era of scientific laboratories, physicians found ways of reading the information that the organism transmits through each of its parts. They frequently checked the tongue to learn about the state of the organism's inner processes; they assessed a person's condition by the smell emitted; their ear was sensitive to the nuances of the voice; they dared to palpate the patient's skin to determine its texture, and also considered the patient's colour. A judo student once told me that her teacher in Japan knew what had happened to her back by the sound of her voice over the phone.

Using a knowledge which is not encompassed by today's conventional medicine, there are experts who by certain stripes and spots in the iris of the eye can determine the changing conditions of every organ in the body, the degree of waste deposits in the intestines, a person's mood and every physical injury sustained in the past. Iridology is a science based on extensive experience, and many books have been written about it.

The pulse also contains a world of information. In Chinese medicine, it is a minimal standard to be able to differentiate between thirty-six types of pulse in the wrist. A certain order within the organism is recognised; every organ in the body is related to a specific layer in the bloodstream. The Chinese physician can gather information from a sensitive probing of pulse changes which take place according to the depth of his pressure on the wrist. A skilled acupuncturist who is highly sensitive to subtleties can determine the degree of deviation from a healthy state of every body function, just by checking the pulse.

In Israel there is a well-known healer named Zvi, who is ninety years old. His astoundingly accurate diagnoses are all based on the appearance of a person's fingernails.

Reflexology is a therapy which is perhaps easier to explain than the ones mentioned above.

Functional reflexology

Walking in a natural environment, over rough uneven ground, involves not only the interaction of movement between the foot and the trunk, but also the dynamics of applying pressure from the feet to the ground, and vice versa. While moving, the body's weight is focused each time at a different area of the sole of the foot. Every such momentary shift of weight aligns all the members of the entire body in a specific arrangement that will accordingly elicit increased pressure onto a specific part of the body. For example: leaning on the outer edge of the right foot will bring the right side of the belly to a somewhat more intense pull than that of the left side, and thus will stimulate the functioning of the liver. This means that in order to achieve stimulating internal massage, the liver needs a right foot that knows how to lean from time to time on its outer side. This is the economic and multi-purpose way of Nature, in which every function serves more than the one, directly visible purpose.

During waking hours, the inner organs are meant to function within a context of mobility, of constant displacement and tilting, derived from the ever-changing stimulation of pressure on the soles of the feet. If a person's feet remain in a stagnant state most of the time, his organs miss out on this hidden, refreshing, inner invigoration.

Indirect negotiation through the neurological partner

Coordination of the back's behaviour also depends on how the pressure of the body's weight is distributed over the sole of the foot. If you wish to locate in your foot the focus which, when pressed, will induce your back to find a posture of relief, shift your weight slowly backward while standing. When you come to lean mostly on your heels, when the toes nearly begin to lift off the floor, you'll surely notice that in order to keep your balance and avoid falling backward, your lower back must begin to round out into a backward convex. The lumbar vertebrae then find, on their own, the way to free themselves from the depression and pop out. At the other end of your spine, your chin then extends further forward.

On the other hand, if you transfer your weight forward onto the big toes, in order to keep your balance you will be obliged to bend your head down a little, and in that way invite the back of the neck to release its entire length and stretch, convexly, while the lower back deepens its concavity.

This response is an inherent pattern repeated with every step taken. You're familiar with it in minute portions as a tilting wave that throws your head back while the small of the back rolls out, and bows your head down to the earth while the curve of the lower back deepens.

The significance of this is that in order to enable the lower back to complete the phase of elongated convexity, a person should step in such a manner that with the imprint of his foot on the ground, there will be an instant when the pressure will focus on the heel area. When the person fails to achieve an effective pressure on the specific zone of the heel, the action of the back is incomplete and lacks the ability to negate the lower back depression, and thus remains dull and limited.

In order to increase pressure on the heel, the ankle has to deepen the angle of its flexion. In a culture of tight shoes, elevators, wheels, and flat floors, people don't make full use of their feet, and can't provide their internal organs and external members with the stimulation they would have received from walking in natural surroundings. In addition, these organs have lost the benefits that were formerly derived from walking on all fours.

Reflexology is a kind of substitute for complete walking. It relates to the dimension of pressure applied to the ground, and it reconstructs this by initiating accurate pressure on specific zones of the sole of the foot. Even when a person is lying in a horizontal position, applying pressure to a specific point on the sole of the foot induces in the nervous system the same experience which would have been generated if the person were standing with his weight focused on that specific pressure point. Through the pressure applied, the brain is stimulated to retrieve the corresponding behavioural ties, locked in its functional memory, which activate the entire body according to that specific stance, and the body responds and becomes aligned in the way that it would through actual standing.

There is a profound message to be found through understanding this link and utilising it. A person whose back is contorted from an injury tends to hold on to his defensive contraction. There is little chance that the organism will voluntarily dismiss the admonition of the threat and take the risk of stretching itself to full length again. Any direct and forceful demand of that sort will meet resistance and setbacks. Alternatively, one can approach the back through its neurological partner — the sole of the foot or the palm of the hand — locating the point which triggers in the back the response of lengthening, and applying pressure to it.

Reconstructing the pressure in this way provides the injured person with the condition he needs. By sustaining the pressure for a period of time which is sufficient for the organism to absorb and respond to it, the back will soon align itself accordingly, ready to extend itself without trauma and without resistance. The only pain felt is at the point of pressure in the foot, and that too can be moderated. The skill is to attain a state in which one still feels the tender vulnerability of the point even though the pressure is decreased. It is beneficial to dwell on this optimum state.

At times the lower back forgets the way to attain the elongating relief, and in the reality of a standing position it isn't resourceful enough to initiate it, not even when the balance is endangered. But when you reach the lower back through the family relations of its neurological network, in a comfortable lying position, the brain recalls the original program and can carry out the adjustment that it could not do while standing in the field of gravity.

The back's effective response draws its power from the primordial experience of millennia of evolution that refined the nervous system to its present form. This power is beyond an individual's personal experience, and applying it summons up powerful resources for bringing about a desired change, in tune with Nature's intentions.

The dimension of sustained pressure

The sensation of being subjected to pressure is basic to full natural movement. The Feldenkrais Method — Awareness Through Movement — aims at movements as free of inner pressure as possible, and intentionally creates hothouse conditions that are also as free as possible from the field of gravity. A low threshold of internal and external pressure is a learning necessity. Only when the pressure is reduced is the brain capable of noticing and assessing the efficiency of every subtle increment of pressure in the movement. Similarly, in order that the brain be free to discover alternatives for movement coordination, it has to disengage from its habitual coping with the force of gravity. Thus the movement lessons are usually carried out when lying down, with the movements floating as if weightless.

During private sessions, though, the practitioner of Functional Integration sometimes addresses the dimension of pressure, and provides a person with the experience of actual pressure, not only to the various points of the foot but also to the head, the vertebrae, the shoulders, the pelvis and the ribs, transmitting pressure throughout the entire skeleton in every possible way and direction. Every such application of pressure triggers a chain of responses and sets off a re-organisation, as if the student were standing on the head, the spine or any other area where pressure is applied and accordingly adjusts the alignment. You could say, then, that one aspect of Functional Integration is multi-reflexology to the entire organism.

You, yourself, can utilise the microcosmic system of the organism to move towards a more ideal functioning, by applying pressure on the sole of the foot. Even if you aren't expert in the various connections between specific zones in the foot and their corresponding body functions, you can assume that any area in which you sense a significant tenderness that can't be justified merely by the pressure, calls for a reminder to adjust to pressure. The tenderness testifies to the neglect of this particular area of the foot, from the point of view of its utilisation, and its capacity to sustain pressure. Most likely, it corresponds to a malfunction in some other part of the body. With your own hand you are capable of providing the foot with its missing experience, and training it to sustain the pressure of bearing weight, by actually pressing on it, and thus affecting the deficient function associated with it.

To apply the pressure, you can use your hand, or an appropriate tool, or the heel of your other foot, as will later be explained. Sometimes the relief brought to the back is so dramatic that the pain can immediately disappear. Irritating aches that over the years have become a permanent part of your life, can suddenly give way to a sensation of emptiness, almost as if something were missing there.

Pressing the eraser end of a pencil on a tender spot of the ankle, or taking a few minutes while lying in bed to press with the heel of one foot into the inner side of the ankle of the other foot, can become for you a self-refreshing routine.

When you hit the inner edge of your heel down on the floor with light strokes, from a kneeling or a standing position, your system registers this as an experience of jumping and will organise itself accordingly — just as in jumping it will compose your posture in the best alignment that you are capable of reaching in your present state.

Auto-reflexology

Sit comfortably. If possible, raise the sole of the foot that's on the same side as the pain in your back, and place it lying on its outer edge on top of the thigh of your other leg, so that you can view the heel and sole.

With your thumbs, begin applying pressure at different points along the area between the heel and the ankle, the ankle and Achilles tendon, the bottom of the heel, and sustain each pressure long enough to observe the response.

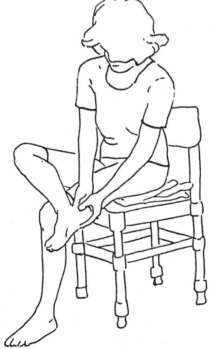

Activating the Heel-Lower Back Neurological Connection
Giving the heel, in a sitting position, an experience of sustaining pressure, elicits in the brain, an organisational pattern of standing that is a way of leaning on the rear of the heel, in which the lower back has to balance the posture and rounds out spontaneously.

In this trial-and-error process, there will be a point where the pain is more acute than would be justified by the pressure. This is a focal point worth staying with longer.

It's very helpful to use a pencil eraser instead of your thumbs. The eraser gives you that semi-hard, semi-soft texture and spares you the strain on your hand-arm-shoulder-back-jaw.

Breathe while pressing.

Heel to heel

Sometimes the condition of your back prevents you from reaching and holding your foot in your hands. Nevertheless, you can still apply the pressure yourself by using one foot to press on the other.

Lie on your back, with knees bent pointing to the ceiling, and feet placed flat on the floor. If you're aware that the right side of your back is the more injured side, tilt your right knee slightly to the right, keeping it bent, and lay the ankle on its outer side. You can support the knee with a pillow and free yourself from carrying the weight of the leg in the air.

Release the Lower Back from the Heel
In a lying position, too, it is possible to elicit the neurological programme that releases the lower back by pressing one heel with the other.

With your left heel, begin stepping on the inner side of the right ankle at various points around the entire area from the heel to the Achilles tendon. Remain for a while in each position and let the left hip rise just a little from the floor, to reinforce the pressure. Do this gently and sensitively, breathing throughout, so that you'll be able to moderate the pressure thus applied by your body weight upon the right ankle.

You can also apply these pressures around the right ankle, using the big toe of your left foot. Thrusting the bent toe provides you with an even more effective force of penetration.

In this way, explore various locations around the right ankle, near the heel, near the lower leg, and especially between the protruding ankle bone and the Achilles tendon. When you feel you've reached a sensitive spot, keep probing various directions for pressure till you find the most effective one. You can deepen the flex of the left ankle, to an angle that is sharper than a straight one, and thrust the left big toe into the right heel in a screw-like, back-and-forth rotating motion, as when putting out a cigarette. When you've found the direction that has the sharpest reaction, remain there for a while.

Extend your legs and rest awhile. Listen to the way you are lying, and to the different sensations in the two sides.

Repeat the entire process several times.

When you're ready, come to a standing position and observe the differences. The foot that received the pressure may feel softer, more flattened out along the entire sole, more in dialogue with the earth. And, most important of all, you may discover that you can go through your daily activities without your back impeding you, as it did before.

Clapping feet

Get down on all fours, on your hands and knees.

Tap the upper side of your right foot on the floor lightly and rhythmically, as it lies with the toes extended backward. Keep your knee in contact with the floor. Feel how the arch and all the many bones of the foot receive a thorough articulating shake.

Raise your right knee to your side, up in the air, with the inner edge of your foot turned to the ground. Like this, lift the right foot slightly from the ground and strike the floor with the inner side of its heel in gentle kicking motions, with the orientation of moving it further away from you.

Get up and notice the difference between the sides in the way you stand. Go through each of the procedures with the other foot.

Come back to kneeling; spread your knees, raise your lower legs into the air and clap the soles of your feet together. In particular, bang one heel into another.

Stand upright and listen to the changes. The soles of your feet, which perhaps usually seemed like inflexible foot-stools, supporting the body above them, may now appear no different from all the rest of your body. An inner flow streams through them, softening them to a suppleness that connects you into a unified entity. Perhaps, now, you are standing less on your feet and more on the ground.

Sense how your back feels with ankles that reclaimed their pressure. The full surprise is waiting for you in walking. Begin to walk around and notice the springiness and the sense of power that revitalises both your ankles and your back.

Thinking in images: a short cut to actualisation

'Your movements are as good as your images.' (from the Tao)

Sometimes the most effective of all ways is the most gentle one. This is a way of movement that is not concrete, but it has full intention, and the full design of the configuration — a movement that takes place in the imagination alone. The imagination tunes the action before it is actually carried out in space. It initiates an inner mobilisation which organises the entire system and prepares it to manifest the image that was formed in the mind. Most adults are in the habit of thinking in terms of words and phrases. When they are about to carry out any act, they usually skip creating a mental image in their brain, and relate only to the semantic verbalisation of the action. Instead of visualising themselves at the height of the successful act, with all its related sensations, they are identified with the cognitive concept of that act. The trap of thinking in words is that at times it carries with it intellectual considerations like worry and fear of failure, that reduce the establishment of a complete and positive ideal.

It is amazing how applying the imagination can be a short cut to success. Just an instant spent in creating a vision of the action as if it has already been successfully manifested, are repaid many times over in terms of the quality of lightness, the simplicity of doing, the precision, the spontaneous capability — achievements which are not easily attainable through other means. Apparently, thinking through images originates in the early stages of development, and is directly nourished from the powerful resources of primal vitality.

Waking dream therapy

There is a Cabalistic spiritual teacher in Jerusalem, Collette Muskat, who developed a whole, rich method of Waking Dream Therapy. With rare elegance, Collette inspires people to transformation by guiding their creative imagination into processes of visualising inner images. Her disciple, Katherine De-Segonzac, who has a practice in New York, knows how to apply the accurate image, tailored to the individual, that will bring about an improvement in the person's posture and in the attitude towards the self that is imbedded in that posture.

One of the assignments she gives to people who have back pain is to imagine that in the space of the stomach, behind the navel, there is a small ball of white light. Then imagine that this ball of light begins to expand and becomes the size of a big ball.

The imagination talks directly with the brain. Without doing anything intentionally, the brain sets itself to clear an actual space for the ball, and you feel how your back unravels its arch and fills out in the delicacy of scattering smoke. The imagery of the ever-growing ball of light induces the back to do what has previously been impossible for it — the lower back is now ready to elongate and move out of the stressful angle at the injured and contracted area of the waist. It does this spontaneously, without resistance and without effort.

Not only the back, but the stomach, too, becomes free of tension. The ball that swells in all directions softens and expands the stomach as well, and reminds the organism of a specific pattern for mobilising the back which does not come at the expense of the stomach. Any cancellation of the hollow of the lower back that costs you the penalty of tightening the stomach, cuts down your vitality and continues feeding the defensive milieu of pain. Learning to activate the lower back and at the same time to neutralise the stomach, so that it doesn't sabotage its functioning, is an advanced level of masterful differentiation. To achieve it intentionally calls for many processes of dealing with many sacred cows. You will find more information concerning the tightening of stomach muscles in the guided processes available on cassettes: head to knee, and back-stomach interaction.

While inspiring the imagination, it is important to avoid being tempted to help enlarge the movement through actual intervention. Even when you feel the first stirrings of movement emerge of their own accord, don't concern yourself with trying to evaluate the achievement, but continue to focus your mental resources on the image in your mind, as all you have to do is just see the picture. It is the image which will carry you to further accomplishment.

You can imagine, see, and sense the span of your shoulders spreading to each side, a further 20 cm in width, and something gentle and subtle will begin leading you to broaden your shoulders to a stable and comfortable width which perhaps you've forgotten was ever possible.

You can imagine your head carried at the top of a neck as long as a mast, that reaches one or two metres high. When you see this picture in your mind's eye, with your eyes closed, you may feel a hidden migration of movement within you towards straightening up on a line that makes you taller and brings you closer to the best possible posture for you at present.

Your nervous system understands the language of imagery and does all that is needed to fulfil the tasks with which you presented it. Whatever you succeed in imagining, you will also succeed in doing with greater ease. It can almost be said that the boundary of your ability to move in space is only as limited as the imagination in your mind.

The master's story

I recall a most instructive lesson on the power of imagery — a story concerning the master himself.

Towards the end of our training in Tel Aviv in 1971, Feldenkrais was injured in his knee and began limping rather severely. It was his sensitive knee, the one which had started him on his research and led him to consolidate his method and bring relief not only to himself but to so many people. One of us gave him a lesson in Functional Integration, but his knee swelled and hurt even more. After that none of us dared to touch the master's knee again. We felt quite frustrated: here we were, nearly at the end of our training, with our dear teacher suffering — and not one amongst us knew how to help him.

One morning he appeared without a limp. 'Moshe', we yelled out, 'What did you do; what helped you?' But Moshe didn't reply straight away. He did not respect impulsive curiosity that was not first dealt with inwardly with sufficient struggle. In a moment of grace, after a few days, he told some of us how he cured his knee.

He sat on a chair with both his legs as bent as they could be, his injured knee that could not bend well stretched further out. He closed his eyes and slowly entered the imagery of squatting, which demands maximal bending and pressure on the knees.

He said that it took him two hours to visualise himself comfortably accepting this crouching position, with every part of him knowing how to assume its role and sense the feeling of actually participating in that form of sitting. When he got up, his injured knee was ready to bend as easily as butter.

We have to be experienced in movement and have a broad awareness in which every detail of the intimate dynamics of the body's functions are fully clear to us, in order to be capable of reconstructing these details in our imagination with such precision. Consider the famous pianist who admitted that his most fruitful concert rehearsals were those that he carried out only in his imagination.

Imagery: prelude to the ideal

You can use imagery by yourself and see in your mind's eye not only a position or structure, but also a movement performing its function, and give it the style and rhythm you desire. You can imagine any task or assignment. When you fail to take a moment to preview in your mind's eye the manifestation of your will and you get involved in the actual doing, you are more likely to be drawn towards compromise and habit. When doing is not fed by a vision, it becomes difficult and problematic — like working exhaustively upstream. It is then even hard for you to assume that elegant solutions that emerge on their own are at all possible.

Awareness Through Movement gives you many opportunities to develop the lever of the imagination within you. You learn to respect the preparatory stage and allow yourself the time to build up the positive. You carry out a small part of the movement — the safe part — and the rest you complete in your imagination, without any part of your body actually continuing to move, and therefore without anything to awaken your resistance. You imagine that the movement flows easily and pleasantly, free of any pain.

In your imagination, you are not subjected to the realities of life, or to the laws of gravity. You can confer grace upon your movements, doing them with pleasure. You let your imagination stroke you from within. You can also imagine how the oxygen enters the cells, colours them with light, and gives them life, or how it enters between the joints and spaces them out. You immediately feel the relief that follows this microscopic process over which you have no control with your voluntary movements.

You give your organism a chance to recall what it felt like when it moved before the onset of pain. It knows; it has experienced this feeling before. When you give yourself the full ideal picture, as much as you dare wish for, its fulfilment begins to happen spontaneously.

Our sages said long ago: 'The end result of doing is implicit in the initial thought'.

Bending — yes, no, or how

The most frustrating movement, when the back hurts, is trying to bend forward. Such a bend makes an extreme demand of lengthening on the area that recoils most from doing so — so you are better off not trying it at all. You probably know how to bend down by bending only your knees, without calling upon your back to elongate in a curve. Indeed, this is the safest mode for you, as long as you are in danger of pain, and haven't yet learned to deal with your back in another way.

To further clarify for yourself the dynamics of a frontal bend, see if you can differentiate between what is taking place at the front of your spine and at its back. At a certain stage in your recovery, when you are ready, you will be able to return the forward bend to your repertoire of life movements, with the help of this differentiation.

Stand or sit comfortably with your eyes closed; imagine your spine as it is seen from the anterior part of the vertebrae, facing the inside of your body.

Visualise the spaces between the vertebrae closing in so that the front facets of the vertebrae come close to each other and fasten into one another.

Visualise the cervical vertebrae, looking at the part facing the throat, closing in together and tightening upon each other. Sense how the entire front of the spine, from the cervical spine to the lumbar, decreases in size as the vertebrae close together.

Imagine that the chest bone is shrinking and sinking; the shoulders seem to come closer to the chest, and the belly is gathered and diminished of its own accord.

Repeat this visualisation several times. Feel how inside you an inner movement begins to take place, adjusting itself to the imagery, without any intentional intervention on your part.

In this subtlety, you may observe what is happening behind the spine: how the part of the vertebrae that faces outward is passively relinquished, releasing its length to spread out, thus making the contracting bend in the front possible.

When you intend to bend forward and give your attention to what transpires behind your back, your system receives a signal to put into action the part on which you are concentrating. If at present, because of your back's sensitivity, its tendency is towards contraction, you are actually increasing this contraction. When your attention, focused on your back, awakens it to be active (which means contracting), it impedes you from bending forward. The trouble is that when your back hurts and you want to bend forward, you know that the back won't allow it, so you anxiously focus your attention on that liable-to-be-painful area of the back, and thus create the impasse.

You may consciously and intentionally shift your attention to the frontal area that controls the frontal bend, and you will release the bending from its rear restriction. The hidden perception, individual to each person, that is beyond the apparent movements, seems so imbedded and inseparable from them that it is hard to imagine that this perception lends itself to differentiation and choice.

Coordinate your visualisation

When you feel ready to complete your back's recovery and introduce it to more of its potential movements, suggest to yourself bending backward as well.

Imagine in your mind's eye the posterior projections of your cervical and thoracic vertebrae, visualising the spaces between them diminishing as they move in closer and are inserted into one another. Listen to the readiness of your chest and the front of your vertebrae to expand to their full spread. Clarify for yourself this different orientation, in which the front is released without resistance, allowing the action behind to work unhindered.

In order to clarify the relationship between the location of your attention and the movement, do the opposite several times. Think of the posterior processes of the vertebrae when you bend forward and see if you feel a difference.

Then visualise your chest bone and try to bend backwards. Do you feel you hinder the movement? Go back to the reference that serves you.

You may improve the function by refreshing the relationship of the eyes with the direction of the movement. Notice where your eyes tend to go. You may look upwards when your back becomes shorter and your head is moving backwards.

You may also lead your eyes in the opposite direction so that you look down, although the course of the movement in the spine and back is upward.

After a few times of correlating one way with the other, raise your eyes to coincide with the movement of the head backwards and observe what the non-conventional differentiation has contributed to the flexibility of the joints of your spine — or better still, to the flexibility of your nervous system.

For a sense of completion return to a forward bend, and compare it with the initial bending. Several such gentle overflowing movements of the back, slightly forward and then backward, when you know how to adjust your hidden intention to the course of the tangible movement in space, help your back to come out of its fear of participating in life.

Through the same methodology you can enhance bending to the sides, which will further contribute to your potential mobility forward and backward.

When bending your torso sideways to the comfortable side (for instance to the right), be mindful, as before, of the side that is shortened — that is, the active one.

Visualise your ribs on the right side coming closer together, the cervical vertebrae closing spaces as the ear projects above the shoulder. All the while, witness how the left side corresponds in passive expanding. Perhaps it still doesn't expand where it is most held; perhaps it opens more space only in the shoulder, in the ribs, in the buttocks. Allow the elongation the time for a process that develops for as long as it continues, and be with the short side. Your progress is made by picking up the manifestations of ease along the way.

Time and again, sense how the right hand slides downward along the right thigh. Notice that the left hand then climbs upward along the left thigh.

Stay for a while in this arrangement, at a level that is comfortable, and shift your weight from one leg to the other several times.

Stay leaning on your left leg and wave your entire torso as it is, like a door on its hinges, forwards and backwards.

Stop and check how the bending to the right works now. Is there a little less resistance?

Lend the injured side the image of the free side

If the pain appears on one side of your body, you may take advantage of this phenomenon and use it to learn about self-mastery. You can turn the free side into a model of recovery, and lend it to the injured side. This process is done in your imagination.

Close your eyes and imagine your impaired region. Locate its boundaries and figure out its form. If it has colour, note what it is. Gather all the details that draw your attention, such as its texture, its inner layout, its size, distances, alignment or angles. Take a deep breath and return to yourself.

With your mind's eye, in the same manner, scan the opposite, uninjured side. See how all the above details are expressed in it. If you have words that describe well the characteristics of each side, add them to your survey.

Direct your attention to the side that doesn't hurt. This side is free of restraint and it can assume any movement or stance, including — if you so wish — the particular condition of the impaired side. Slowly, let the free side imitate the impaired side. In your imagination, grant it the shape, the orientation and the colours you derived from the suffering side. Apply there, one by one, the clues of the disturbance.

Now direct your attention to the painful side. At this stage you may feel as if the impaired side has emptied itself of its program and seems more ready to accept another suggestion. Let the impaired side now imitate the healthy side, as you remember it. Grant it the original colour of the free side, the code of the characteristic word you assigned it; see in it the size, the form as it was originally; imagine the same texture.

You may notice some inner migration, some mobilisation towards reorganisation, in which the impaired side begins to take on the arrangement of freedom and may feel that it is able to behave as if there were no impairment there.

If you wish, you can invite the free side, that is still free to choose, to return to its original state, and in this way you will enjoy a total recovery everywhere.

It is a stunning experience to be able to dissolve longstanding physical limitations on the spear of a thought. You may apply this procedure of swapping roles to any one-sided movement limitation.

It seems that pain is not only physical impairment but also the subordination of your brain to a specific pattern of response following that pain — a kind of vicious circle of cause and effect. The movement experience implies that all you need to do in order to release yourself from the vicious circle of the disturbance is a moment of awareness, in which you see clearly the details of your inner organisation when you react to that disturbance. You faithfully reconstruct those details to the degree of being able to reproduce them in another place. You shift the make-up of the disturbance to the positive and safe side, where you don't risk reinforcing the injury in your self-image. It seems that this awareness is sufficient to bring about an instant of detachment from the inertia of the disturbance programming.

It is interesting that what is required in order to recover is not so much to learn the ideal way, as to track the individual way in which you set yourself up for the disturbance. It is as if the intentional reconstruction of an unwanted act, which is out of your control, gives you control over it.

Letting the free side imitate the injured side puts you in communication with the nervous system, in a direct way which consistently bears predictable results, astonishing in their effect. You may view this phenomena as the superiority of the software of programming over the hardware of the computer itself, or if you wish, the superiority of mind over matter. This phenomena calls for thorough neurological research in order to be explained. Until this explanation comes your way, experience it for yourself and wonder privately at the results.

7

Free Your Back

Relief or true healing?

When you are in pain you are not interested in explanations of the cause of the trouble in the past, or in conflicting opinions and theories about a course of action in the future. When you are in pain you want immediate and effective relief. Right now.

In the previous chapter you found several suggestions concerning how to free yourself of the pain in ways that can also lead you to a true healing process.

What is true healing? Are you considered a healthy person as long as you're not a case for hospitalisation? As long as you aren't absent from work due to illness? When you don't feel any apparent physical limitation? When you can carry out the elementary functions of your existence despite having a limitation? Where do you draw the boundaries of health?

Living fully

Can you define health in positive terms that do not mention sickness? Health, says Feldenkrais, is when you can realise your concealed dreams. You are healthy when your body serves you faithfully, empowering you to participate in life as you would wish, daring you to aspire to be the person that only in moments of exaltation and grace you believe you can be. That could be the meaning of authentic health.

To be interested merely in easing the pain is like looking for a smart lawyer who will cunningly save you from a jail sentence. If he succeeds and you're spared imprisonment, there is no guarantee that you will know how to lead a creative and honest life.

However, if you've reached the threshold of the prison of pain, you do need emergency help, while understanding that it can't substitute for an educational transformation.

Many people are willing to compromise by achieving a state of non-pain alone, and have no aspirations to improve beyond that. This isn't narrow-mindedness or sluggish evasiveness. It is perhaps a lack of faith, coming from a history of suffering that has left no room to believe that life can be more than mere survival. Suffering from back pains is considered by our society as an accepted norm, as long as the victims aren't bedridden or in need of an operation. In matters of health, our society even holds as sacred the determination to hang on to life unconditionally, regardless of every onslaught and deterioration.

This book addresses the people who care not only to manage to live without pain, but to seek a level beyond survival — the people who desire to live fully.

Actually, you don't have a choice. It is only when you are motivated towards health in the broadest sense — self-actualisation — that your local problems clear up. If you deal only with the immediate problem, trying to chop off the tip of its iceberg, it will persist in floating upward, to overcome you with increasing force, as more and more of its parts reach the surface. Moshe used to say: treating the pain turns it into a lifelong problem.

Only a change of climate will make possible the melting of the iceberg, and the climate is the level of integrity of your functioning. In order to heal yourself, you have to learn to modify, not only your entire movement coordination, but also your basic beliefs which underly the very manner of moving which feeds your vulnerability. To change means not only refraining from a certain manner of moving that inflicts damage upon your body, but also — and this may be the hardest part — being willing to explore new non-habitual attitudes and ways of moving.

Organic generosity — a temporary loan

Pain, as in any illness, indicates a blown fuse. Some impediment in the circuit has been building up, and the pain calls out to you that the system can't continue this way any more. Perhaps, for a long while, you were able to draw loans from your estate of well-being, without exceeding your credit limit. This is an advantage of organic generosity. But when you've reached the stage of sensing the pain, your system is sending you a signal that it can no longer lend against your overdraft, perhaps forewarning you of bankruptcy. As in the case of a fusebox, if you put in a fuse with a higher tolerance level, you are endangering the safety of your entire house. Wouldn't a more responsible approach be to investigate what went wrong with the system?

Not why, but how to get out of it

How can you find the source of the pain?

Unfortunately, the human organism is far more complicated than the electric fuse box. Life's creation is engineered with much higher sophistication and intelligence than any complex instruments invented by human thought.

The reasons for your back pains may be intricate, and subject to the history of your unique functional habits, your mental approach and your structural constitution. It is hard to distinguish the primary cause from its outcome. Your ability to precisely single out one specific factor is no greater than your chance of locating the one piece of coloured glass in the kaleidoscope that moved in a certain way and altered the entire pattern.

For you, the useful question is not why did it happen and what caused it, but how can you get out of the trouble?

Helping Nature help you

Fortunately, unlike the circuit of electric current through the fuse box, your complex organism is inherently capable of ridding itself of trouble. You may remind yourself that Nature always strives toward healing — that is its initial intention. In Hebrew the words 'health' and 'creation' come from the same root. Through a slow gravitation towards well-being, Nature bestows upon you, minute by minute, the choice of helping it help you. Your organism is so steadfast in its persistent orientation towards the good, that even when people do every possible thing to sabotage it, placing hardships in its way, punishing it with drugs that repair one thing while perhaps damaging two others, nevertheless its deterioration is slow and wearisome. For humankind, even dying comes hard.

Pain — your guide to reform

Pain bears witness to Nature's longing for recovery. It is the organism's cry for a return to the right path. Your pain can be the teacher, showing you the way back to health, if you know how to read its message beyond the suffering.

Pain is a regulating mechanism, a built-in safety device that sends to you precise signals, steering you away from danger. You're like a blind person making your way through a winding tunnel, where every bump into the wall shows you where you have deviated from the safe path.

Pain indicates to you where not to go and what not to do. In order to find out what to do, you have to be alert and open to discovering it by yourself. Your sensitivity to detect and locate everything that enhances your well-being is your key. Your helping Nature is summed up in your ability to discern differences between changing levels of pleasure. Or actually, in the permission you give yourself to seek indulgence.

Perhaps the first message you receive from pain is 'Stop!'. To stop, not in order to confine yourself within your limitation and feel sorry for yourself, but to stop because you understand that what you've done till now no longer works for you, and that now you have to think of and look out for another direction. In the Feldenkrais approach thinking means new ways of doing.

Non-action as a correction

If pain had words, perhaps you could hear it telling you that all you really need is just rest. Generous, patient rest, free of pressures and commitments to try harder to accomplish the impossible. Sometimes, all that is needed is that you stop using yourself in the manner that's harmful to you, and all the rest of the healing will be done for you by Nature.

Nature's effort to heal you cannot take place under pressure. It is a consistent, delicate and subtle orientation which has its own pace. Any clumsy pressure overshadows and inhibits it for a long while. It's very easy to disturb the healing process, and not so easy to decipher and create the conditions that will allow Nature to set its own renovative course.

You may hesitate in heeding pain's message. Perhaps you regard rest as a surrender and a loss of your state of activity. See if you are consciously willing to accept slowing down as a step in organic honesty. Try it and sense for yourself what rest does for you, and what remains in you afterward.

You want to correct the situation, and you're used to thinking that correction, like any other activity, involves an intentional action. See if you can, at times, regard non-doing as a source of corrective power as well. Come to realise how refraining from action slowly returns you to a neutral state which gives you the chance to start anew in a more appropriate way.

Learning relaxation through learning activity

If your pain is so overwhelming that even if you wanted to relax, your body has already forgotten how to organise itself to find comfort in that rest, you do need further help and preparation towards resting, so that it will be beneficial to you. The easy way of learning how to organise yourself for relaxation is by learning how to organise yourself for optimal balance while in activity. When you are searching for an economic style of moving, for a way of regulating your efforts to be congruent with the activity which you are performing, you become acquainted with the orientation towards relaxation. Your life consists of movement. It is possible for you to follow it with awareness and initiate changes in it. Eventually, what determines your well-being has to do with the level of your functioning when you're active, what you're capable of doing, and at what price or benefit.

How to move — creative searching

How, then, should you move when you're in pain? Should you continue trying to carry out all your daily activities? Do you need to add specific exercises? Is it good for you to walk, swim, sit and bend, or should you avoid doing them all?

These are questions that people ask, questions that ask what should be done and fail to ask how to do it.

Troubles are many and varied. There are no two people whose injuries are the same. Even if their injuries carry the same label, for each person the injury is conditioned by his or her own personal constellation of emotional context, style of functioning and structural constitution — all of which lend themselves to an endless variety of combinations. One person may have a backache that signals sporadically under certain circumstances only, while he lives his normal life with the realisation that something isn't quite right there. Another may be caught in a back spasm and be totally incapable of tying his shoelaces, or thinking of anything else but his back. The only resemblance they have to each other is that both of them got into a habit of using their body in a damaging way, without sensing how they were doing it to themselves.

The trajectory of the beneficial movements is secondary. It's a configuration that's unlike an exercise and more like a search for what can be done for the moment. You can discover this trajectory from within yourself if you listen to what your organism needs at any moment in time.

This search can be undertaken in any condition, from being bedridden after an accident, to mountain climbing. When you let your sensitivity lead the way, when it is important for you to receive a reading of your comfort scale from within yourself and not necessarily to succeed in performing a certain movement to a specified degree, you will slowly discover what is available for you to do, and where you can gently expand it.

Resourcefulness in times of trouble

Primitive traditions have a rich experience of folk medicine that treats injuries, starting from the simple knowledge of medicinal herbs and ending with ceremonies to expel ghosts. The progress of medicine that relies on scientific ways of thinking, on research-based findings of the secrets of chemistry and the surgical knife, did not stop to sift out the superstitions from ancient customs in its attempt to cope with life processes. But is man today, as an individual, really better equipped when facing the problems of loss of health? Does he or she have more criteria by which to judge? Does a person know how to retrieve further resourcefulness from within?

An intelligent person, in our culture, knows just how ignorant one is of professional language which demands years of training in order to be able to master its concepts. One has no choice, then, but to place the understanding and the responsibility for health into the hands of the medical establishment. Hospitals seem to have taken over the role the churches played in the past, as the citizen knows how dependent one is on them for salvation. People weren't raised to think that they are allowed, in times of trouble, to use their intuition as well. They were even brought up to think they shouldn't interfere, or try to understand by themselves.

How relevant is it that individuals dare to help themselves when in trouble? Where is the borderline beyond which it is stupid and dangerous to act alone? This is a dilemma of fine balance. The purpose of this book is to shed light on and broaden one's familiarity with that domain in which one can act for oneself. Along with cultivating one's own sensitivity and awareness, one gains the ability, when asking for medical help, to incorporate this help with greater efficiency.

Reframing your complaint

One of the ways in which to increase self-attunement and plug into the resources of natural sensibilities is to use terminology with caution in defining one's problems. If the name of the illness bears importance for you and you assume that its treatment is contingent upon its name, then you are engaged in something you know very little about, and you haven't got a chance of seeing the entire picture with all its consequences. If you are attached to the name of the illness, reciting and repeating it over and over again to others, especially if it is written, and what's more, in Latin, you confer upon it the power of a spell. Unintentionally, you give up your right to an opinion of your own and you lock yourself into the verdict this label carries.

You will maintain more power if you leave the professional terminology to the medical specialists, who know how to use it. For yourself, try using a language that is founded on your own, unique and direct inner knowledge of yourself, through what you are feeling, through what you are sensing.

Oriented towards functional capability as the major key to well-being, Feldenkrais took special care to reframe the complaints of the people who came to him. When they began reciting the name of the trouble that brought them to him, he would listen and then ask: 'What would you like to be capable of doing that you cannot do now?' Immediately, the conversation would enter a domain of possible action, a direction of hope. People's faces lit up when they were given a part in the search, when they participated in the process in a way they could understand, and ceased being dependent on something they could not change.

Ceasing to think in banal verbal terms and beginning to think with images and authentic, non-verbal sensations is an aim that appears throughout the Feldenkrais Method like an ever-present motif. One can calculate and navigate one's actions by relying on one's senses, without any verbal statement.

Numbers: your private criteria for self-assessment

Whereas words should be handled cautiously, numbers can be very helpful to you.

If you feel pain, give it a number, accurate for the moment. If zero is the ideal condition and ten is unbearable, determine where you are with your pain on this scale. You alone can know the answer better than anyone else. The observation that you go through in order to mark the number in itself places you in a category of being responsible and not a victim, of having a chance instead of feeling hopeless. Uttering the word 'pain' immediately evokes in your mind a complex dead end that is too much for you to deal with. When you say a number you know it is a stage that hints of possible change.

The number you determined for your pain will be a signpost showing you how you are progressing. Pain, like every injury, needs time to heal. The relief you can bring is gentle, subtle and gradual. The way you can help is mainly by knowing how not to aggravate, how not to hinder the process of healing. It is very easy to ignore a degree of relief if one doesn't consciously pay attention to it. When you become more sensitive to fine differences and discover you have passed from number 6 to number 5, you know you are progressing even if it still hurts. This is a source of encouragement to have the patience to persist with the process.

Impairment of your back: impairment of your ability to say no to the world

Viewing the distress of the back against the background of the whole person, is to see the entire picture of what you are in your life, to take into account your functional honesty, to see to what extent you wear yourself down with inner waste of fruitless effort, with movements that are made awkward through aggression. To see your total self is to realise what you do to yourself in time of stress, to what extent your anxiety to achieve your commitments impels you toward useless tension, which neither leaves you nor comes under your control.

Perceiving your suffering back within the context of your total personality also means recognising how your emotional make-up affects the resourcefulness of your body in dealing with life's tasks. If you remember well, you may acknowledge that the very same failing movement which marked the beginning of your back trouble, was accompanied also by frustration, a certain emotional pressure.

Your back is your armour. It is the part through which you say 'no' to the world: 'I won't allow', 'I don't want', 'Don't hurt me'. When you turn your back on someone, your gesture cries out, better than a thousand words can do, your rejection of that person. Recall the polite exit from a church, walking backward, being careful not to imply impertinence. When your back is impaired, actually your ability to say 'no' to the world is also impaired. You feel as if you are denied the capacity to protect yourself against all those things in life you wish to say 'no' to, and to which you perhaps don't even know how to say 'no'.

In this way, you can reach your back from the aspect of your personality. If you can find out what stands behind your back and discover what that unexpressed 'no' is and take care of it, perhaps you will no longer have to burden your back with the suffering of your spirit.

The suppression of improvised solutions: the decline of optimism

Any weakening of your optimism, any doubtful mood, or self-castigation by way of complaints or anxieties, immobilises your creative powers to improvise solutions. Whereas, on your good days, when your optimism is intact, you can safely and gracefully survive through even more difficult physical conditions.

To look beyond the local, painful area of the back, and to see that actually the whole person is hurting about life, is an intricate approach for which not everyone is ready. Most people know that after a motor accident they need to invest in car repair, but won't always admit that the driver also needs re-education. They aren't aware of their deficiencies in the realm of well-being. People adopt a belief that they must conceal all discomforts and tensions inwardly, keeping up a good front, until they no longer see the distress in which they dwell. People walk around with clenched jaws, with tight throats, with fossilised ribs, with legs that have lost their springiness, with a harsh look, yet they believe they are okay because they've continued to meet all their commitments adequately. However, their bodies, whether it is the back or the face, disclose their deprivation of that one thing for which they yearn — never daring to admit it, even to themselves.

Does this mean that you don't have a chance for a sound back, unless you first cease hurting yourself before pain forces you to rest? Does this mean that in order for you to get rid of the pain, you should first give up your ambition to want more out of life, or to the contrary, that you should not make all those small compromises, giving up an appropriate level of comfort, nor accept anything less than that which brings you contentment? Will your back continue to bother you as long as your emotional life is not secure? These are all difficult questions in which cause and effect are interdependent. I would like to approach this dilemma through a case history.

Back pain and the frustrated psyche: mutual captivity

Sara was an energetic doer. She came to me for help because of severe back pains. She indicated the area between her right shoulder-blade and the spine, saying she had incessant pain and a burning sensation.

When I began to touch her, I found that her entire spine was held like an unbendable rod. Every place that I touched reflected a level of stiffness that implied a need to maintain it, as if the woman's very existence depended on her ability to summon up all those muscles to her defence. This was an extensive, all-out defensiveness, which expressed her world view that life is about overcoming by force.

Sara told me how she always kept in shape, and participated in many hikes. All that stopped after she sprained her ankle badly. She didn't give up immediately; she tried forcing herself to overcome this by walking with a painful foot, but her condition just became worse. Now she no longer went out on hikes, and in addition her back began torturing her.

Opening up for a moment during the course of the session, Sara spoke of her aloneness in life, her failing communication with her daughter-in-law despite her good intentions, of her unfulfilled yearning for warmth and sharing with another person, with no forseeable chance of attaining this, and her fears concerning the 'sentence' of old age. It was clear to me that the softness in body comfort which Sara so desperately needed, and for which she came to me, had very little chance to be absorbed within such an emotional state which has no faith that life can meet her needs. She saw no other way of coping than by being even stiffer. I could see how her severe mood stifled her capacity to slacken the way in which she held her body, like armour, and her ability to move in a gratifying way. On the other hand, her physical trouble in all its facets, from head to toe, entrapped her capacity to relate to life with more optimism and with permission for enjoyment. Within this vicious circle, she just kept harming herself more and more.

The harm in persevering

Can you figure out what happens when one continues to walk with an injured ankle with determination to force it to carry on, in spite of the pain? The pelvis recoils with each step when it has to lean on the painful leg; each shoulder is immobilised with anticipation of pain; every rib dares not relinquish its defence to allow a deep breath. What does this persistence to overcome at any cost do to the neck, to the look in the eyes? For the price is paid not only by the area between the shoulder-blades and the back, where the protest is perhaps first heard.

Can you imagine what kind of communication — if any at all — is capable of being established with the environment, given this lack of kindness towards oneself? What can be done to help Sara? Can a session of mobilising the vertebrae reform the struggles of her life, and what can she learn from them? Where to begin so that she can experience relief without pain? Should all the deformations of the body's organisation first be reversed and all the points of tension be totally dissolved? Or will her movements go on failing her unless she first learns to treat herself as she treats her grandchildren, enjoying them as they are, no matter how they are. She knows how to be sensitive and forgiving towards them, with no exaggerated demands. Won't her pains fail to leave her until she is ready to spare herself as she does her grandchildren?

In other words: Do we have to eradicate and repair all physical defects and all destructive emotional attitudes, and only when we become perfect and symmetrical, harmonious and carefree in our body and soul, only then will we have a chance to stop the pain?

My aim in this book is to bring you the message that in any physical condition, at any age or with any trouble, you have the chance to make progress, a lot or a little, towards a functioning of the human body that is more comfortable, more beneficial and more self-restoring.

Functional Integration: response to acceptance

The guidance in Functional Integration which a student can receive from his or her teacher during a private lesson, lying on a table, is transmitted through touch. The mindful teacher, who is organised within himself at a high level of coordination, touches the student with his hands, exploring his body with gentleness and attentiveness. Through the phenomenon of one nervous system resonating to another, the student begins to receive permission to be gentle to him or herself, to be patient, to be aware. Through the attentive touch, which seeks to read the organism at hand and explore in detail its individual ways of moving, the teacher also transmits to the student a respect for being as he or she is.

The feeling of being accepted melts away the constant pressure of defensiveness. With the new trust a climate of openness comes about. The teacher's exploration increasingly becomes a manner of suggesting new options for movement. The lesson does not necessarily start at the problematic focus, but may begin at an area associated with it, where there is a chance that the student will feel that trouble-free movement is feasible. After that quality has been cultivated in the periphery, the teacher can direct suggestions to the core of the problem, searching out for the student the missing trajectory, the mode of coordination that the student does not know how to find alone. The teacher repeats this very slowly in different contexts, putting the student in motion as many times as is necessary for the new option to be accepted by the nervous system. All this takes place through a sensitive dialogue between the teacher and the student, with no words spoken.

If the student experiences the most minute difference in movement behaviour, even though in absolute passivity, that is already an important and revolutionary lesson which is sufficient for one session.

Sara got off the table as if she had just returned from a far journey in a land with different laws. She had been in a place where one was allowed to drop one's regular armour, and to remain without words and without time. Perhaps for the first time in years, life did meet her on her own terms. Someone showed her what was good for her — to a greater extent than she knew how to wish for herself. Her face looked as if all expression had been washed away, like a child that has just awakened from sleep. Her entire way of standing was totally different: softer, more reconciled, more human.

Listening to the positive

Sara made several movements with her shoulder and said that now it really was easier. She continued manipulating her shoulder about in order to make certain that indeed the pain had completely passed. At this stage, it was important for her to describe the nature of her pain when she first came and to demonstrate it by distorting her body. She was not yet ready to give a chance to the taste of the ideal, which had been slowly built up on the table.

Indeed, to adapt to the change, and to know how to reap the benefit in the way one is organised at the end of the session, when the change is so obviously clear, required a process of its own that is no simpler to carry out than creating the change in the first place.

Moshe used to say: The hardest thing to change in people is their belief that they cannot change.

The grandmother in the above case history needed several more sessions, progressing patiently and gradually, before she was ready to get up from the table and listen attentively and curiously to what was now improved and more positive.

Her transformation concerned learning how to learn. I had deep pleasure in seeing her glow with the budding of her new freedom. At first she watched over it with possessive seriousness, until she trusted that it could become a part of her life, just by simply giving it her attention. With her body's new statement, her attitude to life also projected the strength of a person who knows that there are things which it is up to her to change.

The more you try to overcome it, the more it overcomes you

Which part of pain is real and which part is influenced by one's attitude towards it? To what extent does resisting the pain increase one's suffering? To what extent does one augment the consequences of injury when one adds to it one's disappointment, one's fright, one's impatience? What does acceptance of the pain do to it? Is it possible to outsmart pain and develop towards it an attitude of humility?

In answer to these questions, I would like to tell of a personal case history, which I feel has an important message for many people.

My father, who was especially close to me, fell sick with a terminal illness. He was operated on and received drug treatments that perhaps lengthened his life, but oppressed him with suffering and alienation. He asked us to help release him, but at that time no-one knew how to relate to such a request, or even how to listen to it.

He told me how once, at night, his calf muscle was caught in a cramp, and he thought to himself: if only such a cramp could seize his heart, he would pass quickly and elegantly from this world.

A few weeks later, he woke up late at night with a sharp pain in his heart. His whole left side was in spasm from the shoulder to the ribs. He had suffered from a heart attack years before, and he recognised the signs. This time he welcomed the pain; he lay quietly and waited. He didn't wake his wife and he thanked God for hearing his prayer and sending him this attack, to take his soul with the touch of a kiss.

What happened, he told me, was that after a few moments, the attack subsided and passed. My father's suffering was not over. After a while he took a bath, swallowed all the sleeping pills he could find, and left a note of farewell asking us all forgiveness. He'd had a full and satisfying life, he wrote, and he saw no point in destroying his self-image with this illness.

However, this attempt of his didn't succeed either. His wife woke up and summoned help. He was placed in intensive care and even survived through pneumonia. He was forced to live a few more weeks until the disease claimed his life, like a candle that has burnt down to the end.

This ending is certainly nothing new in today's culture; however, the heart attack that passed as if it hadn't occurred, when he wanted it with all his soul, continued to astonish me. Where else can a clearer indication be found of the effect of surrender to pain? Is it possible that one can survive a heart attack simply by not fighting it? Is it possible that it becomes critical only when trying to overcome it? Can it be that the more a person summons physical strength to resist such an attack, the more it is likely to prove fatal?

It seems that, in the power struggle between an innate animal urge and the voluntary wishful thinking of man, the animal urge will always win out. Even if rational man can intellectually accept the idea that it's to his benefit to remain pliant in the face of pain and allow it to be there, he still doesn't know how to carry this out. He who has become accustomed throughout life to achieve everything through effort and overcoming, will not be able in emergency situations to find within himself the quality of surrender in emergency situations.

From this point of view, the educational contribution of Awareness Through Movement is highly valuable in that it familiarises people with moderation. It trains them to cease reacting with maximum effort, and puts them in touch with their capacity to bear with a frustration and to breathe through it — all of which are qualities that may be crucial in times of crisis.

Saying yes to life

Throughout every motion in Awareness Through Movement, the quality is as important as the configuration and the didactic design of the process. When you are seeking movements that are meant to bring relief, the style of moving is even more important. Relief won't come through harsh, swift and tearing movements. Perhaps that's what you've done all your life, but you must admit that it hasn't helped you to arrive at a sound condition, nor did it make you more graceful, nor did it relieve you, for after all, you are suffering.

Take a moment to clarify for yourself if you are truly willing to give up the approach that pretends to create ease through harshness. In order to restore in yourself a quality of softness and lightness, you may need to wrap yourself in an attitude you could perhaps have received only from good parents — parents who don't hold on to theories with preconceived knowledge of what is best for their child, but follow their intuition and always find ways to support a child's well-being with gentleness and mindfulness.

The observation that in certain conditions of sensitive consideration, your back can again perform movements safely and successfully gives rise to new hope for improvement within you. Rehabilitating a movement where there was previously only a clear statement of vetoing life, even if that movement is still small and only partial, is a breakthrough. It is the beginning of saying yes to life.

To once again move safely is like renewing communication in a relationship. The gratifying movement comforts you as in reconciliation, when you realise that not everything is lost, as you had thought. All you need to do is the little bit that is safe, and remain within its bounds. After ten or twenty such micro-movements, which may seem worthless, you will also be able to carry out a wider movement without it triggering the onset of pain.

Your patience for gathering the finer subtleties of well-being

If, in reading the above suggestions, you think that this method of sophisticated sensitivities is not for you, that you haven't the patience for what seems to you exhausting egocentricity or self-indulgence, then this is the very evidence of just how far removed you are from a supportive lifestyle.

Ask yourself honestly where you see any better chances of rehabilitating your dwindling vitality. Does your reluctance to pay attention to the details of your sensations help you to stop being their victim? In the long run, aren't the chronic troubles taking up more time, with less hope of any solution on the horizon?

If you aren't willing to play at varying levels of doing, and tune yourself for patient moderation, you sentence yourself to either all or nothing. Either you continue with insensitive, arbitrary movement that accumulates damage, or you seclude yourself with distrustful abstention, that curtails your participation in life. Either way is frustration. It's believing that there is no way out.

In any vulnerable condition it is possible to find mental resources to learn a style of moving that won't aggravate your pain or your disappointment, that searches out what is available for you in order to reverse the injury pattern and train you to trust that you can be as you were before the trouble. You just have to do what you are doing with less force and speed. In the body, quantity determines quality. With readiness to reduce your involvement in doing and to be aware of the small ever-changing details within you, you will find the path towards relief. Where else do you have at your disposal such a clear laboratory in which to experiment with your creative interaction with well-being?

I heard from a pupil of mine a case history that clearly illustrates this approach. She had an operation after a car accident in which her pelvis was fractured in nine places. All during the recovery period she was in control of her condition through her awareness and sensitivity. She would listen and discover the minutest movement possible for her, and she would repeat it over and over again, very gently. She was engaged in her own private research of herself, when all she had at her disposal was her willingness to experiment and to consider the feedback which her body gave her. 'The doctors couldn't believe how quickly I recovered,' she told me. 'These weren't exercises,' she added: 'You simply imagine where else you can still go, and feel how much is allowed, and then you play with it.'

What you can indeed move

There are quite a few things you can do for yourself, in the same spirit, at least for the time being.

On difficult days, perhaps you can't even tie your shoelaces; however, if you can consciously raise yourself above the anxiety of anticipating punishment for every move, you will discover, for instance, that your shoulders are ready to break free from their rigidity, and bounce slightly when walking. Perhaps you are able to turn your head smoothly and softly from side to side, provided that your motions are minute and unhurried, and above all, sensitive. You may also invite your chest to breath more fully. You can certainly open your mouth wide, and let it resonate to the rhythm of walking.

This act has significant meaning. Within the complexity of organic family ties there is an intimate correspondence of reactions between the pelvis and the jaw. When your back hurts and your pelvis knows it is unsafe for it to sway inconsiderately, the jaw also tends to clench and tighten up. When you consciously convince the jaw to move, as it can do on its own, then due to its traditional ties with the pelvis, the hips will be persuaded to allow more movement too.

When you approach your back indirectly, it is easier for you to dissolve the trauma there. When you mobilise what you can, you create a milieu of natural, flowing movement in which each part is used to interact with every other part. When all the links in all the systems are in gear for functional optimism, then the reluctant part also becomes, at least passively, more ready to give up its recoiling and begins to take part in the general movement.

In any physical condition, you can discover those places that are capable of movement, remote as they may be from the suffering and resisting back, and move them gently, insignificantly, like any other natural movement. You may realise that the idea of moving will slowly diffuse to the back as well. The more you reveal what is possible, wherever possible, the more faint and bearable the pain in your back will become. The improvement may perhaps be very slight and imperceptible, because the trouble is still there, but you are heading in the right direction — training your functioning to shift from confinement to activity, which, in organic language, means recovery.

Handicapped, or a person with a problem ?

Your primary assignment when you are in pain is how not to enter into the 'handicapped' role, and how not to torture yourself because your back is torturing you.

There is a difference between being handicapped and being a person with a problem. When in 1967 Moshe taught his method of Functional Integration to his first group in Tel Aviv, one of the people on whom he demonstrated was a man injured in a car accident. His arm was hanging useless and had lost its motor control. Moshe tried many strategies with him but the nerves were apparently severed, and it was impossible to restore independent movement to this arm. Moshe lessened the side effects of the injury that created a one-sided distortion throughout the rest of his body, and brought him to a more balanced and improved state. But the arm itself was not rehabilitated. This was our first model, and we learned from it a great deal of humility. During the last session with this person, Moshe devoted the entire time of his session to words of farewell. 'I have done all that I know, and more than that I cannot do for you.' These were rare words to hear him say. 'However, know that the friends who rush ahead, out of consideration, to open the door for you, are not your true friends. They will tire of you very quickly and will leave you. But if someone will show you how to make use of your brain, instead of your helpless hand, he is your friend.' 'There are many things you can do,' Moshe continued to say, 'You can love and raise a family, and the deepened sense of responsibility that comes from your injury will strengthen this love.'

Truly, the borderline between a handicapped person and a person with a problem runs somewhere between the thought of what I cannot do and what I can do.

The dominance of limitation

It may seem difficult for you to see that you still have a choice of attitude where physical pain is concerned. The organic fabric works in such a way that even the smallest localised disturbance is broadcast to the entire whole, and is reflected in its total response. When the disturbance reaches the level of pain, it receives dominant priority. This is a necessity that serves survival at a certain stage of injury, that works to enlist the entire network to help in self-defence. If the injured back has a need to immobilise itself, all the other parts of the organism will identify with this message and will react by a tendency to block motion, to a slight or great extent, according to the severity of the injury.

When you are confined, and you find it difficult in the most realistic sense to move without suffering, you can hardly imagine how it is possible not to become a handicapped person whose life is totally dictated by his limitation. Inadvertently, everything will work to generate within you the feeling that you are a prisoner to your pain. Without wanting to, you are drawn into thinking that your body has failed you and you are in a bind.

The organic mechanism is structured in such a way that people will be alert to the negative, to dangers, to life threats. This is the equipment that every living creature needs in order to survive the struggle for existence in Nature. The brain is very efficient when it has to find faults, and according to these faults it determines its course of action — much more so than according to what is satisfying. The recognition of satisfaction can be easily lost if you don't intentionally acknowledge it.

It is like when you uproot weeds in the garden and forget to enjoy the flowers. Indeed, in growing up we received attention for the negative things we did. We tend to consider warnings about what not to do far more than we hear encouraging voices, calling us to dare, to do something that is more promising than the conventional. We even have less terminology for verbalising the positive than we do for the negative. To pay attention to that which is positive is like listening to the silence beneath the noise. It needs training, and education towards a tradition of selectivity.

The option of attitude — the half-full cup

It is still within your human capacity for awareness to choose where to invest your attention. That which you apply awareness to has a chance to grow and strengthen. To concentrate all your attention on your back, where it hurts, makes it irritated with no way out, sets it out of all proportion in your self-image, and gives the problem dominance over anything else, as effectively as does any persistent advertising. On the other hand, if you take time to practice all that is positive in you, then your well-being will also have a chance to assume its proper place and become stronger.

It is your human assignment to transcend the defensive tendency and instead utilise your mental resources to balance the picture.

The most remarkable revelation of human capacity to consciously channel one's view toward the half-full cup I received from Jonathan Cohen.

Jonathan, in his wheelchair, with a body that gives the least support I have ever seen, explains in his book *From Defect to Wholeness* how instead of taking life for granted and being mechanical, the injury demands of him to draw from within himself the mental resources to become creative. Moment by moment, he recreates through his awareness his physical existence as well as his spiritual development. For him, this intentional creativity is the highest meaning of being human.

Through the medium of movement coordination, you have the opportunity to cultivate a conscious orientation towards the positive. In times of pain or limitation, this opportunity is further highlighted. You are capable of learning from pain when you succeed in summoning up a forbearance which leaves you serene and watchful, observing what is happening, determined to learn from it.

Your system resonates to your observations. As you explore your possible options for movement, you gradually annex to your territory of freedom more and more areas from reluctant confinement. You become increasingly capable despite your present problem.

The end that is the beginning

Whatever ways you choose to ease your pain, be it pressure on key points of the neurological network, drugs that may soothe one thing and impair another, elastic belts, supports and mechanical devices, or electrowave therapy and localised heating — whether you undergo an operation in which the injured zone might be permanently fixated so that it is no longer vulnerable, or you receive acupuncture treatment where needles revive electric currents throughout your total organism — in all of these cases you will still have to learn to use your body in a way that won't invite the recurrence of the trouble.

The fact that you are no longer in pain does not yet testify that you are a healthy person.

Recovery comes when you have rehabilitated your capacity to function in a safe and gratifying way, as is necessary for a full life.

Recovery is when, with time, you have to intervene less in order to regain well-being, and a reminder alone will suffice.

Recovery is when you raise your level of immunity, when you enhance your independent ability to deal with increasingly harder challenges without injuring yourself.

Recovery is when you learn something from your injury and you come out of it better than you were before.

As long as you are conditioned by a method, a device, an exercise, you are still in the stages of merely creating relief. As necessary a stage as it is, remind yourself that functional autonomy does not always follow relief inevitably. Functional autonomy is on the horizon, and you can approach it when you are ready to undertake the path to movement efficiency, updating your habits. In order to recover, you require a thorough reformation in your functional integrity.

It is up to you whether you stop mid-way or endeavour to reach the horizon of your potential.

The work of broadening your potential is rejuvenating. The process of introducing alterations in your movement patterns takes you to an early time in your life when your habits were still incomplete and open to change. This new openness to updating your habits gives you the same feeling that was embedded in it then — the feeling of being young.

Mindful Spontaneity

For information about Awareness Through Movement, Ruthy Alon
on cassettes, videos, workshops and professional trainings in the
Feldenkrais Method, readers should contact:

UK
Moshedo
16 Cascade Avenue
Muswell Hill
London, N 10

USA
Feldenkrais Resources
PO Box 2067
Berkeley
California 94702

AUSTRALIA
Me Lazy Productions
PO Box 108
Broadmeadow
NSW 2292

Movement Nature Meant
PO Box 158
Coraki
NSW 2471

ISRAEL
Ruthy Alon
A-27 Ein Karem
Jerusalem 90872

Bibliography

Bertonoff, D., *Journey to the World of Movement*, Reshafim, Israel, 1984

Capra, F., *The Turning Point*, Fontana, London, 1982

Feldenkrais, Moshe, *Awareness Through Movement*, Harper & Row, San Francisco, 1972, Penguin, 1984

Feldenkrais, Moshe, *The Potent Self — a guide to spontaneity*, Harper & Row, San Francisco, 1985

Feldenkrais, Moshe, *The Elusive Obvious*, Meta, California, 1981

Feldenkrais, Moshe, *The Master Moves*, Meta, California, 1985

Feldenkrais, Moshe, *The Case of Nora*, Harper & Row, San Francisco, 1977

Feldenkrais, Moshe, *Body and Mature Behaviour*, Routledge & Kegan Paul, London, reprinted by ALEF Israel May 1988 — a study of muscle and behaviour first published 1949 ALEF Publishers Ltd 49, Nachmani St Tel-aviv

Fynn, *Mr. God, This is Anna*, Ballantine, New York, 1988

Heggie, J., *Running with the Whole Body*, Rodale Press, Emmaus, Pennsylvania, 1986

Kurtz, R. and Prestera, H., *The Body Reveals*, Harper & Row, New York, 1984

Leonard, G., *The Ultimate Athlete*, Avon Books, New York, 1979

Mowat, F., *Never Cry Wolf*, Bantam, New York, 1984

Pearce, J.C., *Magical Child*, Bantam, New York, 1981

Pearce, J.C., *The Bond of Power*, Dutton, New York, 1981

Sacks, O., *The Man who Mistook His Wife for a Hat*, Harper & Row, New York, 1987

Sacks, O., *A Leg to Stand On*, Harper & Row, New York, 1987